Monturiol's Dream

Monturiol's Dream

THE EXTRAORDINARY STORY
OF THE SUBMARINE INVENTOR
WHO WANTED TO SAVE THE WORLD

Matthew Stewart

PANTHEON BOOKS, NEW YORK

Pantheon Books and colophon are registered trademarks of Random House, Inc.

Library of Congress Cataloging-in-Publication Data

Stewart, Matthew.
Monturiol's dream : the extraordinary story of the submarine inventor who wanted to save the world / Matthew Stewart.
p.   cm.
Includes index.
ISBN 0-375-41439-8
1. Monturiol, Narciso, 1819–1885.   2. Marine engineers—Spain—Catalonia—Biography.   3. Naval architects—Spain—Catalonia—Biography.
4. Submarines (Ships)—Spain—History—19th century. 5. Inventors—Spain—Catalonia—Biography.   6. Catalonia (Spain)—Biography.   I. Title.

VM140.M78S74 2004   .623.8'12045'092—dc22   2003062368
[B]

www.pantheonbooks.com

Printed in the United States of America

First American Edition

2   4   6   8   9   7   5   3   1

For Katherine and Sophia

Contents

Contents

List of Illustrations

Monturiol's Dream

Prologue

The Vision

Lives do not have plots. For the most part, they accumulate events day by day like a stack of old newspapers. But sometimes someone glimpses a fixed point in the flux of things, a hard certainty around which the rest of life turns like the pages of a good novel. Narcís Monturiol believed he had discovered the point of his life on the rocky shores of the Cap de Creus when he saved the life of a coral diver and conceived of a craft capable of taking humankind safely

The Cap de Creus

under the sea. Everything he had been and everything he hoped to be made sense to him in light of this fantastic vision. The submarine "is the soul of my life," he declared. "Without it my earthly existence would have no purpose."

The Cap de Creus—the Cape of the Crosses—lies at the end of a ragged peninsula on the northernmost coast of Spanish Catalonia. The rocky bed of the cape has withstood the erosion that has eaten into the softer coastline surrounding it. A wind called the tramontana blows down constantly from the nearby Pyrenees mountains and sweeps across the peninsula to the sea. Local lore has it that the wind can drive people insane—which explains the high incidence of eccentricity and deviant behavior in the area, or so they say. Where the land meets the water, the wind and the waves have performed a certain kind of magic, carving surreal curves and ghostly shapes in the stone.

Just off the shore, at depths of 10 to 40 meters, coral covers the submerged bed of rocks like a prickly blanket of crushed glass, coloring the sea bottom in patches of crimson, rusty red, rose, tangerine, caramel, and bone-white. The coral is the work of millions of tiny animals, whose mineral-rich secretions accumulate over years to form these motley, plantlike stones. In the age before plastics, humans placed extraordinary value on coral. Smaller chips were prized for earrings, necklaces, bracelets, and other jewelry. The rare, larger pieces of one to three centimeters in diameter were used to make elaborate candelabras and commanded exorbitant prices. Crimson was the favored hue, especially in the markets of South Asia, where much of the coral was sold. The coral of the Cap de Creus was long considered the finest in Spain and possibly the best in the Mediterranean.

At the peak of the coral age, coral diving was the chief source of employment in the fishing village of Cadaqués, an afternoon's walk down the coast from the Cap de Creus. Typically, the divers worked in teams. They would suspend a basket from a boat, and then each would take his turn to plunge as much as 20 meters underwater. In the few minutes that he could hold his breath, the

*Coral in the nineteenth century: "Report on the Florida Reefs,"
1880, based on field studies by the renowned biologist Louis Agassiz.*

diver would chip off bits of razor-sharp coral and drop them into
the basket. It was a hazardous way to make a living. The risk of
drowning or injury on the rocks and coral was substantial; the
occasional shark attack only made matters worse. "Often the diver
does not return, or else comes to the surface mutilated or dying,"

Coral diving, 1859

said a reporter of the time, "his blood giving to the waves the color of precisely the product he coveted."

One day on the shores of the Cap de Creus, Narcís Monturiol came upon a group of divers huddled around the inert body of one of their fellows. The fishermen flailed their stricken colleague frantically, trying to beat the seawater out of his lungs, but to no avail. Narcís being Narcís, he couldn't just *stand* there; he rushed in among the crowd to help. He grabbed the man by the feet, lifted him up so that his head pointed down, and allowed the force of gravity to pull the water out. The diver spluttered back to consciousness, still clutching the red gold it had nearly cost him his life to acquire.

It was around this time that Monturiol first conceived of the possibility of a craft capable of navigating underwater. Later, as he walked the same stretch of the cape in the company of a close friend, he revealed his secret ambition to build such a vessel. He called it a *fish boat*—an "*Ictí-neo*," he said, using the ancient Greek terms for *fish* and *boat*. We would have called it a submarine.

✦   ✦   ✦

Narcís Monturiol was not your usual submarine inventor. In 1856, when he first announced his underwater plans, he was already thirty-seven years old, and his résumé was not promising. He had published a number of journals, all of which were now banned; he had helped to organize a radical political party, most of whose members were now in jail or exile; and he was currently wanted by the police. In other words, he was pretty much your typical utopian socialist revolutionary. By training he was a lawyer, though he never practiced at the bar. When the money ran low, he took up portrait painting to make ends meet. Although time would eventually prove that his technological genius was in the global class, at the outset of his project he could offer no formal credentials in science of any sort. He taught himself everything he knew. He found time for research mainly in brief periods of exile that resulted from failed revolutions. His prior inventions included a device for cutting and printing student notebooks, a cigarette-rolling machine, and some untested ideas for the fabrication of potato starch.

He was of slim build, not very tall, with a slightly pinched nose, firm, purposeful lips, and clear blue eyes "of an irresistible penetration," or so they said. Bushy eyebrows, an airy coif, a generous beard that at midlife retreated into billowing sideburns, and a thick mustache framed his face with abundant peppery locks that gradually turned salty with the passage of time.

Yet there was something about the out-of-control hair or maybe the mesmerizing gaze that inspired enduring confidence and affection among his contemporaries. One friend described him as a man "of great virtue, a treasure of kindnesses . . . who considered all people his brothers: he wanted men to esteem each other mutually, and dreamed of the best of all possible worlds, ruled by the laws of love and fraternity." His manners were refined, his speech was precise and often elegant, yet his demeanor was simple and unpretentious. Friendly and agreeable in society, he exuded "a modesty so natural and spontaneous that all those who engaged with him respected him and loved him every day more." Another writer declared—as though it were an obvious and uncomplicated truth—that Monturiol was "one of the most noble and glorious representatives of humanity."

There was an aura about Monturiol, an air of quasi-religiosity. One commentator went so far as to call him "a Christian from the first centuries." Of course, as a card-carrying utopian communist, Monturiol wasn't exactly the churchgoing type. Yet at times he could be so moral as to seem moralistic, so virtuous as to seem prudish. When he discovered that a friend was a philanderer, for example, he removed the friend's portrait from his dining room and relegated it to the most obscure corner of his study. That would teach him. His favorite novel was *Don Quixote*, an eerily prescient choice for such a tragicomic dreamer. Before allowing his children to read about the bewildering adventures of that errant knight, however, he scrupulously excised all the many naughty bits from Cervantes' novel. The prospective submariner may have been a godless communist, but it cannot be said that he didn't uphold family values.

In short, Monturiol lacked all the obvious qualifications for the task he set himself—save one. Behind the sea-swept eyes and the windblown career, as his contemporaries sensed, was a rocklike integrity of character, a passionate firmness of mind. And that was enough, it seems. When he announced his improbable plan to journey to the bottom of the sea, his countrymen risked their money, their time, and in some cases their lives in order to join him in the extraordinary venture.

Nor was it your usual submarine that Monturiol had in mind. As a rule, the pioneers of underwater navigation conceived of the submarine as a delivery system for weapons of war. Monturiol was the exception. He was on a mission to save the human race.

He thought he'd start by saving the coral divers of the world. In future, he hoped, divers would harvest coral in the safety and comfort of a hermetically sealed vessel. He further imagined that the submarine would open up all sorts of opportunities for the landlocked working classes—perhaps deep-sea fishing, salvage operations, underwater farming, who knows? Above all, the submarine was, for him, a tool of science. He longed to *see* what lay hidden beneath the blanket of ignorance that covered three-quarters of the earth's surface. He had only a vague idea of just *what* he might see down there, but he was sure that whatever it was would be of profound importance.

A string of scientific questions addled his restless mind. Do deepwater animals rely on oxygen as do surface animals? Do deepwater plants depend on sunlight as do surface plants, or do they make use of some other source of energy? Are there any plant or animal products worth retrieving from the deep? What health risks are there to human beings in spending a long time in underwater chambers, away from natural air, the electrical currents of the atmosphere, and the sun's rays? Conversely, are there any diseases that might be cured by such an underwater isolation therapy? Is the ocean floor made up of the same minerals as the rest of the earth's crust? What kinds of currents wash through the deep? In what ways do these currents interact with waves on the surface and winds in the atmosphere? What are the causes of hurricanes, whirlpools, and waves? In a word, what differences are there and what relationships exist between the deep ocean world and the everyday surface world?

The quest for answers amounted to more than idle curiosity. Revealing the mysteries of the deep, for Monturiol, was really about the liberation of humankind. He sought to mobilize the masses of the world—or, at the very least, the masses of Barcelona—in a quest to liberate humanity from, as he put it, "the fetters that keep it subject to the limited atmosphere on earth." Like many of the prominent thinkers of his time, he believed in Progress with a capital *P*: the idea that the accumulation of scientific knowledge and the advance of social justice were one and the same thing. Strange as it may sound to our ears, his submarine project was a continuation of revolutionary politics by underwater means.

Monturiol was unique among submarine inventors not just in his motives but also in the scope of his technological ambition. In general, his military-minded predecessors aimed to build vessels capable of diving just deep enough to hide from surface surveillance and of staying down just long enough to inflict damage on enemy warships. Monturiol conceived of a much grander technological challenge. He envisioned a craft capable of descending to any depth, even to the very bottom of the ocean; capable of moving around underwater at will; capable of sustaining human life indefinitely in the inhospitable environment of the deep; and enabling humankind to interact with the watery environment in all the many ways—seeing, hearing, grabbing—available on the surface. What he intended to build was, in a certain sense, the world's first *true* submarine.

If his concept of the submarine was daring, his idea about the nature of the project in which he was involved was bolder still. Most inventors devise their machines to serve a specific and limited purpose: to catch mice more efficiently, to toast bread on both sides simultaneously, to sink enemy ships. Not Monturiol. He began with a vision, the vision of a true submarine, and assumed that the full utility of his invention would become evident only *after* it was built. He set out to create a machine that could do something absolutely marvelous, something extraordinary, something incredibly difficult—simply because he believed it could be done. The submarine was his Mount Everest, and his noninstrumental approach marked out his labors as the work of genius. His project belongs to the category of pure science—or, more precisely, *pure technology*.

Living as we do in the age of the submarine, it takes some effort to imagine the fear and loathing experienced in earlier times at the prospect of slipping beneath the surface of the sea. Monturiol's Mount Everest was a terrifying abyss populated with unnameable monsters and roiled by voracious whirlpools. Only the very brave or the very reckless dared to seal themselves inside these underwater contraptions, which typically took the shape of a coffin—and all too often assumed the function of one as well. The very idea of descending into eternal darkness in this way seemed gruesome, unnatural, and possibly evil. The advent of the true submarine, as Monturiol sensed, would require more than a few technical breakthroughs in naval architecture. It called for a comprehensive change in the way people thought about locomotion, human survival, and the watery world. It demanded the kind of alteration in the paradigm of knowledge that happens when projects in pure technology succeed. In short, it would represent an act of *radical progress*.

Monturiol was a man of unexpected talents. He was, for example, a stylish portrait painter. He also had a penchant for poetry. Shortly after beholding the vision of a true submarine, he burst into verse:

Fiery are my cares,
Toilsome is my cause
To know what hides unseen
In this mysterious sea.

To view perchance its depths,
Its forests of coral;
To see perchance the wrecks
Of such bold ships that sailed
And in great terror fled
At the roar of the hurricane.

The cause perhaps to discover
The source of stormy seas,
For if the deep says naught to others
Perhaps it will speak to me.

Poor heart that trembles,
Desist not from your cause!
Conquer the fear, for glory
Is yours when you return.

Come, my heart, be strong;
The boat awaits you yet
With its wingèd tail of iron
And its crystalline eyes.

In its body air is born,
The air that cradles life,
On its nose there is a star
That floods the world with light.

There is no more complete expression of Monturiol, the man himself, than in these lines: romantic visions of hurricanes and shipwrecks, mystical meditations on the mysteries of the deep, seriously
anthropomorphic feelings about his submarine machine, self-
encouragement that teeters on the edge of self-martyrdom, and
lyrical flights that probe the boundaries of good taste. To explore
the ocean deep was, for Monturiol, much more than a job or occupation. It was the story of his life.

It is a remarkable ambition to want to expand the frontiers of
human knowledge, even if it is possibly a bit foolhardy to find the
meaning of life in a submarine. And it is surely a noble thing to
hope to improve the lot of one's fellow humans, even if it is probably rather optimistic to expect to save the world by means of a submarine. But that was Narcís Monturiol: remarkable, ambitious,
foolhardy, noble, and delusionally optimistic. Not to say quixotic.

Amazingly, Monturiol would build his submarine. And it would be
the finest submarine of its day, the world's first true submarine. But
it would never become quite the thing he imagined that day on the
rocky shores of the Cap de Creus. His underwater utopia, needless
to say, never came to be. Although subaquatic technology continued to make impressive progress after his pioneering efforts, it
would soon embark in a direction that seemed very different from
that which he had forecast. As for the inventor himself, there would
be a harder lesson still. Like Prometheus of Greek myth—the
demigod who brought humankind the gift of fire, only to be
damned by the gods to an eternity on the rocks with his innards
splayed open for the vultures—Monturiol would learn that fate is
not always kind to humanity's benefactors, and that the same qual-
ities which make a man a revolutionary genius can also be the
source of his downfall. Inevitably, the vision he beheld on the Cape

of the Crosses—the vision that gave meaning to his life—would hang forever beyond his reach.

Even so, as seems appropriate for such an unlikely hero, the great submarine inventor would indeed leave a lasting mark on life as we know it, and he would leave it in the most unexpected places. As his dream machine wended its way along the bumpy paths of the real world, it would have its greatest effects on life on dry land, in its home city of Barcelona. Like the last drop of water that precipitates a flash flood, Monturiol's submarine would carve out a new course of history for Catalonia's capital. It would shape the city's new and distinctive culture; it would determine the way the city's inhabitants responded to the challenges of modern life; and, astonishingly, it would even leave its trace on the streets of the city itself. The fragments of Monturiol's dream coalesced in his wake, conspiring to make his home city, if not quite utopia, a better, richer place. The story of Monturiol is in part the story of this place: a city and a state of mind defined by its often compelling, sometimes quixotic, and always illuminating reflections on the nature and meaning of modernity.

Monturiol's tortuous life and posthumous career would challenge not just his assumptions about the nature of progress but also, or so I hope, our own. He, on the one hand, made no distinction between *technological* progress—the accumulation of know-how—and *moral* progress—the advance of social justice. After a century of bitter experience with modern warfare, we know better. We, on the other hand, after decades of planned innovation and continuous improvements in fuel efficiency, now tend to assume that technological progress, at least, follows a predictable course; that its benefits are self-evident; and that the only way to ensure its perpetuation is to appeal to the self-interest of those who would pursue it. Monturiol's story will show by example that the causes, direction, and consequences of technological progress are far less predictable than we imagine. It will show that the link between technological and moral progress is neither the simple unity postulated by utopians nor the exhaustive disjunction imagined by dystopians, and that, in the space between utopia and its antithesis, there is still room for hope for improvement in the human condition. And it will show that some of the time, at least, everything depends on the extraordinary individual who wants to save the world.

Monturiol's dream is as much about an ideal as it is about a time and place. His vision is a beacon for what might have been and what perhaps one day could be. It stands for a submarine very different from the submarines our world has come to know, a hope for progress grounded in something more than the conventional wisdom, and a kind of heroism that was as rare in its time as it is now. Like any decent ideal, it keeps at a respectable distance from the present state of affairs, receding as one approaches, marking the end of a process that by its nature must remain perpetually unfinished.

Part I

The Making of a Submariner

A portrait of the inventor as a young man

One

The Fires of Youth

Narcís Monturiol i Estarriol was born in 1819 in Figueres, the capital of the Alt Empordà, the northernmost region of Spanish Catalonia.* The family's home and principal place of business lay on a small street just off the central town square. The Alt Empordà stretches out from Figueres into the peninsula that includes the Cap de Creus and the fishing village of Cadaqués. There, among the mountains, forests, and rocky cliffs by the sea, Narcís spent the vacations of his youth.

Narcís's father was a cooper. His job was to make the hermetically sealed barrels that would contain the abundant wines, oil, and milk of the Empordàn countryside. In an arrangement typical of the time, Narcís's mother represented the religious faction of the family. It was her duty to pray for her son's "condemned soul" whenever he strayed from the path of true faith. She would have many occasions to pray during the course of her long life.

The family included five children. Narcís's elder brother, Joaquím, was the *hereu*—the heir—in the family. In accordance with the rigid inheritance laws of the land, he would eventually take over the cooperage business. As the second son of a devout mother, Narcís was destined from childhood for the priesthood.

---

*According to Spanish and Catalan custom, surnames are composed of the father's family name and the mother's (from her father's side). When abbreviated, it is the mother's family name that disappears first.

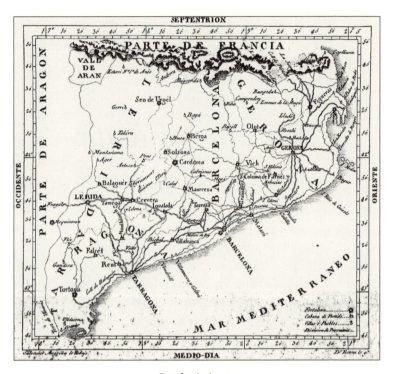

Catalonia in 1823

At the age of ten, Narcís built a wooden model of a clock. It couldn't tell time, but it certainly looked the part, or so his parents thought. Sensing that their boy possessed an uncommon mind, Mr. and Mrs. Monturiol scrimped and saved to pay for his college education. When Narcís turned eleven, they packed his bags with all his things and all their hopes and tearfully put him on a coach for the University of Cervera, far away in the mountains surrounding the interior provincial capital of Lleida. He was enrolled in courses on Latin, Greek, and all the other subjects that would normally go into the making of a local parish priest.

Despite his mother's prayers, however, Narcís had little intention of entering the Church. Rather, he showed interest in the sciences and the mechanical arts. He also developed a reputation among his fellow students as a warmhearted spirit. So, perhaps naturally, he chose to study medicine, where he might apply his analytical skills to helping others.

The death of the king of Spain disrupted his plans. Ferdinand VII had been a monarch in the old uncompromising sense of the word. The nature of his vision for Spain may be gleaned from the fact that he numbered among his proudest achievements the establishment of a national school for bullfighters in Madrid. In 1833, when Ferdinand finally departed for that great bullring in the sky, he took with him the last great hope for absolutism in Spain.

Upon the king's death, Spain divided itself in two over the matter of succession. In one corner sat Ferdinand's three-year-old daughter, Isabel, in the grasping hands of his widow, Maria Cristina. Liberals throughout Spain seized on the regency of Maria Cristina as an opportunity to begin a transition to a representative and constitutional form of government. Maria Cristina herself was hardly an enlightened political thinker. She proved to be liberal principally in her choice of secret consort: an ex-sergeant and shopkeeper, who was her accomplice in a number of unwanted pregnancies. Her chief ambition was to secure the throne for her one legitimate child, Isabel. When Maria Cristina's support for the progressive cause wavered, the liberals kept her in line by threatening to expose the unbecoming details of her morganatic union.

Over in the other corner, representing those who had no wish to give up the medieval lifestyle, sat the dead king's brother, Carlos. The clergy of the Catholic Church championed Carlos from their pulpits in tens of thousands of village churches across Spain. He returned the favor by promising to create a theocratic state founded on fundamentalist principles of absolute intolerance. Hordes of peasants, egged on by their parish priests, took up arms on behalf of Carlos.

For the next seven years, Spain suffered through its first civil war. Allowing for the inevitable complexities of history, the dividing lines were clear enough. The cities stood for progress, and the villages stood for the Middle Ages. It was a struggle between the new and the old, between the literate and the faithful, between pens and pitchforks. The identities of Spain's leaders for the next generation were made in the course of the conflict. The generals who would trade coups and countercoups over the next thirty years, the liberal politicians who would campaign for democratic reforms, the revolutionaries who would fight for justice, even the writers and the odd inventor who hoped to change the world—all won their medals, made their names, and formed their opinions in the heat of the seven-year civil war.

In the sweltering summer of 1835, Barcelona erupted in riots. While liberal politicians sought to unseat the reactionaries, the working classes—unhappy with the whole political process—set fire to a number of convents and factories. The authorities sent in the army. But the masses were in an exceptionally surly mood, so they killed the commanding general, dragged his body through the streets, and then burned it too.

The distant rumbles from Barcelona carried all the way up into the hills of Cervera, and politics captured Narcís's imagination—not to let go for some time. He had little difficulty deciding whose side to take in the epic political struggle. His origins in the class of urban artisans, his career as a student, and his youth itself would have made him a natural progressive anyway, even if his generous disposition had not already made the choice inevitable. In a burst of revolutionary fervor, he switched from medicine to law, figuring that the bar would provide a better platform from which to change society, and applied for a transfer from Cervera to the University of Barcelona, because he wanted to be where the action was.

Once in Barcelona, Narcís took up digs with a fellow student in a tiny top-floor studio apartment on a narrow lane near the center of the city. In order to earn his keep, he tutored his landlord's daughter, a clever and sprightly girl ten years his junior.

Narcís went out and bought some law books and registered with the law school, but that was about as far as his legal career went. He promptly set the books aside and fell in with all the wrong friends: revolutionary journalists, student demonstrators,

Barcelona burning

radicalized workers. He threw himself into the fight for social justice. He took up smoking.

It was a furtive, caffeine-driven life, brimming with whispered discussions and clandestine meetings in the cafés and private houses of Barcelona. The topic of the day was the overthrow of the existing political order. For the young Narcís, Barcelona was a problem to be solved. He was sixteen years old.

Two

The Problem of Barcelona

"A city is like an ancient hieroglyph," or so said Ildefons Cerdà i Sunyer, a young civil engineer and friend of Monturiol, as he surveyed the city of Barcelona in the middle years of the nineteenth century. Properly deciphered, the roads and alleys, bricks and stones, and buildings and monuments tell the story of a city's people. It is a story that, as Cerdà put it, spans "the past with its traditions, the present with its vested interests, and the future with its noble aspirations and initiatives."

The past with its traditions figured prominently in the hieroglyph of nineteenth-century Barcelona. Dominating the city center was the greatest concentration of Gothic architecture in Europe. In the first half of the fourteenth century, Barcelona was the seat of the Catalan empire, a mercantile dominion that extended across the Mediterranean to the Balearic Islands, Sardinia, Sicily, parts of the Italian peninsula, and even out to Greece and Turkey. The wealth of conquest poured in through the port of Barcelona and congealed in the form of spectacular cathedrals, hospitals, convents, and a ring of thick stone walls, ten meters high, that turned the city into an impregnable bastion. But by the second half of the fourteenth century it was all over. The Venetians, the Ottomans, and others divvied up Barcelona's Mediterranean holdings. Then the central powers of the Iberian peninsula in Madrid began to draw a reluctant Catalonia into their orbit. Barcelona never regained its imperial grandeur, so it never had the occasion to replace

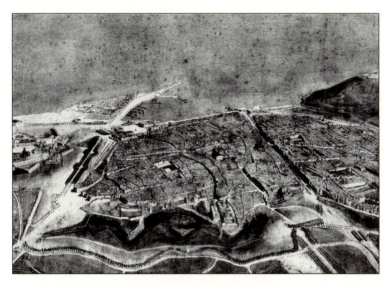

A bird's-eye view of Barcelona

its medieval structures. Instead, the elaborately carved piles of Gothic glory remained, like a stone-gray memory of the city's all too brief moment in the sun.

On the northern side of town, occupying an area nearly a third as large as the city itself, lay the star-shaped fortress of the Ciutadella, a monument to Barcelona's final futile attempt to free itself from its tutelage to Madrid. In the early eighteenth century, Catalonia chose the wrong side in the Spanish War of Succession. (Siding with history's losers soon became a Catalan national habit.) As punishment for this act of retrospective treachery, the man who eventually did succeed to the throne, Felipe V, effectively destroyed the state of Catalonia. Then he razed an entire neighborhood of Barcelona and slapped this gigantic citadel atop the remains. In order to house the displaced neighbors, the chastised city built a narrow grid of tenements on the triangular peninsula that lines the northern boundary of the harbor. The Barceloneta, as it is called, became the home of the city's seafaring population and was the only neighborhood of Barcelona that lay outside its walls. Over on the southern side of the harbor, high atop a craggy cliff, the peeved

Felipe reinforced the panoptic fortress of Montjuic. The fortress supposedly guarded the entrance to the port, but more often than not it cast a glowering eye over the querulous city instead. "Catalonia is best ruled by the stick," a Spanish general famously explained.

Barcelona, the general might have added, is best ruled by its walls. In order to contain the obnoxious Catalans, the central government in Madrid decided to confine the city of Barcelona to the space defined by its medieval ramparts. Outside the stone curtain was little but farmland and meadows, vacant lots stretching toward the nearby mountains like an open stage. Inside, the city squirmed and chafed under house arrest. By the middle of the nineteenth century, Barcelona was a city besieged by its own walls.

Trapped within this topography of oppression, Barcelona turned inward and devoted its restless energy to the pursuit of private gain. Under the blind eye of its military guardians, the city surreptitiously lit the flames of the industrial revolution. The smokestacks of steam-powered factories sprouted like smoldering barnacles inside the walls of the ancient urb. By mid-century, Catalonia had become the industrial heartland of Spain and the fourth largest textile manufacturer in the world, after only the United States, the United Kingdom, and France.

As their experiment with industrialization progressed, Catalans won fame and even notoriety for their *seny*: their practical penny-pinching common sense. This *seny* was canny, full of cunning, what we might call smarts. It was reason with a small *r*, the kind of intelligence that survives the muddy mess of real reality. *Seny* built the machines and factories that turned the city into a giant profit-making enterprise, because *seny* was mainly about money. The very name of the peseta, Spain's currency until 2002, was an invention of the tight-fisted Catalans, or so it was said. *Barcelona és bona quan la bossa sona*, began a standard refrain: Barcelona is great when the purse jingles.

As mechanization spread to the agricultural sector, thousands of landless peasants streamed in from the countryside to fill the factory jobs. Between 1825 and 1850, the population of Barcelona nearly doubled, to approximately 200,000, while the geographical size of the city remained largely unchanged. The buildings grew taller, the streets darker, and the air thicker. At 859 inhabitants per hectare, the population density of Barcelona was double that of Paris and four times that of Dickensian London. In the crush for space, new archways covered the streets and overhanging floors pushed out on top of each other, to the point where inhabitants of the upper stories could sometimes reach outside their windows and touch their neighbors' laundry.

Life inside the hieroglyph was cramped, smelly, and short. Ildefons Cerdà, the civil engineer, grew livid as he described the living conditions of the new working masses, which

> cannot be described as housing that meets the standards established by civilization. This is no more and no less than the stacking of rational human beings on shelves, one on top of the other. The air, the light, the space, the water that nature has provided around us in such abundance . . . are disbursed in the dwellings of the rich as well as those of the poor with a niggardliness that is truly criminal.

Actually, Cerdà elaborated, the dwellings of the rich were different from those of the poor. According to his meticulously tabulated statistics, the rich had an average of 3.6 cubic meters of space per person in their bedrooms, for example, whereas the poor had to make do with as little as 0.9—hardly enough to lie down in. Furthermore, Cerdà exclaimed indignantly, after developers reduced room size for the poor, they took "the next logical step" and reduced the number of rooms. In a typical unit, they put a bed in the sitting room and thus saved themselves an unnecessary bedroom. Then they took out the larder, since poor people "had no food to put in it," and they eliminated the dining room as well, on the theory that whatever food was available could be eaten straight from the stovetop in the kitchen. Next, they decided that the lavatory didn't require a separate room, it only required a drain; so they put it in the kitchen to save on plumbing. Upon further reflection, they concluded that a group of poor families in a single apartment building didn't really need separate kitchens, so they built a common kitchen to serve multiple apartments. Naturally, the astute developers put the lavatory next to the common kitchen, in the stairwell, where it might "perfume every dwelling."

In the crowded bed-sitting rooms of Barcelona, physical privacy was a scarce commodity. "Rare is the Barcelonan," commented one observer, "who before learning to speak has not already learned graphically the manner in which he was conceived." Cerdà writes, with biting sarcasm, "Decorum, hygiene, all are trifles that should have no place in construction."

The statistics support the rage. Cerdà's carefully aligned rows and columns of numbers show a significant correlation between life expectancy and the floor on which an individual lived; the higher the floor, the shorter the life span. In the days before elevators, top floors were always reserved for the poor.

The average Barcelona worker started his or her career as a toddler of seven, put in fourteen-hour days handling steam-powered looms and toxic dyes, received wages calibrated to the absolute minimum of subsistence, and then died at 23.5 years of age. The average member of the bourgeoisie lived over half as long again—although that brought his or her life expectancy to a mere 36.5 years. Diseases such as cholera periodically swept through the filth of the city's dark and fetid lanes and thus performed a macabre service of population control.

It should hardly come as a surprise, then, that Barcelona during the first half of the nineteenth century periodically went up in flames. About every six years or so, the masses would vent their rage in frightening outbursts of violence. Typically, these would involve the torching of convents and factories. The uprisings invariably ended with the application of equal and opposite force by the Spanish army.

When they weren't up in arms, many of the people of Barcelona responded to their pestilent way of life by pining for an earlier, simpler time. Most of them, after all, had only recently emigrated from rural areas, and most still had relatives in ancient villages they thought of as home. One historian famously observed that the basic unit of Catalan history was not the individual but the home—and left unstated the clear assumption that such a home was always to be found somewhere in the misty hills and meadows of the back of beyond.

Catalonia always imagined itself as a nation of the soil. Its heart lay in the mountains, the vineyards, the groves, and the pastures of its bountiful countryside. This is why Catalan culture always had a rough and earthy edge. No account would be complete, in fact, if it failed to remark on the Catalans' absorbing interest in all matters scatological. Catalans would cheerfully discuss flatulence, excretion, and the many varieties of fecal matter with anyone who cared to listen. Unique among Christians, they included within their nativity scenes a homegrown figurine called *el caganer*—literally, *the shitter*—a friendly shepherd taking a break on his way to pay his respects to the baby Jesus. The Catalans' equal and opposite obsession with food arose from the same earthy sensibility. After chewing over the scatological issues, a typical Catalan might next talk for hours about the quality of the ingredients of his last meal: the wines, the latest batch of olive oil, the berries and mushrooms, the grilled rabbit meat, and the infinite variety of *botifarra*, or country sausages. "Eat well and shit forcefully," goes an ancient Catalan saying, "and you need have no fear of death."

The spirit of the countryside was for Barcelonans something mystical, a striking counterpoint to their notorious *seny*. Indeed, every now and then, otherwise sensible Barcelonans were known to lapse into fits of Dionysian rapture. The Catalan word is *rauxa*. In the feverous grips of *rauxa*, a Barcelonan would typically see God and then come back raving about a heroic past, about a time free from external coercion, and a place almost certainly situated in an idyllic countryside surrounded by forests and mountains and rocky cliffs along the shore. Wafting above the gritty reality of urban life were vaporous visions of a long-lost Eden by the sea.

Oblivious to such fantasies, however, the blinkered city of Barcelona hurtled into the future, which eventually arrived in 1848 in the form of Spain's first steam-powered train. The orthogonal lines of the railroad created a shocking contrast to the sinuous forms of the ancient hieroglyph. To many observers, those railroad tracks looked like the very lines of Reason (with a capital *R*), destined to bring order and happiness to the unruly tangle of life in Barcelona. The "magnificent sight" of these new machines, said Cerdà, sent his "spirits soaring to the loftiest reflections on the social order." Like others, he was convinced that this and other modern technologies would lead to the establishment of "a new, vigorous, and fertile civilization, one that will radically transform humanity's way of being."

The railroads, like the textile mills, were indeed beginning to transform Barcelona, but they hadn't yet made much of a dent in humanity's way of being. As Cerdà could see, this new technology had yet to be integrated into the fabric of the city. He described with a mixture of awe and horror what happens when a mighty steam train dumps its human cargo on the edge of a medieval city. A multitude of "all ages, all sexes, all conditions . . . looking like a whole town on the move" spills through the gleaming doors of the new station onto the dark and winding lanes of the old city, only to become anxious, bewildered, and lost in the transition from the new mode of transport to an old way of being. Technology had made the familiar into something strange; it had turned individual human experience into something alien. The most advanced city in Spain was also, at some level, the most inhuman.

For those who could decipher it, the hieroglyph of Barcelona at mid-century spelled trouble. Incarcerated in its own walls, immersed in squalor, oscillating between mean-spirited *seny* and surrealistic *rauxa*, steaming blindly into an uncertain future— Barcelona was a problem crying out for a solution. The problem was, in essence, the same one that faced the rest of western civilization as it underwent its grueling initiation rites in urbanization and industrialization: What is progress? And where is it taking us? How should society mediate the new sets of interests that emerge out of economic, social, and technological change? How can one ensure that advances in science and technology con-

A dark and fetid lane in old Barcelona: Carrer Sant Domènec del Call, 2002. Monturiol lived on this street for a time during the 1860s.

tribute to the improvement of the human condition rather than to its deterioration? In a word, what is the right approach to modernity?

There was no shortage of solutions on offer, however fantastical. Against the gloomy backdrop of a real dystopia, bright visions of a utopian alternative appeared in stark relief. Visions of some alternative future, of an anti-Barcelona, a city that would be everything the existing city was not—spacious, green, clean, and at peace—arose from the twisted streets like a photographic negative of the material Barcelona. Regionalist sentiments fused with progressive ideals to create optimal conditions for the breeding of revolutionaries. Some would seek to overthrow the entire political order, others would aim to change a thing or two, while others would focus their energies on the world of culture and the arts. But among the many dreamers Barcelona produced at the time, none could dream as much or as well, or with such consequences, as the young Narcís Monturiol.

Three

Urban Guerrilla

Monturiol was in his element. He navigated the dank lanes and smoky cafés of Barcelona like a fish in a pond, searching through the stagnant murk for like-minded creatures who would help him imagine a different future.

As it happens, the people who wanted to change the world didn't all know one another. For security purposes, in fact, the progressives of Barcelona never met more than a handful at a time, and maintained only indirect contact with similarly concerned groups throughout the city. One day, as Monturiol later recounted, the conspirators determined to find out just how many fellow radicals there were in Barcelona. They spread the word that all republicans should carry specially colored lanterns that night to identify themselves. Monturiol and his pals set off into the darkness and counted up the lanterns in the different neighborhoods. On returning to their haunt, they were amazed to discover that there were at least forty-eight coreligionists in the city. The late-night nicotine-fueled seminar groups were beginning to turn into a movement.

The leader of the pack was a man by the name of Abdó Terrades. Born in 1812, Terrades, like Monturiol, hailed from Figueres. An intensely energetic and gregarious man, Terrades was also smart and fiercely determined to fight for social justice—two attributes that were bound to get him into trouble in nineteenth-century Spain. While still in his twenties in Figueres, Terrades came across a disturbed young man who, having just read *Don Quixote*, came to believe that he was the real King Micómicon (a *mico* is a monkey). Terrades organized a court for this new king of dementia, appointed himself chief minister, and for two years issued a stream of royal decrees, much to the amusement of his fellow Figuerencs. The authorities, however, were not so amused by all this monkeying around, and they booted the young prankster out of the country.

While in exile in the southern French town of Toulouse, Terrades managed to get himself arrested, along with a group of fellow agitators, on rather implausible charges of seditious, immoral, and otherwise mean-spirited behavior. Terrades got off the charges—surely a lapse in judgment on the part of the French authorities—and returned to Spain with clandestine literature under his cloak, radical political ideas in his head, and revolutionary vengeance in his heart.

He set about organizing local militia groups; wrote the lyrics for "La Campana," the musical anthem of all progressive Catalans to this day; and launched *El Republicano*, a magazine that would for a time become the standard-bearer of the Catalan left. He was elected mayor of Figueres three times in rapid succession, but each time the central government overturned the election. On the fourth go, the government asked him to swear allegiance to the crown. Terrades refused. On the fifth, Terrades finally consented to accept victory and take the foul oath because, he said, it wasn't fair to leave the people of Figueres without a mayor. He became Catalonia's first true socialist.

Under Terrades's guidance, Monturiol joined the staff of *El Republicano* as a writer and signed up for the militia. The two men formed a tight bond of friendship. Terrades would show Monturiol how to realize himself as a man, or at least as a social revolutionary. Collectively, Monturiol and the circle of Young Turks who accreted around the mesmerizing aura of Terrades would form the nucleus of the progressive movement that would ultimately shake the political foundations of Barcelona and Spain in the latter half of the nineteenth century.

✦   ✦   ✦

The reactionaries lost the first Spanish civil war, but the liberals didn't exactly win either. The hostilities came to an end with the regency of General Baldomero Espartero y Fernández. The infant Isabel, now ten years old, ascended to the throne, but her scheming mother was packed off to France while the general ruled the roost. It was an arrangement typical of the time. In nineteenth-century Spain, the generals usually called the shots. Sometimes they would side with the liberals, other times they would side with the reactionaries. Often, the same general would switch from one side to the other with head-spinning ease, because mainly the generals represented themselves. The Spanish army, unlike most of its European counterparts, filled its ranks from the lower-middle classes. Its officers depended on patronage for their livelihoods and would fight for any government that promised to protect their right to serve it.

Although nominally a defender of the liberal cause, General Espartero would soon prove to be liberal only in comparison with the theocratic medievalists he defeated. The youngest of eight children of a humble wagonmaker, Espartero always had the air of a spoiled child. He married a highborn lady and, after further conquests of a military nature, came to think of himself as the Caesar of his day. Unfortunately, his actions in office provided little evidence to support this exalted self-image. In truth, he was a ham-handed politician and through a series of tactical blunders managed to offend everybody to the right *and* to the left.

In 1842, Terrades, Monturiol, and their republican comrades lambasted the "pseudo-liberal" Espartero regime in the pages of *El Republicano*. The pseudo-liberals, not surprisingly, reacted in a rather illiberal way: They imprisoned most of the magazine's editorial board and ransacked Terrades's house, sparking widespread outrage. Terrades and Monturiol escaped arrest. Real revolutionary violence was not long in coming.

Shortly after the Terrades break-in, a group of workers returning from a Sunday picnic tried to sneak some extra bottles of wine through the city gates. Technically, they should have paid an excise tax on the wine. The police stopped them and confiscated their tipple. An angry mob came to the rescue of the bibulous workers. In the ensuing fray, a soldier was killed. As the military readied its response, the local commanding general was heard to say, "Spain can live well enough without Catalonia." His words spread mouth to mouth, and soon the entire city was seething with indignation.

Terrades, Monturiol, and company seized the day. A group of republican sympathizers marched on the city's central square and occupied the city hall. Terrades's militia joined in the rebellion and helped chase the Spanish army out of the city and into the twin fortresses of Montjuic and the Ciutadella. On November 15, 1842, the newly emancipated city of Barcelona declared itself against General Espartero. Militiamen from nearby cities began to pour in to support the rebels.

For a heady fortnight it seemed that Catalonia would rise up from the slumber of centuries and fly away to freedom. Motivating some of the rebels, no doubt, was a nascent sense of Catalan separatism. This particular form of regionalism, however, was emphatically not shared by Monturiol and his revolutionary friends. Their aim was to liberate all of humankind, beginning with the Barcelonans, continuing with the rest of the Spaniards, and ending, possibly, with the Chinese.

General Espartero, in any case, intended to stop the rot in Barcelona. On his orders, the Spanish army troops wheeled the guns of the fortresses around and shelled the city center. They damaged and destroyed hundreds of buildings, but at least they managed to restore the social order. The dents in some of the medieval buildings in Barcelona's Gothic quarter can still be seen.

The bombardment did little to cool local tempers. The following summer, the city boiled over once again. The radicals took to the streets, singing fighting songs, including one memorable ditty in which they promised to "fry up" the useless aristocracy in a "well-seasoned paella." The military government—clearly in no mood to be sautéed—doused the rebels' fire with more cannon shot. In the meantime, though, the revolutionary fever had spread to Girona, Figueres, and other major towns in Catalonia.

Chaos in the streets of Barcelona, 1842: The flying chairs and flowerpots may be taken as a fair representation of public attitudes toward central authority.

Monturiol was all places at once. He was on the front lines when Barcelona was liberated and remained there as the bombs fell. After the government took back the city, he moved up north to Girona. There, at the age of twenty-four, he became editor in chief of the journal *El Centralista*, whence he fired off salvos of revolutionary rhetoric. The journal lasted four weeks, or about as long as it took government troops to overrun Girona and shut the presses down. The renegade journalist then retreated to his hometown of Figueres. By this time his leadership skills had earned him considerable recognition and respect from his fellow fighters, and he was promoted to captain of the First Company of Figueres. Figueres was the last town to surrender, after withstanding a two-month siege.

Although the government forces soon reestablished a grim order in the land, the commotion in Catalonia shook Espartero off his pedestal. Forced to resign from his regency, the fallen general fled Spain aboard a British cruiser.

The progressives' joy at relieving Spain of Espartero promptly turned to dismay, however, when they took a closer look at his replacement. General Ramón María Narváez y Campos was, by all accounts, a reactionary by instinct. His mind was unencumbered by complex political theories. He believed only in *la mano dura,* the hard hand. "I have no enemies," he reportedly said on his deathbed. "I have had them all shot."

Espartero's problem, Narváez figured, was that he had been too soft. So, soon after he became prime minister in May 1844, Narváez put the firing squads to work, and the number of active republicans in Spain subsequently diminished considerably. The militias were forcibly disarmed and disbanded. The reins of government would remain in Narváez's hard hands, with few and brief interludes, for the next ten years. He would rule in the name of Queen Isabel II, who had come of age on her thirteenth birthday in October 1843 and was now monarch of Spain in her own right.

Terrades got off with a jail term, and Monturiol avoided arrest by hurrying off to the fishing village of Cadaqués. Joining him in exile was a comrade in arms, Martí Carlé. Carlé was the twenty-four-year-old Monturiol's first disciple, in a manner of speaking. He hung on Monturiol's every word, served as his accomplice in many a revolutionary deed, and made a habit of following his mentor wherever he went. The two spent long hours walking and talking along the rocky shores of the Cap de Creus. Mostly, Monturiol talked about the fate of the nation, and Carlé listened. Along the way, they witnessed the grueling labors of the coral divers.

Monturiol was in a fragile state. The memories from the trenches of urban warfare haunted him; the sight of coral divers practicing their perilous art unnerved him more. When one day he came upon a group of frenzied fishermen, slamming the body of a drowning diver in hopes of dislodging the water from his lungs, it was too much for him to take. He had to stop the carnage; he had to save the diver.

Shortly thereafter the troubled revolutionary and his faithful follower set off for another hike from Cadaqués. Carlé brought along his rifle and suggested that they hunt for rabbits along the way to the Cape of the Crosses. Monturiol recoiled with horror at the sight of the gun. He could no longer bear anything having to do with guns, he said, and refused to join in the hunt. The two walked for a time in silence. When they reached the Cap de Creus, Carlé went off in search of dinner while Monturiol sat down on a flat rock overlooking the sea and gazed at the ships rounding the cape.

He had a lot to think about. Terrades and other militants had argued that physical violence was a justifiable means to revolutionary ends—reasoning like Lenin, no doubt, that you have to break some eggs to make an omelet. Monturiol remained devoted as ever to the republican cause, but he could not reconcile himself to the prospect of using armed force in pursuit of political goals. After much agitated reflection on the matter, he finally found a peaceful resting place in his thoughts: "I am a revolutionary," he would declare, "but a pacifist revolutionary, a revolutionary of ideas, a revolutionary of consciousnesses. I am the enemy of violence." He was determined to make a revolutionary omelet without harming a single egg.

While sitting on that rock by the sea, though, the reborn revolutionary of consciousnesses nurtured other, still more unsettling thoughts. As he watched the ships round the cape where the coral divers practiced their trade, he began to imagine a vessel capable of traveling *under* rather than *on* the surface of the sea. He pictured joyful coral divers, happily going about their labors in the quiet comfort of a watertight container. He pictured himself gliding beneath the waves in such a craft, in philosophical repose, ensconced in a world of utter tranquillity. So strange were these thoughts, however, that for more than a decade he told no one about them, out of fear that he might be thought a lunatic.

By early 1844, the political waters had calmed enough for Monturiol to return from exile. The authorities were keeping a watchful eye on him, however, so he decided to maintain a low profile. He went to Madrid, where he planned to complete his long-neglected

*A flat rock on the Cap de Creus: Could this be the rock on which
Monturiol conceived of the submarine?*

legal studies. Once in the capital, he rapidly blew through the
allowance his mother sent him and was forced to train as a cashier
to make spending money. But he did finally manage to get his
diploma.

In 1845 he returned to Barcelona, where he never got around to
practicing law. Instead, he published a thoughtful essay against the
death penalty, which at the time was wielded by all governments
with gruesome spectacularity. It was the opening salvo in a long
nonviolent campaign to change the world. In 1846 he set up a publishing house, La Libreria Oriental, in partnership with the ever-
loyal Martí Carlé. So long as the reactionaries ruled in Madrid,
Monturiol would be publishing one journal after another in the
name of radical pacifism, fending off the censors, periodically flee-
ing into exile, and otherwise living the life of a peaceful revolutionary in a time and a place that wasn't quite ready for either
revolution or peace.

Four

The Mother of the Family

Meanwhile, Monturiol's sprightly young pupil, the landlord's daughter, had blossomed into a vivacious woman with dancing brown eyes, an enigmatic smile, and radically progressive political views. They were wedded in 1846. She was sixteen; he was twenty-six. They remained happily married throughout the ups and downs of his long and agitated life. The marriage produced eight children, three of whom died in infancy.

Monturiol was the kind of husband and father who gives those occupations a proud name. Much to the disappointment of would-be psychobiographers and other scandalmongers, everything recorded about his family life paints a picture of happiness, virtue, and love. The many letters he exchanged with his wife and children over the years were, in the words of an early chronicler and acquaintance, "masterpieces of tenderness." In trying times Monturiol would write, "What a consolation it is to have children and a wife so good!" Long after his death, when she was well into her seventies, his eldest daughter, Anna—he called her Anita—would write that "[e]ven more than a father, he was a friend to his family, one of those friends for whom one feels an immense respect; yet to whom we confide, without even being aware of it, all of our thoughts, all of our feelings."

In 1846, overcome with postnuptial bliss, Monturiol founded a revolutionary journal to promote a decidedly feminist version of

Emilia Monturiol i Mata

family values. The journal was called *La Madre de Familia*. "For us the family is the most sacred thing," he wrote in the introductory issue. He promised to defend women against the "tyranny" of men. "The necessity of your education," he told his presumptively female readers, "is imperative."

Monturiol's feminism marked him as a true radical. In his day, the struggle for women's rights distinguished the revolutionaries from the mere liberals—who also favored political equality but on the assumption that equality would be distributed only among propertied males like themselves. Charles Fourier, a French utopian of the time who went about as far out on a left-leaning limb as one can go (in his ideal world, seawater would be converted to lemonade), spoke for all radicals when he said that the degree of the emancipation of the women is the natural measure of general emancipation in any society.

Unfortunately, the degree of emancipation of the women, in Barcelona in particular, was not great. Many could not read, and those who could apparently could not persuade their husbands to pay for the subscriptions to Monturiol's journal. *La Madre de Familia* closed down after eight weeks.

The would-be defender of womankind was crestfallen. In the farewell issue of *La Madre* he frankly admitted that the failure of the journal affected him "profoundly" and awakened in him "sad and disconsolate thoughts" about the "level of civilization" in Barcelona. He berated the city's unenlightened menfolk: "The heads of families . . . are ignorant of woman to the point of keeping her in a degrading situation."

But he didn't sulk for long. Within a month he was plotting his comeback as a revolutionary of consciousnesses. In his speedy rebound to good spirits, Monturiol exhibited the kind of resilience that would bring him bouncing back up from innumerable setbacks to come. His pessimism in the aftermath of failures could be as black as the bottom of the sea, but it was no match for his natural radiant optimism.

By curious coincidence, marriage overtook Queen Isabel II in the same year of 1846. She too was sixteen years old. The prospects for her union, however, were not so happy. The generals thought it expedient that Isabel marry her cousin, Francisco de Asís, an insigficant wisp of a man. She detested him. On the other hand, she was no prize herself. Judging from her portraits, the American writer Washington Irving was not unkind when he said she had a "rough and mealy look." Isabel's failure to find satisfaction in matrimony led her to embark on a series of ill-concealed affairs. She compensated for her sins by developing a religious paranoia, a pressing need to justify her private life, and a constant fear of eternal damnation. She surrounded herself with the kind of people who could salve her troubled psyche, the most notorious of whom

Queen Isabel II, with a distinctly come-hither look

was a nun, Sor Patrocinio, whose stigmata—self-inflicted Christ-like wounds to the hand—supposedly bled at any offense to the Catholic faith. In the queen's household, to be sure, there were many such offenses, and over time they would add up to a serious political crisis, with unexpected ramifications for all concerned in our story.

Five

The Brotherhood

On the rebound from *La Madre de Familia,* Monturiol launched a new journal in 1847 to promote the advancement of all sexes of the human race. He called it *La Fraternidad.* Its motto: "From each according to his capabilities; to each according to his needs." In other words, Monturiol effectively declared himself a communist. The journal's pacifist credentials were underscored in a line that ran beneath the title: "We anathematize force; our propaganda is peaceful." That is, he declared himself a peace-loving communist.

The prospectus for *La Fraternidad* decried the present state of the world, in which social injustice was to be found "in all places and in all social classes." The new periodical, it announced, would

> moralize and educate its readers and bring to the public all the great, generous, and philanthropic ideas that tend toward the improvement and perfection of all the social classes and toward the common goal of education and enlightenment and loving each other like brothers.

Here, as throughout the rest of his career as a social revolutionary, Monturiol showed a disarming ingenuousness in his politics. He took it on faith that humankind is inherently virtuous and that all people would come together in a brotherhood of love if only they were properly educated. His diagnosis of social evils was as innocent as his proposed remedy: "Isolation and selfishness are the problem; association and brotherly love are the solution."

In issue no. 2 of *La Fraternidad*, in any case, the journal seemed to move toward a somewhat more concrete agenda. Now, according to the lead article, the aim was to provide a unifying voice for all the many socialists in Spain and thereby contribute to the formation of a single coherent party of the left.

Monturiol did not conceal his fervent hope that the larger part of humanity would soon join him in this new brotherhood. He promised to publish subscription figures, so that the faithful could see how their numbers grew. In the event, subscription climbed from a few dozen to about 350 issues per week. Assuming that each copy had four readers, it seems that the brotherhood of the human race peaked at about 1,400 members.

What Monturiol's brotherhood lacked in numbers, it made up for in passionate intensity. Monturiol emerged as a charismatic leader. The "freshness and vigor" of his ideas, combined with an "affectionateness" that was never "loud" but rather "reserved, concentrated, and from the heart," as one comrade later testified, inevitably put him at the center of the movement. Not yet thirty years old, he came to be recognized as one of a triumvirate of propagandists for the progressive cause in Barcelona. The other two were his mentor, the irascible Abdó Terrades, and a Young Turk named Francisco de Paula Coelho, a member of Terrades's *El Republicano* group. Among the three, Monturiol stood out for his pacifism and his feminism. In other words, he was the dreamer.

The brotherhood formed a tight circle around Monturiol. They sang songs together, shared intimate secrets, and became lifelong friends. Many of Barcelona's young utopians would follow Monturiol even as he took them on ventures that ran far afield of revolutionary journalism. Some would achieve prominence in their own right. Together, they would plant the seeds for the regeneration of Barcelona in the latter half of the century.

Monturiol's Fraternity included Francisco J. Orellana, a writer who later found fame as a journalist, essayist, and lyricist of revolutionary anthems. Francesc Sunyer i Capdevila, a young doctor from Figueres, and Joan Tutau, another Figuerenc, would eventually occupy political positions of some distinction. Ramón Martí i Alsina (1826–1894) would become a famous painter. The two most talented of Monturiol's comrades, though, formed a curious pair: a musician and an engineer who would spread the word of Monturiol in unlikely ways.

Josep Anselm Clavé was a barrel-shaped, boisterously mustachioed communist with an exceptional ear for melody. Born to a modest family in Barcelona in 1825, he spent his youth busking in bars and cafés to earn a living. His commitment to the working classes came straight from personal experience. He composed a number of catchy worker-friendly songs, with titles like "The Fishermen" and "The Seamstress." His aim was to put to music something about the real experience of the working classes, and thus raise revolutionary consciousness. He also provided the melody for "La Campana," the socialist anthem whose lyrics were the work of Abdó Terrades. When Monturiol's Fraternity took to song, it was usually Clavé's tunes they were singing.

Like Monturiol, Clavé believed that voluntary associations— free from the power of the ruling institutions of society—were the only way to provide a truly liberating education. So he hit upon the idea of forming voluntary associations of choral singers. He set up his first choral society in 1845, when he was only twenty. The oppressed of the land would sing their way to communism, or so the brotherhood hoped.

Ildefons Cerdà, on the other hand, was not the singing type. Unlike Clavé, Cerdà was the scion of a wealthy liberal bourgeois family. He grew up near the mountain town of Vic, in a *casa pairal*—the kind of country seat that all good Catalan families in the nineteenth century could claim and that in our times have been snapped up by an urban bourgeoisie grasping for ancestral roots. The Cerdà country home was a magnificent stone mansion blessed with an abundance of space, fresh air, beautiful forests, and spectacular views of some nearby cliffs. Against his family's wishes, Ildefons left this earthly paradise as a teenager to study civil engi-

A portrait of the musician as a busker:
Josep Anselm Clavé at the age of twenty-six

neering, in Barcelona and then Madrid. Upon graduation, he took
a job with the prestigious Corps of Civil Engineers.

Cerdà was pure *seny*. As a friend later put it, he was "an
algebraic man"; he "thought like a sage, demonstrated like a mathematician, and felt like a child." He soon developed a monomaniacal passion for his work. For him, designing roads and bridges was
just about everything that life had to offer. Most of his acquaintances assumed he had no personal life. Recently, however, some of
his diaries have surfaced. One entry, scratched in with pencil—
unlike the usual, meticulously inked entries—reads: "16 or 18
August 1848, Got married." Farther down, another entry reads: "27
May 1864. Major family thunderstorm. Clothilde [his wife] leaves

*Ildefons Cerdà i Sunyer. In a century known
for its mustaches, Cerdà's stood out beyond the
rest and earned him teasing nicknames among
the café set in Barcelona.*

for Madrid." That they got divorced is hardly surprising, given that he couldn't even remember the date of their wedding.

As a young man, Cerdà's politics were of the liberal sort practiced by his parents; he was a "bourgeois reformist," a biographer says. Monturiol changed all that. Although the engineer kept his distance from the singing brothers, he did form a close friendship with Monturiol. Together, they tackled the great texts of radical political theory. By the time they finished, Cerdà had become a communist too.

Inspired in part by Monturiol, Cerdà began to see that there was more to life than designing roads and bridges; one could design entire cities. While still in his early thirties, he conceived of a whole new discipline of urban planning—a field that would bring together statistics, sociology, demographics, psychology, geography, engineering, and architecture to create flourishing new urban environments. He coined the word *urbanization* to denote the process of creating cities. The object of his fascination henceforth would be "this vast swirling ocean of persons, of things, of interests of every sort, of a thousand different elements . . . this marvelous and exceedingly complex whole we call a city."

If Cerdà was a man of pure *seny*, however, Monturiol remained a man of pure *rauxa*, of exalted passion. In issue no. 5, dated December 3, 1847, subscribers to *La Fraternidad* came across this startling notice. "READ THE FOLLOWING LINES WELL," it began:

> We now promise to reveal (in issue 7 or 8, that is, within the month), repeat, we solemnly promise to reveal the REMEDY that will eliminate all social evils at the root; and this remedy, we do not doubt, sooner or later, will be universally adopted. We are so profoundly convinced that our communication will remedy all social evils . . . that we will give the maximum publicity possible to our *revelation*.

Tell your friends, the paper urged.

Issue no. 6 kept up the suspense: Just wait! the brotherhood said. Matters were finally clarified, to the extent possible, in issue no. 8, of December 26, 1847. The remedy to all social evils, it turns out, consisted of an article lifted from an obscure French journal, an article about some new earthly paradise, a place called Icaria, to be built and managed by a man *La Fraternidad* called "the Great Reformer of the nineteenth century" and "the holiest man since Jesus Christ"—a short, plump, and preternaturally cheerful man, in fact, who was once, for a brief and now long-forgotten moment in time, the most celebrated and influential communist in Europe: the incomparable Étienne Cabet.

Monturiol would never be the same again. Étienne Cabet provided the framework within which he ordered his past and built

LA FRATERNIDAD.

PERIÓDICO DIRIGIDO POR MONTURIOL.

El primer derecho es el de EXISTENCIA, el primer deber es el TRABAJO.

EN LAS SIGUIENTES LÍNEAS.

LA FRATERNIDAD.

PERIÓDICO DE REORGANIZACIÓN SOCIAL,

DIRIGIDO, BAJO LOS AUSPCIOS DE M. CABET, POR MONTURI

Ansiarmatizamos la fuerza: nuestra propaganda es pacífica.

El primer derecho es el de EXISTENCIA, el primer deber es el TRABAJO.

GRANDE EMIGRACIÓN para ir á fundar en América el COMUNISMO ICARIAN

CIÓN FRANCESA.

La Fraternidad, *issue nos. 5 and 18. The changing subtitle of Monturiol's weekly reflects the dramatic revelation of its allegiance to Étienne Cabet. Issue no. 5, in which the paper announced its forthcoming publication of the remedy for all social evils, describes itself as a "journal directed by Monturiol." By issue no. 18, this has become "journal of social reorganization, directed, under the auspices of M. Cabet, by Monturiol." Note, however, that no. 18—the journal's last—was dominated by the recent revolution in France, an event that would dramatically change the fortunes of both Cabet and his fan club in Barcelona.*

the rest of his life. In Cabet's philosophy, he found the archetype for all his visions of an ideal world. In Cabet himself, he found the model of an ideal human being. Étienne Cabet has since been condemned to the crowded margins of history, but in 1847, when history was only a sheaf of blank pages fluttering off into the future, he was, for Monturiol and Barcelona's young utopians, a destiny.

Six

A Word from the Prophet Étienne

Étienne Cabet was born in 1788 in Dijon, also the son of a cooper. He became a successful lawyer and entered the political stage somewhere on the left, although still conspicuously robed in the traditional garb of the liberal bourgeoisie. The impression he made was chiefly that of a corpulent, jovial, and annoyingly garrulous man. Had he not reached the second half of his life, a friend noted, Cabet would have been seen by most as merely "a lawyer, politically inclined, restless, impassioned, narrow-minded, with no education beyond that of his profession, and even so, limited, and superficial." Nonetheless, it seems he was a little too far to the left and perhaps a little too impassioned for the ruling authorities, and in 1835 he was sentenced to exile.

In the winter of 1835–36, at the age of forty-seven, Cabet passed through his dark night of the soul. He was broke, lonely, depressed, and living in London. He sought refuge from the cold and damp in the reading room of the British Library, where he buried himself in Plato's *Republic* and Thomas More's *Utopia*. In the evenings, he held long conversations with Robert Owen (1771–1858), a wealthy industrialist who had risen from a hardscrabble childhood in the textile mills of northern England. Owen had become a radically progressive force in the British economy. He fought passionately against his fellow industrialists to ban child labor—at least, for children under ten years of age. He built a model village for his workers, which he endowed with such forward-thinking features

Étienne Cabet in November 1848,
on the eve of his departure for Icaria

as paved roads, decent housing, adequate sanitation, and education for the workers' families.

Whether on account of his inspiring talks with Owen or as a
result of his daily spells at the library, Cabet regained his natural
good cheer and discovered the truth about human society. Slavery
in the ancient world, serfdom in the medieval world, and the class
system in the modern world, he suddenly realized, were three sides
of the same coin: oppression of the many by the few. Communism

was the only answer. From that point forward, Cabet exuded an eerie air of certainty, as though he had locked his mind in place and thrown away the key. He dashed out a best seller, *Voyage to Icaria*, in which a fictional English lord describes Cabet's own kind of communist utopia. In 1839 the French authorities, perhaps foolishly, allowed Cabet to return to France. He came home in triumph, declaring, "Yes, OK, I am a communist! I am a communist like Socrates, Plato, and Jesus Christ!"

As this last outburst suggests, Cabet's communism was hardly an exclusive affair. In what may be taken as either a brilliant propaganda move or the sign of a weak mind, Cabet insisted that not only Socrates, Plato, and Christ but also Immanuel Kant, John Locke, Napoleon, and just about everybody else of note who ever breathed a word about human equality were, as a matter of fact, communists.

In his potboiler, Cabet describes how communism came to Icaria through the deeds of its founding hero, Icar. Icar was an unbelievably good person from birth. As an infant, he gave his own jacket to a friend who was cold. As a teenager, he charged into burning buildings to rescue old ladies. Icar joined the priesthood, but quit when he saw that the Church did not adhere to Christ's communist teachings. He became the leader of the "revolution and reform party." After a conveniently brief two-day revolt in which the people of Icaria overthrew the corrupt King Corug, Icar was named dictator by universal acclamation. He wisely put in place a fifty-year transition process to communism. Although he died in the year sixteen to great national sorrow, the people of Icaria were so inspired by his example that they achieved communism by year thirty, and thereafter dispensed with the dictatorship. After his death, some of his followers compared Icar to Christ. But, Cabet modestly intones, there was no hard evidence of divine intervention, so he must be classed merely "a Genius Benefactor of humanity." There was more than a little semiautobiographical fantasy in Cabet's book.

In the world that Icar built, egalitarianism is ruthlessly inscribed in topography. Icaria is divided into a hundred provinces of equal size and population. Each province is composed of ten communes of equal size and population, and each commune contains eight equal villages. Icara, the capital city of Icaria—oddly, Cabet could not imagine a utopia that did not have an answer to Paris—is a circle crisscrossed by a regular grid of fifty avenues on a side and divided into sixty *quartiers* of equal size. Each *quartier* has its own school, hospital, temple, and assorted other buildings of various types. Enormous swaths of gardens run along all the avenues and behind every house—Icarians love their gardens. Thus, in Icara, the urban experience is pleasant, efficient, green, and everywhere the same for everyone. The division of geographical space in Icaria reflects the division of spoils in any system that deserves the name of communism; all goods are shared, and shared alike.

Individuals in Icaria are defined by their membership in family, geographical group, and profession. All wear uniforms, but, Cabet assures us, there is plenty of variety in clothing, as each occupation and place has its own color scheme and style. Icaria is family-friendly; adultery and experimental lifestyles are definitely not encouraged. Icaria is also open to various religious orientations. Although Cabet never embraced the church, he did surmise, not without reason, that the Sermon on the Mount is a communist tract. In Cabet's view, education is "the base and foundation of society." Icarians receive instruction on all things from birth— indeed, before birth, if you count the prenatal workshops.

Women, in particular, are specifically included in all activities in Icaria; Cabet, like Monturiol, was a feminist of the pro-family variety. He claimed to have written his book with a female audience in mind. "Above all, we desire the complete emancipation of woman," he declared to his Spanish supporters, "assuring her in her rights and happiness. Mother of the human race, hope for the future, font of all pleasures of the heart; whether as wife, daughter, mother, or sister . . . women will convert this earth into a paradise of humanity."

But Icaria is not your standard back-to-nature earthly paradise. Everywhere you go in Icaria, says our breathless English lord, you see "immense machines." Railroads crisscross the country, and the locomotives even make use of a special mystery fuel that allows them to surpass in power the puny English trains. Flying machines fill the skies, and marvelous steamships ply the waters. There are plenty of factories in Icaria, but—like Owen's, perhaps—they are "clean, brightly painted, and well-lighted."

The utopians of the first half of the nineteenth century were, as a rule, avid fans of science and technology. Henri de Saint-Simon (1760–1825), usually considered the first in the line of utopian socialists, wanted to found a whole new society on the basis of calculations to be derived from Newton's law of gravity. In fact, he adored Newton so much that he planned to canonize him as the patron saint of a new religion of science. Auguste Comte—who remained Saint-Simon's disciple until he decided he was a genius himself—argued that humankind was in the process of emerging from the ages of religion and metaphysics and was now entering its third and final phase, the age of science. For these and like-minded thinkers, the physical sciences were the roots of a new tree of knowledge. Sitting atop the tree, Comte insisted, was a new science called sociology. And just as soon as the tree blossomed—that is to say, just as soon as his books received the readership they deserved—the philosopher-sociologists could climb back down its branches and order society in the best of all possible ways.

All these utopian thinkers were, in one way or another, taking a page out of the philosopher Hegel's book. In the days before Karl Marx co-opted the field of social metaphysics, it was Hegel who presented the most enduring vision of a world whose increasing complexity and interdependence could end only in a singular, all-knowing, morally perfect being called world-spirit.

Cabet was of the same school of thought, if rather more blunt in his words. Of the railroad in Icaria he says simply, "Providence sends it and shouts to the aristocracy, 'Out! Out! The steam coach is coming! Away! Away! Make way for democracy!'" For Cabet, technological progress and social progress went everywhere together, like two seats on the same train.

Cabet may not have been a literary genius, but he did have a significant impact on the politics and thought of his day. His message

VOYAGE

en

ICARIE

par

M. CABET.

—

FRATERNITÉ.

Tous pour chacun.   Chacun pour tous

—   ☷   —

SOLIDARITÉ   AMOUR   ÉDUCATION
ÉGALITÉ—LIBERTÉ   JUSTICE   INTELLIGENCE—RAISON
ÉLIGIBILITÉ   SECOURS MUTUEL   MORALITÉ
UNITÉ   ASSURANCE UNIVERSELLE   ORDRE
PAIX.   ORGANISATION DU TRAVAIL   UNION.
—   MACHINES AU PROFIT DE TOUS   —
AUGMENTATION DE LA PRODUCTION
RÉPARTITION ÉQUITABLE DES PRODUITS
SUPPRESSION DE LA MISÈRE
AMELIORATIONS CROISSANTES
Premier droit,   MARIAGE ET FAMILLE   Premier devoir,
Vivre.   PROGRÈS CONTINUEL   Travailler.
—   ABONDANCE   —
ARTS.

À chacun   ☷   De chacun
suivant ses besoins.   suivant ses forces.

BONHEUR COMMUN.

———

PARIS
AU BUREAU DU POPULAIRE, RUE JEAN-JACQUES-ROUSSEAU, 14.
Dans les Departements et à l'Etranger, chez les Correspondants du POPULAIRE
1848

Title page of Voyage en Icarie. *Cabet seems to have believed that putting his principles into this geometric pattern would make them more persuasive.*

was simple, relentless, and widely heard: All classes should unite as one, they should unite peacefully rather than through violence, and they should name Étienne dictator by universal acclamation in order to lead the fifty-year transition to pure communism.

More effective than his *Voyage to Icaria* in getting the message out was his weekly paper *Le Populaire*. Cabet pioneered the tabloid format: big pages, big print, the liberal use of exclamation marks, and short, punchy articles consisting mainly of true-life stories of hardship and exploitation. His weekly didn't say much of substance that the other left-wing journals of the time didn't say better, but it far outstripped them in circulation.

Cabet exulted in the power that his mastery of the media brought him. According to one contemporary, "He possessed a talent for organization to a high degree and hid, under the exterior of a communicative bonhomie, the instinct and even the qualification for power." Setting the standard for many leftists to come, he proved far harsher with like-minded competitors on the left than with his reactionary opponents on the right. As his network of Icarian organizations grew through the 1840s and spread to include tens of thousands nationwide and in other lands, Cabet began to show unmistakable signs of a messiah complex. He adopted the paternalistic pose of one who is certain of his own omniscience. He faced prospective self-sacrifice with an eerie grin. His apostles described him as "the living martyr of our epoch." Some addressed him as Father Cabet. Others, clearly unencumbered by a sense of irony or good taste, simply called him the Redeemer.

By the late 1840s, however, planet Cabet was spinning farther and farther away from the center of French political life. Dogged by critics to the right and to the left, Étienne saw his chances of being named dictator waning. In the face of appeals from competing utopians, his flock was getting uppity and confused. Then, in the May 1847 issue of *Le Populaire*, Cabet unleashed a thunderbolt and lit up a shining path into the future for the troubled Icarian movement.

Typically, he began by citing the words of Christ: "If thou art persecuted in one city, get thee to another." No longer would he seek to convert the corrupt regime of France into Icaria, Cabet declared. Rather, he and any who cared to follow him would build a new paradise on earth from the ground up—at a remote and undisclosed location, he added suspensefully. He sent out an appeal for volunteers to join him on a voyage to Icaria in real time.

Cabetians around the world were abuzz with nervous excitement. Much speculation centered on the topic of just where utopia was to be located. Despite Cabet's public assurances, it seems, he wasn't too sure himself on the subject. Behind the scenes, he scouted around frantically for a territory that would live up to the promises already issued. On the advice of his friend Robert Owen—who by now had accumulated his own pockmarked track record in building utopias—he settled on northern Texas, a land with "a heavenly climate, a soil that would produce, with scarcely any labor, an unparalleled fruitage." He negotiated an agreement with the Texans that would allow the Icarians to claim one million acres of land, or so he told his readers.

"We can count on ten to twenty thousand Icarians, and very soon with one hundred thousand, and maybe with millions," Cabet boasted. (His math was often fuzzy.) Eventually he settled on a plan to dispatch an "advance guard" consisting of "several hundred" Icarians, to be followed by "one thousand to one thousand five hundred" within a year.

In the summer of 1847, Cabet occupied himself drafting a *Contrat Social* for his proposed community. According to the *Contrat*, the new Icaria was to be a society of complete equals. All property would be held in common. Each individual would contribute to the community according to his abilities; each would receive according to his needs. It was communism, pure and simple.

For those mindful of such details, it should be noted that the *Contrat* was literally a contract, fully enforceable under French law. Among the terms and conditions was a subscription fee. Prospective Icarians were asked to cough up 600 francs—a not inconsiderable sum in those days—which caused some grumbling among the more extreme groups of supporters, who thought it unseemly that the price of admission to communism should be so high. Another clause that drew some attention stipulated that Cabet would be the "Managing Director" of Icaria for a term of ten years. How could it be, the extremists groused, that in a communist state one individual should be more equal than the rest?

For Cabet, everything was on the line. Critics on the left hammered him for seeking to escape from the demands of revolutionary politics in France. They worried that any mistakes on the part

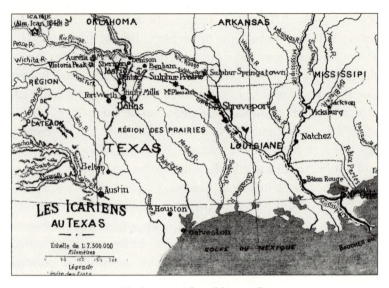

The location of earthly paradise

of the Icarians would damage the credibility of the communist cause at home. Critics on the right exulted in the hope that they would never have to hear from Cabet and his noisome followers again. Cynics of all stripes took it that Cabet had finally crossed the line that divides the visionary from the lunatic. To set up a utopian ideal in the mind as an object of aspiration is noble, they conceded, but to set it up in Texas is insane.

Seven

From Barcelona to Paradise

No such doubts troubled the Barcelona parish of the church of Cabet. "At last the happy moment has arrived for the realization of the Destiny of Humankind," *La Fraternidad* effused in issue no. 10, of January 9, 1848. "From today, communism will be the universal science. . . . The universal era begins with the foundation of ICARIA. The 20th of January is the date fixed for the regeneration of the World."

Monturiol was a true believer. He did not come to utopian communism out of a calculus of self-interest or class interest. His choice was not a tactical one, nor was it based on some belief in the historical inevitability of communism. Rather, he was genuinely convinced that he had found the answer to humanity's many problems, and he was desperate to share the good news.

His conversion to the Icarian movement was sudden, instinctive, and overwhelming, like a divine revelation. Cabet's first announcement came in May of 1847, and the trip was planned for January 1848. That Monturiol declared himself a Cabetian and ardent supporter of the voyage as late as December 1847 suggests that he saw God sometime in November. There was something innocent about Monturiol's ecstatic profession of faith, something childlike in the search for salvation and the palpable longing for a new messiah.

In any case, Monturiol's epiphany proved contagious, and soon his band of followers were infected with the same schwarmerei. In the few weeks that remained before the Icarian vanguard was to depart for Texas, the brotherhood threw itself into a frenetic whirl of activity. Francisco J. Orellana wrote a grandiloquent Icarian hymn titled "Cry of Love and Peace"; Francesc Sunyer i Capdevila penned some articles and contributed his savings to the cause; and Clavé composed yet more proletarian ditties. Monturiol, in collaboration with Orellana, oversaw the translation of Cabet's major works, beginning with the serial publication of a Spanish version of *Voyage en Icarie*. But the chief mission of the feverous Fraternity in these few weeks was to recruit and finance the candidacy of one of their very own to become a member of the Icarian vanguard.

Joan Rovira, a twenty-four-year-old doctor from a coastal region to the south of Barcelona, was the perfect candidate. "My heart tells me . . . that today we begin a new era of virtue and happiness," he wrote in a letter published in *La Fraternidad*:

> No longer will you have games, nor diversions, nor superfluous expenditures; everything will be economy, order, and brotherliness; your looks and your thoughts and actions will no longer be directed to anything other than Icaria, to Icaria, brothers, to our beloved Icaria.

Everything was indeed *economy*, as the brothers scrounged to cover the whopping 600-franc admission fee required to get Rovira into the Icarian vanguard. Monturiol himself put up one of the largest contributions; even his wife, Emilia, chipped in a few reales.

With great sense of purpose, Rovira sold "everything, everything." He tore himself away from his tearful pregnant wife and made his way to Barcelona, where he embraced his brothers, and then on to Paris. There he met up with his fellow travelers. They numbered sixty-nine in total—rather short of Cabet's promised several hundred—but the large rounding error did not stop Rovira from becoming even more ardent in his views. In a letter to the Fraternity he gushed:

> The enthusiasm, conviction, knowledge, and virtue of every one of the individuals, and the spirit of fraternity that animates

them, is so great, so fervid, that the skeptics are confounded and change their views on the possibility of realizing a model society.

Rovira offered even kinder words for M. Cabet himself, whom he described as "the true image of fraternity," a man whose wizened visage "inspires a profound veneration."

At eleven o'clock in the night of January 29, the sixty-nine members of the Icarian vanguard set off from Paris for the French port of Le Havre. A tumultuous crowd of 3,000 supporters thronged the streets to bid them farewell. In Le Havre there followed an elaborate banquet in honor of the vanguard, attended by hundreds of local Cabetians. The sixty-nine wore uniforms especially designed for the occasion: all-black tunics topped with white hats. They sang in hearty chorus the "Chant de Départ," an anthem selected in a competition among their far-flung supporters. After the singing, each took an elaborate oath to abide by the *Contrat Social*, the founding document of their new community. As he surveyed the assembled utopians, Cabet avowed that he "could not doubt the regeneration of the human race." He promised to join the vanguard in America with uncounted hordes of supporters later in the year. On the evening of February 2, the sixty-nine boarded the waiting ship two-by-two (plus one). The following morning, they set off for earthly paradise.

The enthusiasm of the people present on that day in Le Havre and of the wider public of their supporters in France and Spain can hardly be overestimated. To many, it seemed that the answer to the manifest evils of modern industrial life lay just on the other side of the Atlantic, a mere six weeks away. Their timing would prove to be the least of their miscalculations.

Three weeks later, on February 24, 1848, while the Icarians were somewhere in the middle of the Atlantic, Paris tumbled into a revolution of its own. The streets devolved into shouting barricades, the national guard refused to fire on the demonstrators, and a republic was declared. The dominoes fell swiftly across Europe. Munich fell on March fourth, Vienna on the thirteenth, Budapest on the fifteenth, Venice and Cracow on the eighteenth. On the nineteenth, the revolution even reached a pair of unpronounceable cities in the Ukraine—possibly the most remote location on the continent. The winter of 1848 gave way, in the words of a German contemporary, to "the springtime of the peoples."

Monturiol and his comrades were elated by the news. If even the Ukraine was in on the revolution, they figured, surely Spain could not be far behind. They forgot about the Icarian voyagers for the moment and pinned their hopes on the home front. In issue no. 18, Monturiol published a pair of articles on the revolutions, articles that were sober enough in tone but unmistakably hopeful that the dominoes would soon knock down the old order in Spain as well.

Unfortunately, the revolution got held up at the Pyrenees; reactionary forces remained firmly in command in Spain. After Monturiol's inflammatory articles reached the newsstands, the police set off to shut the Fraternity down. Tipped off about the impending raid, Barcelona's utopians hurriedly dismantled their presses and whisked them out the office door piece by piece. They scurried through the back alleys of medieval Barcelona, one step ahead of the law, and set up shop at a new undisclosed location, whence they hoped to continue their antisocial ways. A few days later, however, the police caught up with them and confiscated the weapons of verbal warfare.

In the political tempest, Monturiol managed to slip through the authorities' net. He collected Emilia and their daughter, Anita, and darted up to the north. He deposited them at his mother's house in Figueres and continued on to the southern French town of Perpignan. There he was joined by his trusty sidekick, Martí Carlé, and his revolutionary artist friend, Ramón Martí i Alsina.

For the next year, Monturiol lived the life of an impoverished exile, scrounging for daily bread, huddling with fellow exiles to chew over the same bitter words, and poring over correspondence with other persecuted souls in the movement. He kept in close contact with his old mentor, Abdó Terrades, who was plotting the overthrow of the Spanish government from his own exile in Toulouse and Paris. In order to keep communications confidential, Monturiol corresponded under the appropriately pacifist nom de guerre of Plácido Thomas. Through his comrade Francesc Sunyer i Capdevila, who remained in Barcelona, Thomas aka Monturiol organized the publication of yet more incendiary material. This time it was a journal called, provocatively, *El Credo Comunista*. It was a red rag to a bull. The authorities, predictably enraged at the prospect of a magazine with such an offensive title, came down hard on poor Sunyer. They shut down the journal and locked him up.

In Perpignan, Monturiol pined for his family. Emilia—pregnant for the second time—mailed him a sketch of two-year-old Anita. "When I saw her image," Narcís wrote back, "tears leaped from my eyes, and I kissed it with all the warmth in my heart." He cried still more at the thought that his daughter might not recognize him on his return, placing the blame for his family's suffering squarely "on the tyrants who oppress our country."

In the misery of exile, Monturiol's dreams of paradise only grew more fervent. Utopia, as always, was just the other side of despair. Soon there will be "an Icaria on earth," he told Emilia. Not since Jesus Christ entered Jerusalem, he added, had there been such an opportunity to save souls. The second coming, he seemed to think, was just one revolution away. In the meantime, he urged Emilia, we must learn to "resign" ourselves to fate, for that is the path to salvation.

Emilia apparently took the message to heart. In his next letter back to her, Narcís congratulated her for having resigned herself to their current plight. She must have been doing a lot of reading in her spare time, for he also commended her for her diligent study of "the doctrine that we profess and preach." He acknowledged that the family's situation would not have been so dire had he never embarked on his communist ventures. But when he thought about "how many men we have made just, how many generous sentiments we have awakened in the hearts of men," he knew it was all worthwhile. "No, my dear Emilia, even if we should have to go and beg for bread in the streets, even if this should make me a martyr, never will I stop experiencing the satisfaction I feel in these moments." He would soon make a habit of declaring his readiness for martyrdom.

In July, Narcís slipped into Spain to visit his beloved wife and daughter. While he was planning the trip, Emilia worried that the police might catch him on the way in. He assured her he would travel only by night and would therefore run no danger whatsoever—which was almost certainly untrue. They shared only one day together. The following month, Emilia gave birth to their second child, a son, in Figueres. A fretful Narcís learned the joyful news by post. Later that year, the new mother and her two infants slipped into France for a few days to cheer up the lonely father of the family.

Notwithstanding his own wretched circumstances, Monturiol had not forgotten about his friend Rovira, the highly wrought Icarian, from whom there was as yet no word. Actually, his boundless capacity for humanitarian compassion was now focused on Rovira's wife, Candelaria, who remained in Barcelona—penniless, pregnant, and alone. He pleaded with his friends that they arrange to transfer to her an ounce (or two, if at all possible) of gold. "What I suffer, what I have suffered, and what I will suffer until I know that she has received the money is unspeakable," he exclaimed. Upon receiving the gold, Candelaria thanked Monturiol effusively: "My heart is full of gratitude, and now more than ever . . . do I wish to bring your heart close to mine as a sister."

In October 1848, "sister" Candelaria visited Monturiol in France on her way to join the Icarians in the New World. She took with her a bouncing baby and a frantic enthusiasm for a new life in Texas. As the prospects of revolution at home sank, the hopes for earthly utopia abroad were flying ever higher among Barcelona's exiled Icarians.

Over in paradise, however, fate was busy rearranging plans that had not been particularly well laid to begin with. When the Icarians arrived in New Orleans, they learned that the hundreds of miles of river that separated their Eden from New Orleans was, contrary to earlier reports, entirely unnavigable, so they set off on a grueling march through uncharted wilderness. Like many inexperienced tourists, they had brought too much luggage and not enough money. By the time they arrived at their corner of northern Texas, they had little luggage and no money. Then it turned out that, owing to the vagaries of Texan law and the complex terms of the deal negotiated by Cabet, the million acres they thought were theirs could be claimed only to the extent that they built viable houses on it—at a rate of 320 acres per house, all before a deadline of July 1. Feverishly, they slapped together thirty-two shacks before the deadline, which gave them title to a paltry 10,240 of the promised one million acres, and even then their land was spread over the territory in a bizarre checkerboard pattern. Next, they turned to planting a crop on their checkerboard squares, but the plows promptly broke on the unforgiving prairie soil. By the end of the scorching mosquito-filled summer of 1848, with no crop to harvest and no chance of surviving the winter, the advance guard gave up on earthly paradise and straggled back to New Orleans. Several were lost along the way to disease and injury.

In early 1849, Cabet himself, along with two hundred of the promised "one thousand to one thousand five hundred" Icarian reinforcements, sailed from France and showed up in New Orleans. Among them were the hopeful Candelaria and her infant child. Candelaria's reunion with her husband, however, did not unfold well. Joan Rovira was beside himself. The grotesque mismanagement that characterized the real voyage to Icaria had undone his faith in communism and in Cabet. He confronted Cabet, who swatted the "irritating" Catalan away like a mosquito. Rovira fell into a deep depression. In that bitter winter of 1849, at twenty-five years of age, in the presence of his wife and child, Rovira put a gun to his head and took his own life.

Cabet and his followers remained in New Orleans for some months, bickering about the future of Icaria. Cabet pinned the blame for his own spectacularly bad management on the leader of the advance guard, a longtime lieutenant named Adolphe

Gouhenant, whom he accused of conspiring with "the Jesuits" on an "infernal mission" to sabotage Icaria. (After his excommunication from the Icarian movement, by the way, Gouhenant went on to pursue his own version of the American dream: He became the owner of a successful string of saloons in Texas.) Cabet persuaded the remaining Icarians to join him on the voyage to a new locale, a place in Illinois called Nauvoo, where he had purchased a more manageable plot of land. Nauvoo had already developed a track record in this kind of thing; a group of Mormons had only recently left town on their way to claiming the state of Utah. So the weary Icarians gathered their communal possessions and made their way north, along the Mississippi, to Illinois.

Eight

The Father of the Family

Back in the Old World, the regent of Catalonia declared an amnesty for political undesirables in June 1849. Although it was unclear whether the amnesty extended to those as undesirable as himself, Monturiol took the risk, sprinted back to his enchanted Barcelona, and once again launched a journal. This time it was called *El Padre de Familia: Semanario de educación y moral.*

In this latest journal, Monturiol advocated a wide range of initiatives to improve society. He did not aim for the immediate overthrow of the existing political order, as other revolutionaries might have done. Instead, he sought out opportunities of any size and shape for the betterment of the human condition. He wrote long articles about the right way to bring up children. He proposed the establishment of cooperatives for the construction of workers' housing, a practice later adopted in some places in modern Spain. He argued that workers' families should cook their meals together in common kitchens—the potential savings on groceries and firewood, according to the detailed estimates he provided, were mouthwatering.

One article dealt with a problem that presumably vexed many readers of *The Father of the Family*: What do you tell your young working son when he comes home and says he wants to destroy the machines that deprive workers of their jobs? Answer: Put the matter in context; explain that the machines will also provide workers with better jobs and better products in the future; and that to destroy them is to deny progress, which is as bad as committing suicide. Monturiol, like Cabet, believed firmly in the moral beneficence of technological progress.

On paper, *El Padre de Familia* was, just as the title suggested, all about exhorting people to become better, kinder, and more loving human beings. Underneath the moralizing, though, there was a subtle but forceful political message. "And thus it is," Monturiol averred, "that, in explaining the duties between father and son, between husband and wife, between brother and brother, and between principals and dependents, we also explain the duties between governors and the governed." About seven months of this was all the governors of Barcelona could take. They charged Monturiol with promoting "materialism"—a crime so heinous that, according to their way of thinking, it could be set right only by paying a fine of 50,000 reales. Now, 50,000 reales was a lot of money in those days, enough to buy a two-course lunch with wine for 30,000 people. The fine was so preposterously beyond Monturiol's means that it effectively shut down the journal—which was undoubtedly the intention.

At the time, Monturiol was also at work on a compendium of the teachings of the great thinkers in Western history: Plato, the evangelists, and sundry medieval theologians. He intended to demonstrate, in good Cabetian fashion, that all the philosophers of the past were, in fact, utopian communists *avant la lettre*. When the authorities quashed his journal, they also cut short his book project. Monturiol somehow managed to publish a truncated edition, with a note dashed out at the end indignantly explaining to the reader why the book was only half as long as it should have been: "Our aim was to educate humanity," he declaimed, "but the Reaction has triumphed, and *El Padre de Familia* will be condemned just as were *La Fraternidad*, *El Credo Comunista*, and the continuation of *Voyage to Icaria*."

The outcome was predictable enough, and yet, curiously, Monturiol could not help but take the matter to heart. He could not help but feel the injustice and suffer—suffer even on behalf of those who committed it in ignorance of their own self-interest as human beings. A dozen years of revolutionary agitation had yet to harden his soul, which still rose and fell in waves of uncontrollable emotion every time the just cause advanced or retreated.

By 1850, the old order was back in power throughout Europe, and onetime revolutionaries were either dead or silenced. The fact that the revolution had passed right by Spain did not stop the warlords in Madrid from adopting ever more repressive tactics. For the next four years, Monturiol's political activity would lie suppressed under a heavy blanket of police surveillance.

In the aftermath of the *El Padre* debacle, Monturiol had little room to maneuver. Technically, the government could have thrown him in jail at any moment for failing to pay the fine. But their real agenda was to silence him, so once publication of *El Padre* ceased, the authorities simply allowed his case to linger in a quietly menacing way. Francisco de Paula Coelho, one of the members of the triumvirate of progressive leaders that included Monturiol, was not so lucky. One night in 1851, a right-wing death squad hunted him down in the streets of Barcelona and beat him senseless. He died where he fell.

Though Monturiol was muzzled, his Fraternity lived on in song—literally. In 1850, brother Clavé established his second choral group and called it La Fraternidad. After some months in rehearsals, Clavé's musical brotherhood began to give public performances in the gardens off the Passeig de Gracia. Enormous fun was had by all, often into the wee hours of the morning. But the ever-vigilant authorities shut down the performances two years later, on the grounds that "the working classes should occupy themselves with working, and not singing and dancing."

Nine

Cosmic Awakenings

Facing insurmountable obstacles in his political ventures, the restless Monturiol set off in search of other challenges facing the human race. He took to reading the most up-to-date textbooks in physics, chemistry, and biology. The package of volumes that eventually made all the difference in his life bore the daunting title *Cosmos*. Its author was Alexander von Humboldt (1769–1859), a German scientist and explorer, who in his youth had climbed the Andes and the Alps in search of exotic flora and fauna and well into his seventies was still the golden boy of early-nineteenth-century science.

Humboldt was one of history's great synthesizers. He had no time for those who would divide learning into the squabbling fiefdoms of specialized disciplines. He had a "horror of the single fact," said his brother, an eminent linguist. His multivolume work opened with the galaxies, the stars, and the solar system; moved down through the atmosphere, the weather, electricity, magnetism, volcanoes, fossils, and the oceans; devoted special attention to the distribution of plant and animal life on earth; and concluded with a gloss on human history. The mind has an obligation—a moral obligation, in a sense—to discover the underlying unity of all things, he said. This underlying unity is in fact the order of things; the term *cosmos* refers not to the phenomenal world itself, as is often supposed, he pointed out, but to the singular order that produces it. According to this holistic approach, the universe is like a giant ball of thread: Find the right place to pull, and all its secrets unravel of a piece. *Cosmos* was, in brief, the Theory of Everything, circa 1845.

Like the romantic philosophers of nature who preceded him, Humboldt celebrated the importance of aesthetic apprehension in understanding nature. His pictorial representations of natural phenomena were breathtaking; his writing was self-consciously literary. Unlike the *Naturphilosophen*, however, Humboldt also stressed the centrality of empirical observation in science. There was no shortcut to absolute knowledge, he said; the royal road to wisdom crosses the path of everything that blooms and everything that moves. In Kantian terms, what Humboldt preached was the need in science for both intellect—the faculty of concepts that unify experience—and sensibility—the faculty of intuitions.

What science did *not* need in order to explain the workings of the world, Humboldt suggested by omission, was God. His conservative critics, naturally, were scandalized by his presumption in describing the order of things without including the slightest reference to the Supreme Orderer. More sympathetic readers, however, understood that his intention was not to take a theological position one way or the other; rather, his point was that theology only gets in the way of true science.

Humboldt's world came equipped with a seductive vision of historical progress. "The single idea emerging from history," he wrote, is "the concept of humanization, the tendency to break down the barriers of prejudice and religion, and the belief in mankind as one large community capable of evolving its inherent capabilities." Every age pursues an understanding of the unity of nature, he said, and each age's theory of the universe is the sum of all the worldviews that came before. For Humboldt, the historical expansion of cosmic consciousness closely matched the geographical expansion of European knowledge. Columbus's discovery of the Americas, for example, was one of the epochal events of modern science. The process of cosmic awakening is without end, said Humboldt, and our own theory of the cosmos will one day yield to an even more comprehensive one.

Most appealing for Monturiol was the implicit political message. For Humboldt, the progress of science and the advance of social justice were two stars in the same constellation of human destiny. He believed—like Plato—that knowledge was just another word for virtue and that the accumulation and dissemination of scientific knowledge could only lead to a more perfect society. Although he wasn't a banner-waving communist, Humboldt was a supporter of liberal causes. In an age characterized by racial prejudice, he had the temerity to write, "There are no inferior races. All are destined equally to attain freedom." He offered *Cosmos* as part of a project of scientific education, one he hoped would ultimately unite all social classes in the quest to rid the world of ignorance and oppression. He wrote his multivolume masterwork in a popular, accessible style, so that it might cast the beneficent wisdom of science over as wide a public as possible.

And the program seemed to be working: *Cosmos* was a runaway best seller. One admirer claimed, improbably, that it had outsold every other book but the Bible. "Were the republic of letters to . . . choose a sovereign, the intellectual sceptre would be offered to Alexander von Humboldt," wrote another reviewer. Historians since have seen fit to dignify the first half of the nineteenth century as the Age of Humboldtian Science.

Inspired by Humboldt's hopeful vision of cosmic progress, Monturiol took his first tentative steps as an inventor in 1851, at thirty-two years of age. As he pulled out a notebook in which to sketch some ideas on potentially world-saving inventions, the first thing that drew his attention was apparently the notebook itself. He could see it had been cut to shape by hand. Throughout Spain, students of all ages used similar hand-cut notebooks. As many as 400,000 were consumed every month in the classrooms. There had to be a better way. Monturiol figured that with a more efficiently produced notebook, he could reduce the cost of schooling and make a profit at the same time. He drew up designs for a machine that would cut and fold the notebooks from a continuous roll of paper. Feed the machine a roll, turn the crank, and out comes a complete notebook. He calculated that if he ramped up production to 100,000 books per month, he would recoup his initial investment within two weeks. His indefatigable optimism, it seems, carried over into his business planning.

He formed a partnership with one of his revolutionary buddies from the north, Josep Oliu, to exploit the invention. The machine seemed to work but, unfortunately, Monturiol's business plan didn't. Monturiol & Oliu made a number of notebooks, but Monturiol himself didn't make any money—not the first (or last) time that a utopian communist business venture would fail to turn a profit.

Monturiol was especially proud of his next invention: a cigarette-rolling machine. At the time, tobacco factories employed hundreds of cigarette girls: working women with nimble fingers who could roll thousands of cigarettes in a day. Monturiol built a device that would free these women from such dreary toil and make a better cigarette to boot. Put tobacco into a funnel at the top, supply a roll of special paper, turn a hand crank, and out comes a perfectly cylindrical cigarette. Monturiol, in any case, enjoyed the new smokes tremendously. He hoped to sell the machine to cigarette factories, but the industry did not seem to be ready for such a dramatic reengineering of business processes. While he waited for market conditions to change, he kept the machine in his house for personal use. Around this time, he also conceived of a means for the manufacture of starch from potatoes. The achievement, however, seems to have been confined to the kitchen sink.

Even under oppressive political circumstances, Monturiol the activist was still soldiering on. In 1853 he founded El Quarto, a secret society to promote the publication of subversive literature—so named because its members agreed to collect a quarter (*quarto*) of a peseta weekly from all their friends and donate the proceeds to the cause. Fifty-nine brave souls stepped forth to join the society. Monturiol managed to get out one pamphlet, a tract by a leftist professor proving that the church fathers were communists after all. When the authorities got wind of the matter, however, the fifty-nine members quietly melted back into the bushes, and the *quartos* stopped coming in.

Monturiol had now been slapped roundly on both cheeks. With both his political and his technological ventures in stinging retreat, he considered pulling out of Spain altogether and decided to apply for membership in the Illinois chapter of Icaria. Astonishingly, the tragic end of Rovira had not yet extinguished the torch he carried for the Cabetian cause. To be sure, the reports on life and death in utopia were dismaying. Yet, perhaps because the stories filtered back in vague and contradictory versions, the full horror of the Rovira episode seems to have escaped him. In any case, Monturiol's worldview as a committed communist, like that of many true believers, showed impressive resilience in the face of dissonant facts. In his letter to Cabet, he was chiefly concerned to secure a place in the Icarian community for his wife and children.

While Monturiol waited for a reply, his family, sadly, suffered a decline in numbers. Emilia had given birth three times thus far during the course of their marriage. But the son born during Monturiol's exile in France died after thirteen months of life, and a daughter born shortly thereafter died in 1854, in her fourth year. Only the first-born child, Anita, now seven, remained.

It took a year for the mail to ferry Monturiol's application to Cabet and return the latter's favorable reply. But by then, in mid-1854, the specter of revolution had once again come to haunt Barcelona, and Monturiol decided that his homeland had the better claim on his services.

Ten

The Virtual Revolution

The revolution of 1848 finally arrived in Spain in the summer of 1854. Like the trains, politics in nineteenth-century Spain usually ran behind schedule. On the platform this time were all the stars of the seven-year civil war that had ended a decade and a half previously—a collection of generals and politicians who would continue to trade places for another decade and a half and whose antics would ultimately decide the fate of a revolutionary submarine.

On June 28, General Leopoldo O'Donnell and a few other heroes of the civil war issued a *pronunciamiento* indicating their displeasure with the status quo—by which they meant the other generals who happened to be in power at the time. O'Donnell was a dour, clear-headed, and ambitious man who believed in the monarchy and in the efficient exercise of power—preferably by himself. He wasn't a reactionary, but he wasn't much of a progressive, either. On June 30, O'Donnell and crew simulated battle with government forces—the fighting was long on drama and short on physical violence—and declared victory. But O'Donnell's coup inadvertently knocked the lid off the social order, and events soon bubbled out of his control.

Progressive politicians rallied to claim the revolution in the name of their cause. Still more radicalized street leaders took advantage of the turmoil above to make the revolution their own. On July 14, an unruly mob careened through Barcelona and set fire to factories and convents. A few days later, fellow radicals stormed through Madrid. Power fell to the streets; the iron hand of authority was nowhere to be seen. The strength of the republican movement—after a decade of repression—astonished the political classes.

O'Donnell had little choice but to ride the horse that history sent him; he allied himself with the progressives. Specifically, he called in General Espartero, who, according to the convoluted logic of nineteenth-century Spanish politics, had returned to Spain as the standard-bearer of the progressive cause. O'Donnell, by the way, was not particularly happy with this turn of events. He didn't much care for Espartero, under whose earlier regency he had been forced to live in exile. And it grieved him that his perfectly respectable coup should have suddenly taken on the unseemly overtones of a progressive revolution. Nonetheless, by August, a new regime took power, and the so-called Progressive Biennium was under way. Espartero played the role of president, O'Donnell occupied the all-powerful post of defense minister, and a new congress of deputies acted as the legislature of the government.

In Barcelona, a new civil governor took office on August 11. Pascual Madoz e Ibañez (1806–1870) was the archetypal progressive politician of the time. When he wasn't politicking, he was practicing law, and when he wasn't practicing law, he was writing literary novels and poems and otherwise expressing himself as a man of great sensitivity and advanced ideas. While in political exile in France during the tumultuous 1830s, he had picked up the new science of statistics from pioneers like Adolphe Quételet and brought it back with him to Spain, where he wrote and published a shelf-bending sixteen-volume *Geographical, Statistical, and Historical Dictionary of Spain.* Once in office in Barcelona, Madoz immediately began to lobby for the dismantling of the stone walls that confined the city.

Madoz found a critical ally in the new captain general who took over as the military commander of Catalonia. General Domingo Dulce y Garay was General O'Donnell's right-hand man. A native of the mountainous Rioja region of Spain and a hero from the days of the Carlist wars of succession, he was tough and leathery on the outside but smart and even a little tender on the inside. He was far more committed than his mentor to the progressive cause. He arrived in Barcelona on August 14, ready to extend the new rulers' sway over Catalonia, and saw immediately that the balance of power favored the revolutionary populace. On the day after his arrival, in a show of goodwill toward Pascual Madoz and the people of the street, General Dulce gave Barcelona the one thing it wanted most: permission to tear down the walls that encircled the city.

During August and September, a band of cholera microbes exploited the social chaos and swept through the dank and filthy lanes of the old city. The revolution took a break while many of the city's inhabitants fled to the hills. Of those who remained, 6,000 died in the epidemic. In October, the germs retreated and the citizenry returned from the hills, swabbed the streets clean of detritus, and resumed the business of revolution.

Monturiol felt he was made for the moment. His revolutionary journalism had helped sustain the republican underground for the past ten years. Now republicanism had emerged into broad daylight to claim the streets. Fired with the enthusiasm of the July uprising, Monturiol returned to the city in October and threw himself wholeheartedly into the fight for a new political order.

In November, Monturiol got his first taste of public oratory on a grand scale. Thousands of progressives gathered for the inaugural meeting of the Republican Party. It was the first-ever such meeting in Barcelona's history—a long way from the days in which forty-eight republicans signaled to each other in secret with color-coded lanterns. Leaders of the movement showered the crowd with passionate speeches. Among the celebrated speakers was Monturiol himself.

For nearly an hour he railed against the Catholic Church, which he accused of robbing the poor, stoking the fanaticism of the Carlists, and otherwise impeding the progress of humankind. He called for a separation of church and state, arguing that there should be no official religion in Spain, that all religions should be tolerated equally, and that the state rather than the church should handle marriage and birth certification. He championed what he called "freedom of conscience": the liberty "to think, create, speak, write, publish, print, discuss, teach, to meet and associate, to elect governors and legislatures, to work, to acquire property, and to exercise a profession." He excoriated the "Espartero–O'Donnell dictatorship"; dictatorship, he said, represented the denial of the principle of liberty for which the revolution was fought. In an interesting indication of his growing political maturity, Monturiol specifically set aside his communist objectives, at least for the time being. Theirs was "the age of liberalism," he said, "not the age of communism." The utopian visionary was gradually evolving into a real politician. It was, in retrospect, a remarkable speech—considering the time and place in which it was uttered.

It went over well. According to a pamphlet later distributed, "Many señores rose to congratulate señor Monturiol for his beautiful discourse. There was applause and a general show of approval." On the musician Clavé's suggestion, the gathered republicans then elected a committee of eight to lead their party in the transition to a democratic Barcelona. Monturiol was nominated and elected to the committee. When the rally ended, the new leaders of the republican movement and 700 of the faithful marched en masse to the grave of Francisco de Paula Coelho—the member of the progressive triumvirate who had been assassinated in 1851.

In subsequent days, Monturiol threw himself into political activism. He collaborated with labor leaders, commanders of the newly reinstated militia, and politicians to advance the progressive cause in Barcelona. His hopes for a better tomorrow for Spain were burning brightly.

Things were going quite well on the home front, too. Emilia produced a second daughter, Adelaida, whose birth helped the couple recover from their earlier losses. Monturiol, always the family man, undoubtedly adhered to Spanish custom and took time off from the revolution every afternoon to relax over lunch with his wife and two daughters.

✦　　✦　　✦

Throughout the autumn of 1854, it seemed that destiny would side with the progressives. The citizens' militia, not the army, assumed responsibility for maintaining order in the streets. In January 1855, 80,000 workers in Catalonia joined a general union for the first time, under the leadership of José Barceló, a friend and political intimate of Monturiol. At the national level, progressives managed to institute a series of economic reforms that would set the stage for a capitalist boom. In piecemeal and halting fashion, they rationalized the nation's systems of railroads, banking, highways, telegraphs, and electricity. Pascual Madoz, the enlightened governor of Barcelona, moved up to higher office in Madrid as minister of finance. He put forward a dramatic reform package, aimed at freeing the economy from the dead hand of the church state.

By the middle of 1855, however, it was clear that destiny was going to take the other side. Conservatives led by General O'Donnell wrested the machinery of government from the progressives. Espartero was the first to go. Once again, he had himself to blame. Led by cheering crowds to believe that he was above party and politics, the general had repeatedly offended everybody, on the right and on the left. His hot air was no match for O'Donnell's cold schemes, and in the scuffle he lost his post as president. Meanwhile, newly minted minister of finance Madoz realized that O'Donnell and his queen were no longer in a forward-thinking frame of mind, so he resigned, his reform package largely ignored. Determined to nip the labor movement in the bud, O'Donnell sent a new and much more mean-spirited captain general to Barcelona.

In June 1855 this new military commander of Catalonia, General Zapatero, banned most labor unions and then, just to be on the safe side, executed the labor leader José Barceló. Outraged workers staged a general strike. On the afternoon of July 3, thousands of strikers marched down to the plaza in front of the city hall, where they placed a large banner proclaiming UNION OR DEATH. After the workers left the square, the city authorities took down the banner and locked it away inside the city hall. Upon hearing of the desecra-

Captain Ildefons Cerdà

tion of their standard, the strikers poured back in through the city streets and collected once again in the plaza. Panting and chanting, they demanded their flag back. The mayor refused. A battalion of sappers from the citizens' militia appeared on the scene. The enraged strikers brandished sticks and stones. The sappers nervously gripped their rifles. It seemed certain that the town square of Barcelona would soon be running with blood.

Then the battalion commander—fortyish, tall, balding, austere, and seriously mustachioed—stepped into the fray and demanded calm. "What is it that you want?" he asked the workers' ringleaders. "Our flag," they replied. Seeing no reason why blood should spill over such an insignificant item, the commander marched into the city hall on his own, took the flag, and returned it to the workers. It was a bold and grossly insubordinate act, but it worked. The strikers took their flag and paraded proudly through the streets, singing their favorite workers' anthems, and the city was spared another round of violence. The battalion commander, as it happens, was Monturiol's friend Ildefons Cerdà i Sunyer, the utopian civil engineer.

As revolutionary activism provoked ever greater reaction from the authorities, Monturiol turned again to revolutionary journalism. During the spring of 1856 he rounded up the old Fraternity brothers—Martí Carlé, Francesc Sunyer, and Josep Anselm Clavé, among others—and prepared to publish a new weekly under the incendiary title *La Propaganda Democratica*.

But it was not to be. In Madrid, right-wing forces had found their way into all the major posts of government. In July, General O'Donnell disbanded congress and took personal charge of the government, thus bringing an official end to a Progressive Biennium that had in any case ceased to progress. But the reactionaries were not satisfied with the vigor of O'Donnell's repression. At a ball in honor of her twenty-sixth birthday, Queen Isabel indicated her political preference by spurning O'Donnell's offer to dance and asking instead for the infamous hand of General Ramón Narváez. By October, the man with the *mano dura* was back in the saddle again.

When the new authorities got wind of Monturiol's journalistic endeavors, they hunted down the usual suspects and awarded all they found with prison or exile. Cerdà, whose antics with the flag as a militia commander made him a very suspicious character, wound up in the jailhouse of the Ciutadella for a day. Released the following morning, he ran off to Paris, where he remained for nearly three months.*

A squadron of police hustled Clavé and his brother to the offices of the captain general of Catalonia. The general abruptly told them they had a choice: They could either go into exile or be

---

*In Paris, Cerdà got to know Baron Haussmann, the man who was at that moment redrawing the map of the city with wide avenues and triumphant circles. Although the two apparently got along, Cerdà was later highly critical of the redevelopment of Paris. The wholesale destruction of central neighborhoods—without adequate provision of housing for displaced families—violated his sense of justice. The absence of any real scientific grounding offended his sense of reason. Haussmann's plan was, Cerdà said, merely an exercise in administrative fiat.

shot. The Clavé brothers were not the kind to take such an affront sitting down. In the heat of the argument, they injudiciously chose to engage in fisticuffs with the general and his assistants. The police hauled the pugnacious pair off to the Ciutadella, where they cooled their heels in prison for a few days. The general then relented and ordered them shipped off into exile on the island of Mallorca.

As Clavé was boarding the ship that would take him away from home, Monturiol's wife Emilia rushed up to him in tears. Clavé asked what had happened to Narcís. "They came for him," she said, "but he saved himself." He had fled north yet again to Cadaqués, in the company of the ever-loyal Martí Carlé. Clavé embraced Emilia on the docks, and then she hurried away to bundle her seven- and two-year-old daughters into a coach for the bumpy ride to her mother-in-law's house in Figueres.

The persecution did not let up. While still hiding in exile, Monturiol often slipped into Figueres to dine with his family. One day at lunchtime some policemen showed up at his mother's house. Emilia answered the door. The police stepped in and asked for Narcís.

"He is not at home," she replied.

"And that man sitting at the table, who is he?"

"That's his brother," she said.

Monturiol, without bothering to get up, tipped his head affably and said, "At your service."

Apparently deceived by their cool demeanor, the police retreated.

If the Progressive Biennium ended badly for Monturiol, it did at least provide one unanticipated benefit: It prevented him from taking up Cabet's invitation to join the Icarians in America.

Life in Nauvoo encountered its first minor disruption in 1850, when Cabet was forced to shuttle off to France to answer charges of mismanagement from some disgruntled Icarians before a French court. He got off on appeal and returned to Nauvoo. The crops, at least, were flourishing in Illinois, and the Icarians seemed to be having better luck with their utopian designs. In 1853, Cabet generously offered to relinquish his dictatorship in favor of an elected board. The following year, however, he decided he wanted to be dictator again after all, against the wishes of the elected board. His followers split acrimoniously over the issue. They dragged the matter before the Illinois state courts, which showed no particular interest in resolving fratricidal disputes among utopian communists. In 1856, a majority in the Icarian community finally voted to expel Cabet from the world he himself had created. He and a minority group left to set up their own commune in St. Louis. They took with them the name and global branding potential of *Icaria,* while the so-called rebels kept the farm.

Of all the setbacks in his long career, Cabet said, none pained him so much as this rejection by his own followers. Soon after the split, on November 8, 1856, a blood vessel burst in his troubled brain and he died. Icaria would never recover. Its offshoots splintered several more times and dwindled in size until the very last twig died off somewhere in the American Northwest in 1896.

Cabet's voyage to Icaria proved to be his final tragicomic act on the stage of world history. At about the time that Cabet and his followers first set sail for America, Marx and Engels published the *Communist Manifesto.* Communism would never be the same. In place of Cabet's attempt to unite all the classes, communism would henceforth identify itself exclusively with the working class. In place of his pacifism, it would organize for violent revolution. In place of his primitive Christianity, it would base itself on materialism and atheism. Marx would throw Cabet and a motley assortment of other thinkers—Fourier, the crackpot who wanted to organize the world into millions of *phalanastries* (communes of 1,700 people sharing all their love and money); Saint-Simon, the man who dreamed of a new society founded on religious worship of Newton's law of gravity; and the remarkable Robert Owen—into a single dirty bag, label it Utopian Socialism, and toss it into the dustbin of history, where it has remained ever since. When Engels published *Socialism: Utopian and Scientific* several decades later, it seemed to many that he was kicking a mangy cur that had stopped breathing long ago.

◆   ◆   ◆

Back on the rough coast of Cadaqués, Monturiol was in desperate financial straits. Once again, he had no visible means of support. In order to make ends meet, remarkably, he became a portrait painter. He took lessons on the subject from Ramón Martí i Alsina, the artist with whom he had shared some time in exile in Perpignan in 1848. Martí i Alsina was a friend and member of the inner circle of Barcelona's ex-Icarian revolutionaries. He was responsible for the two existing portraits of Monturiol (pages 15 and 109) and the one of Emilia (page 40). A close friend of Cerdà, he painted a portrait of the great urban planner (page 48), and also produced a fetching landscape of Cerdà's ancestral home, Mas Sardà, near Vic. At the time he took on Monturiol as a pupil, he was a professor of art. But his tenure would not last. Bored with the still life of the academy, he stepped outdoors and developed a naturalist style of painting, focusing on landscapes. His work would eventually make him famous—posthumously, for the most part—but it didn't go down well with his fellow professors.

Most of Martí's instruction took place through correspondence, as master and pupil were living in different places. Nonetheless, Monturiol showed real verve as an artist and began to generate commissions from the gentry of Girona, Figueres, and other major towns in northern Catalonia. The portrait reproduced on page 87 certainly reflects appreciable talent and skill. He did not, however, show any inclination to make art his vocation. He was what one might call a subsistence painter—a journeyman or a hack, content if his work provided enough to keep food on the table.

The year 1856 was the cruelest year for Monturiol, the kind of year when all pathways of the past seem to lead straight to the edge of a cliff, and ahead there is only a void. On the heels of Cabet's death came the news that Abdó Terrades, too, was dead of natural causes at the age of forty-three. Monturiol was thus the last surviving member of the triumvirate that had once figured so prominently on the stage of Barcelonan politics. His career as a

Portrait of an unknown gentleman

utopian revolutionary was over. The erstwhile would-be leader of all peoples was now thirty-seven years old, painting overly flattering portraits of small-town big shots in exchange for daily wages, and living alone, in exile, on a rocky cape in the remotest part of Catalonia.

The ignominious finale of the Progressive Biennium in Spain capped off the series of failed revolutions throughout Europe. In the twelve sullen years that followed, Queen Isabel II and a rotating cast of warlords would dominate the stage of Spanish politics. The people's militia was forcibly disarmed and disbanded and republican parties outlawed. To many, the romantic ideals of the 1840s and early 1850s seemed like a futile illusion.

But visions die hard, and utopia had some life in it yet. To be sure, Monturiol's hopes for political reform had come to grief on the rocks of reaction. Yet that doesn't mean his youthful passion was uselessly spent. After all, every utopia begins with at least one good idea. And even in the history of thought, the law of unintended consequences often decides the course of events. Monturiol's impossible dreams would have such unintended consequences on Barcelona—and, indirectly, on the rest of the world. Utopia went underground, where it spread its roots, biding its time until it could emerge with even greater strength to claim its day in the sun.

Eleven

The End of Utopia

When the stone walls of Barcelona were ordered down in the heat of the revolution of 1854, history handed Ildefons Cerdà the task that would define his life. Outside the soon-to-be-demolished walls of Barcelona there was little but empty space, waiting like a blank canvas for the artist's hand. The city could now build its Extension—in Castilian, *Ensanche*; in Catalan, *Eixample*. It was the perfect opportunity for a man who would make a science of urban planning and perhaps the ultimate challenge for any utopian.

A more high-minded person might have started the project with some reflections on history, contemporary culture, and aesthetics. Not Cerdà. Cerdà was on a mission from Saint Isaac Newton: He was going to build a new city from the ground up on the basis of pure science. There was no space in his logic for historical accident. He would lay his design for the new city around the existing Barcelona as though the old cathedral city were merely an inconvenient stain on the map.

He took a small fortune out of his large inheritance and hired seventy-five men to gather data for the most detailed study of an existing city ever performed in his day. He surveyed the buildings inside the city and the land outside. Mostly, he investigated the actual living conditions of Barcelona's cramped inhabitants. Then he tabulated the results, making use of the new science of statistics imported from France by Pascual Madoz.

In 1856, Cerdà published a *Statistical Monograph on the Working Class in Barcelona.* (This is the source for all the life-expectancy and density figures we have on Barcelona of the time.) In that work, a fiery rage seethes beneath the cool numbers. He shows a table of death rates in Spanish and European cities and notes with chagrin that Barcelona is at the top of the list. The cause, he concludes, is the unbearable density of those 859 inhabitants per hectare—roughly 175 people per half acre.

Armed with this impressive collection of facts—or, at least, statistics—Cerdà approached the design of the Eixample as though it were a problem in higher mathematics. He developed complex formulas to derive the optimal size of blocks and streets. He quantified the number of square meters of garden space, the cubic meters of air, and the hours of direct sunlight required to sustain the average citizen in good spirits. He had a boundless faith in the power of reason to deduce the equation of human happiness. He intended to show by "the faultless logic of numbers" that his plan alone was the answer to Barcelona's future.

No detail of the new city was too fine to consider for the workaholic Cerdà. He drew up plans for sample houses to be constructed on his new blocks, specifying the location of everything from the closets to the kitchen sink. He made a point of insisting on two handrails on staircases rather than the customary one, for safety's sake. He provided diagrams for the appropriate kind of window blinds. He designed a variety of kiosks to occupy the intersections of his new streets. He made more than sixty drafts of his master plan, each drawn by his own hand to the highest professional standard. There is no trace of erasures; he never made a mistake.

Cerdà was clearly all *seny.* Everything added up, everything was practical. And yet, if there is a single word that best describes the plan that finally emerged from Cerdà's prodigious calculus, it would have to be *Icaria.*

Just as Icaria was divided into hundreds of units of equal size and population, so Cerdà's new Barcelona would be divided into hundreds of blocks of equal size and population.

Just as Icaria eschewed any real center, so Cerdà's Barcelona would have no center. Three diagonal avenues joined a few key areas in the existing geography, but even their intersection was for Cerdà merely an abstract point with no centralizing function.

Just as Icara, the capital of Icaria, was divided into sixty equal *quartiers,* each with its own school, hospital, and temple, so Cerdà called each of the 120 five-by-five groups of blocks in his city a *ward* and endowed each with its own school, church, nursery, almshouse, and public space. In Cerdà's plan, furthermore, each ten-by-ten *district* would have a market, and each twenty-by-twenty *sector* would have two parks, a hospital, and a section reserved for governmental and industrial buildings.

Just as Icara had wide swaths of gardens running among all the houses, so Cerdà designed his blocks to be split down the middle by abundant foliage. Cerdà's complex mathematical formulas, furthermore, somehow proved that the streets of the new Barcelona would have to be exceptionally wide—as much as 80 meters—thus making room for more trees, sunlight, and air. In a final flourish of his drafting pencil, Cerdà shaved off the corners of each of his blocks to allow more visibility at the intersections and create still more open space for the city's inhabitants. The unusual blocks became the octagonal signature of his plan for the future of Barcelona.

The parallels between Cerdà's Eixample and Icaria were the result of neither coincidence nor imitation, but rather followed from his attempt to realize the Icarian ideals of liberty and equality in an urban space. Cerdà declared that his formulas were calibrated to maximize the "independence of the individual in the home; independence of the house within the urb; independence of the various kinds of movement in the urban street." He hoped to replace the topography of oppression that characterized the old Barcelona with a new topography of freedom. He guaranteed equality by refusing to interrupt his relentless grid of octagons with any privileged spaces, any centers of a ceremonial nature or otherwise. Cerdà's Eixample would be everywhere the same for everyone. It would be the ultimate egalitarian city. Insofar as the distribution of public goods was concerned, Cerdà's plan was, in the words of a contemporary journalist, "truly communist."

Like Icaria, Cerdà's new city was to be a kind of anti-Barcelona. It was everything the existing city was not: spacious, green, and clean. Cerdà's stated aim was not just to "urbanize the rural," as he said, but to "ruralize the urban"—that is, to create a new kind of rural-urban space utterly unlike the old city. If one were to look behind Icaria for the ultimate source of this image of an anti-Barcelonan utopia, the answer would seem to come straight from Cerdà's past. The spacious leafy blocks of the "ruralized" city were in fact a re-creation of sorts of the country paradise Ildefons had enjoyed in his childhood in the mountains near Vic. Utopia was a transfiguration of the idyll of his youth. This is why Cerdà insisted, with otherwise bizarre passion, that the true etymological root for *manzana* (block) was not *manzana* (apple), but the Latin *mansus*, meaning house, from which derived also the English *mansion* and the Catalan *mas* or *masia*—precisely the term used to refer to the Cerdà family home, Mas Sardà.

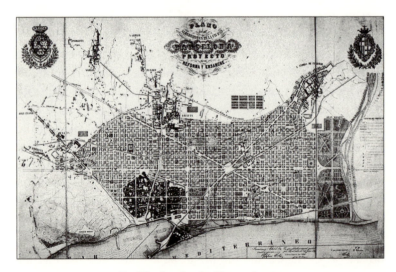

Cerdà's plan for the Eixample, 1859

And yet it would not be accurate to describe Cerdà's plan as utopian and leave it at that. The plan was, if nothing else, entirely practicable in every detail, down to the window blinds. More important, it was a plan that explicitly rejected the utopian delusion that all aspects of the future can be controlled in advance through design. Cerdà repeatedly stressed that his specific layout of the blocks was provisional and that what mattered was the *thought* behind the project, as he put it—that is, its guiding principles and the theoretical evidence on which they were based. He also understood clearly that his urban plan was merely one small piece of the future of Barcelona. It was a framework that would have to be filled in by the city and its inhabitants, through their own spontaneous initiatives.

If he ascribed any great importance to the minutiae of his plan, Cerdà said, it was only because, sometimes, small efforts add up to big change. It is worth citing him on the point, in a passage that curiously anticipates the essence of modern theories of chaos:

> Great effects do not always arise from great causes. Small causes, especially when they provide mutual support and assistance, often manage to produce effects of the greatest significance, as much within the physical as in the moral order. The challenge, in such cases, lies in finding and identifying these small causes and knowing how to give them the importance they deserve.

His own plan—the layout of a city's streets—was, according to this understanding, one such small cause that, if accomplished adroitly, would one day produce effects of the greatest significance.

But if the plan wasn't utopian in the old sense of the word, it nonetheless unambiguously preserved the ideals of an old utopia—specifically, the utopia of Cabet, as purveyed by Monturiol. Without the vision of earthly paradise painted by Monturiol and his fellow Icarians, Cerdà's plan would have had no coherence; it would never have come to be what it was.

Cerdà was, if the expression may be pardoned, a post-utopian. In terms of a Catalan dialectic: Cerdà tamed Monturiol's *rauxa*

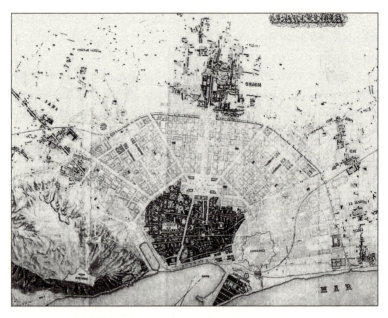

Antoni Rovira i Trias's plan for the Eixample, 1859

with a healthy dose of *seny*. Cerdà himself said, "I am both a revolutionary and a conservative, a reformist and a traditionalist." His goal was to preserve the hopes and ideals of the brotherhood while shedding the delusions of omnipotence that too often led from revolution to dictatorship. In short, Cerdà's Barcelona was designed to avoid the tyranny of utopia in favor of a republic of the possible.

Cerdà was not the only person in Barcelona with ideas about the layout of the city's new Extension. In the years following the decree of 1854, the city's finest architects vied with one another to design the new Barcelona. Soon there were nearly a dozen radically distinct but competing visions on the market.

Antoni Rovira i Trias, a celebrity architect of the time and the darling of Barcelona's ruling elite, produced a design that looked something like a cascade of starbursts. Wide avenues radiated out from the old city—the authentic center of Barcelona—to end in triumphant circles that served as secondary centers, sprouting still more radial avenues. Rovira's motto was *The trace of a city is the work of time before it is the work of the architect.* He wrote the motto in French to give it some class. Other architects and engineers showed similar—if not necessarily so histrionic—deference to the existing city topography in their plans for the Extension.

It was Rovira, not Cerdà, who was the clear local favorite. Utopia—or "post-utopia"—still faced a considerable amount of unreconstituted politics before it could be sure of leaving its mark on the future of Barcelona.

Twelve

The Submarine Dream

On a warm and windy summer morning in 1856, Monturiol set off from Cadaqués for a walk along the shore to the Cap de Creus in the company of his friend Martí Carlé and the latter's son, Victor, who later wrote an account of the ramblers' conversation. Waves from a rough sea smashed into the headland. By lunchtime the hikers had made it to the tip of the cape, where they admired a recently installed ultramodern lighthouse. It was late afternoon as they began to pick their way back among the lengthening shadows of the westward mountains. At a certain point along the trail, Monturiol stopped. He pointed to a flat rock by the sea and turned to face Carlé.

"Do you remember that rock?" he asked.

Carlé stared at the rock mutely. Then he said he didn't understand what Monturiol meant by the question.

"Do you remember," Monturiol asked, "how thirteen years ago, when you went hunting for rabbits, I refused to go because I couldn't bear to use a rifle again? I sat down on that rock and gazed at the sea."

"Of course I remember," replied Carlé.

"Well, as it happens, while I was sitting on that rock watching the ships go round the cape, I asked myself why, if ships can go *on* the surface, why couldn't there be a ship that goes under the surface of the water?"

"Are you serious?" Carlé asked.

"Yes," said Monturiol, "very serious." His glance rested on Carlé for a moment more. "And I know such a ship is possible because it already exists, here, in my head."

Carlé paused to digest the idea. "Tell me," he said. "How is it that you, who have always been my friend and shared everything with me, never told me about this before?"

"Because I knew we would never find the money to build such a craft. And really, because I knew everybody would believe I was a madman for thinking such thoughts."

As the idea began to sink in, however, Carlé responded with unexpected enthusiasm. He urged Monturiol to pursue his dream of underwater travel and assured him that such an idea was bound to find support from other friends and members of the public.

So it was that the vision Monturiol had harbored in his brain for so many years finally came out into the world and, in coming out, became the object of his desire. From that day forward, Monturiol's abundant passion was consecrated to the realization of the extraordinary vision of a ship that could navigate underwater.

That vision was stunningly detailed and ambitious from the moment of its conception. Monturiol made clear in his first writings on the subject that he imagined a craft that would take humankind to the very bottom of the ocean (at least eventually). It would propel itself underwater in all directions, without any link to the land or to the surface. It would interact with the world of the deep in a variety of ways—retrieving objects, depositing them, allowing its passengers to see what was down there—"just as if man were in his own natural element." Most impressively, it would be able to shelter its crew underwater indefinitely, without being in contact with the atmosphere. In his earliest writings on the matter, Monturiol suggested that his aqueous vehicle would extract the oxygen dissolved in seawater with artificial gills, just like a fish.

He even had a name ready for his imaginary craft. "*Ictíneo*," he said, a combination of the ancient Greek words for *fish* (*icthus*) and *boat* (*naus*). The *Ictíneo*, then, would be a fishlike boat:

Its form is that of a fish, and like a fish it has its motor in the tail, fins to control its direction, and swimming bladders and ballast to maintain an equilibrium with the water from the moment it submerges.

But there was a curious double meaning hidden in the name of the *Ictíneo*. "For those who do not accept the change of *naus* into *neo*," he wrote, "the *Ictíneo* is a 'new fish.' As such," he went on, "the word *Ictíneo* defines perfectly my submarine, which is nothing other than an *artificial fish*." In other words, strange as it may sound, Monturiol envisioned the submarine as something like a new species of subaquatic life. More than a fishlike boat, it would be a boatlike fish.

In subsequent months, Monturiol walked away from his revolutionary past. He avoided contact with fellow agitators, withdrew entirely from political activism, and distanced himself from the utopian schemes of Cabet. To be sure, he never abandoned the ideals of his youth, and he remained an unwavering supporter of the progressive cause in Spanish politics. But he now had no time to spare. He had a sole purpose in life.

This remarkable transformation from utopian communist to submarine inventor—possibly unique in the modern history of science and culture—certainly calls for some explaining. Of course, there will always remain some measure of mystery as to why someone in Monturiol's place and time should suddenly want more than anything to build a fishlike boatlike thing. Yet there is a certain logic to the story, even if that logic must inevitably follow a path that diverges from that of pure reason.

Monturiol's first argument on behalf of the submarine was that it would make life better for at least some of the working classes of the world: namely, the coral divers. Rather than risk life and limb in their labors, divers of the future would cruise to the sea bottom in comfort and extract its bounty with the turn of a knob. Fishermen in search of pearls, amber, sponges, and so on also stood to benefit. Thus, the revolutionary's youthful ambition to liberate the working classes of the world now manifested itself in his plan to improve the working conditions of some of its more hard-pressed members. It also seems that Monturiol viewed his submarine project as a prototype for efforts to improve the conditions of the landlocked workers of the world. From the start, he intended to organize the submarine project as an association of committed, working-class types. Like his musical friend Clavé, he believed that such spontaneous collectives, free from the interference of the state and other large institutions, could form the basis for a new civil society, perhaps even a shadow government. While one group looked into submarines, another might look into, for example, airplanes. As a matter of fact, at about the same time that he conceived of a vessel capable of navigating the depths like a fish, Monturiol also imagined a machine capable of flying through the air like a bird. Such a flying machine would also, presumably, alleviate the sufferings of other kinds of workers—stagecoach drivers, mailmen, hunters, farmers, who knows? Just as Clavé's choirs were intended to replicate throughout the land, uniting the working classes in song, Monturiol's technological associations were intended to breed and multiply, uniting the oppressed in the quest for a better life.

Monturiol was also convinced that the submarine would open up any number of opportunities for underwater employment. He pointed out that certain kinds of algae produce fibers that could be used in textiles, and he imagined fleets of *Ictíneo*s harvesting the stuff in vast undersea plantations. He hypothesized that there would be many unusual minerals in the deep, which could possibly be used for the production of new metals by land-based industry. He proposed that submarines be used to lay undersea telegraph cables, linking the world together in a global communications network. He suggested that the submarine—or possibly a mixed-use vessel—might become the preferred means for transporting people across the seas, for it would be able to shelter its passengers from dangerous storms by taking refuge in the deep. He thought that submarines could earn spending money by engaging in deep-sea salvage operations and possibly also in deep-sea fishing.

Even more enticing than the potential economic uses of the submarine, for Monturiol, were the scientific applications. The nature of the earth's crust; the source of ocean currents, waves, and the weather; the biology of ocean life; the behavior of magnetic and electrical fields—all this and more, he maintained, would be revealed by his submarine. In a burst of scientific fervor, he wrote:

> The hour has come to explore the abysses of the sea, those infinite deserts covered with eternal storms that blight the imagination of man with supreme terrors; those hidden depths that human ignorance has populated with nameless monsters, with ferocious whirlpools that devour all that they encounter and lure with their autumnal fury even surface vessels. Now is the hour that reason should triumph over fear and that science should conquer a part of the world hitherto unknown.

Monturiol believed that scientific knowledge could accumulate in only one direction. He adhered to a law-based conception of the cosmos, according to which the universal order consists of the equations that prescribe the behavior of all phenomena—a conception that seduced all the great minds of Western thought since Newton, even if perhaps it might now be ripe for overcoming. According to this line of thought, scientific knowledge advances like a pyramid of stones until it finally touches the sky:

> The Universe is subject to laws that it cannot but obey; human intelligence cannot forgo the study of these laws, for it has the need to know them; every law that man discovers gives him power over Nature; if man were to know them all, he would master the Universe completely.

The laws of underwater nature Monturiol hoped to discover would represent another block added to the edifice of human knowledge, an edifice that would ultimately transform ordinary mortals into the masters of the universe.

Monturiol's passion for science was no accident of talent or circumstance; it sprang from deep within his past as a social revolutionary. All the utopian socialists, from Saint-Simon to Cabet, celebrated the beneficence of technological progress. Just as Cabet argued that the railroads would bring in democracy and haul out the aristocracy, so Monturiol now came to believe that he had conceived of an even more liberational technology, one that would spread democracy across the seas. The submarine would serve as the pilot vessel on humankind's journey toward utopia. (This kind of thinking, by the way, is alive and well as we speak: The gurus who trumpet the democratic virtues of the Internet, for example, attribute to the electronic web the same kind of power that Cabet ascribed to the railroad network.)

But it was Alexander von Humboldt who provided Monturiol with the sturdiest intellectual foundations for his project in revolutionary science. Thanks to Humboldt's mesmerizing vision of cosmic progress, the Catalan revolutionary came to believe that the path to social justice was a side road along the highway of scientific progress and that utopia had more to gain from the scientific education of humankind than it did from piecemeal political reforms.

Like Humboldt, Monturiol saw the expansion of knowledge and the geographic extension of humanity as virtually the same thing. He, too, idolized Columbus. Now, like a subaquatic conquistador, he intended to add the oceans to humankind's dominion. He believed in the giant ball of thread; he believed that if he found the right place to pull he could unravel the secrets of the cosmos. The bottom of the sea was where he hoped to pick up that thread. This is why Monturiol could abandon partisan activism for deepsea exploration and still see himself as ever more committed to the redemption of humankind. He "campaigned with the public for support for the *Ictíneo*," he wrote with unfeigned sincerity, because "humanity has the greatest interest in its realization."

In all these arguments in favor of underwater navigation, one can't help but see a strange mix of passion and sense. On the one hand, it seems that Monturiol—hitherto the archetypal man of *rauxa*—was touched with a newfound *seny*. He did not maintain that his particular contributions to subaquatic science would result in a remedy for "all social evils," as he earlier claimed for his utopian schemes. He was only going to save the coral divers of the world, and then maybe a few other working types. Although, in theory, he still aimed at cosmic consciousness, in practice he set about only to improve oceanography. He dropped Cabet's top-down approach of planning and controlling everything in favor of a bottom-up approach, based on understanding one small thing very well. He believed that in the submarine he had found one of those *small causes*—to use Cerdà's words—that can have "effects of the greatest significance."

Monturiol's trajectory followed Cerdà's in reverse. The arc of his life took him from a youth of *rauxa* in the direction of an adulthood of *seny*. In the end, though, Monturiol's thinking was post-utopian in the same way as Cerdà's. Though still committed to the utopian idea of progress, he now envisioned the perfection of human knowledge as an ideal, something like the asymptote of the line of history. Every addition to the store of human know-how would bring humankind closer to this ideal, yet no particular advance would necessarily create an ideal reality.

On the other hand, a submarine is a mysterious thing, and the conviction that underwater navigation is the key to human happiness is something stranger still. Despite the many reasonable conjectures Monturiol made about the possible utility of the submarine, it seems obvious that what came first in his mind was the vision—the vision of an artificial fish—and all the arguments in its favor arose after the fact. His conversion to the cause of ocean science was sudden and overwhelming, like the utopian revelations of the past. Indeed, if there is a single key to the lingering puzzle of Monturiol's fateful transformation, a single word that unravels the logic of the dream, it would have to be (as with Cerdà's plan for Barcelona) *Icaria*.

In an oddly metaphorical way, the submarine was an embodiment of the Icarian ideal of liberty. In Monturiol's mind, the idea of an underwater contraption with cables attached to a ship or to dry land, or tubes supplying air from the surface, was anathema. The submarine was nothing if not a perfectly free being, capable of moving about on its own, without external support, just like a fish. In his treatises on underwater navigation, Monturiol would make a number of otherwise bewildering claims to the effect that the submarine would "liberate humankind" from "the fetters of the earth's atmosphere."

For Monturiol, the submarine also somehow signified the Icarian ideal of brotherhood. There is no obvious reason to think that a subaquatic vessel should necessarily carry more than one person (or even that it should carry anybody at all). Yet the former editor of *La Fraternidad* always imagined that the submarine would require a crew—not just one individual—and that it would rely on coordinated human muscle power to propel itself through the water. In his vision, the submarine would be home for a harmonious human collective. He anticipated that underwater life would involve the same kind of camaraderie he had experienced in putting out his underground journals. The old Fraternity would live on, he secretly believed, in the safety of the deep.

In a more abstract way, Monturiol seemed to suppose that his submarine world would prefigure the ultimate arrival of a philosophical utopia on dry land. Consider these thoughts on the art of underwater navigation:

> Great is the enterprise of submarine navigation; for it sustains the life of the man isolated from Nature, without participating in Her benign influence. . . . Because, far from the sun and the atmosphere, far from the fields and meadows, it solves the problem of living in the midst of chaos.

Living in the midst of chaos is in a sense the problem we all face in this imperfect world. Utopias, on the other hand, are always ordered from the ground up according to the principles of pure reason. Monturiol's underwater fantasy was just such a perfectly constructed world. His submarine would enclose, in effect, a society grounded in nothing but human intelligence, his very own Icaria.

Monturiol's insistence on describing his submarine as a fish exposed the metaphysical underbelly of his ambition. To draw an analogy between a submarine and a fish makes sense. To call a submarine a new species of fish, on the other hand, is to upend the fundamental ontology of subaquatic life. Monturiol secretly imagined that a machine capable of moving about autonomously underwater—once it reached the requisite degree of complexity, self-sufficiency, and self-organization—would actually come to life. Only later in his career did he acknowledge both the extent of his ambition and the limits of his achievement:

> In vain has man looked for God in the past. The truly free Power lies in what is to come. Just as we are free and powerful in creating our machines, just so will other beings—more complex than we—be free and powerful in creating organisms far superior to man. We do not know how to create anything more than mechanisms and so, naturally, we are mechanics; others will come who are by nature biologists, and others . . . others whom we cannot imagine.

Monturiol was Prometheus. He believed that the advent of a "truly free Power"—the transfiguration of man into god—was the logical destination of human enlightenment. Like Mary Shelley's Dr. Frankenstein, his aim was to create life itself. In Monturiol's case, of course, it was to be an artificial fish, at least in the first instance, rather than a humanoid.

The new life-form Monturiol envisioned was in many ways a photographic negative of this life and of everything that is wrong with it. His utopia of the deep was, in the manner of Cerdà's plan for the Eixample, everything that the city of Barcelona was not. In place of Barcelona's oppressive walls and fortresses, it offered the freedom to roam the sea at will, without limits. In the face of brutal class warfare on land, it promised a harmonious brotherhood of the deep. Instead of cramped and pestilent tenements, it provided a secure and comfortable home with purified air. Monturiol's underwater dream was, at some level, an imaginary new future for the city of Barcelona.

And, as with Cerdà, this longing for the future sheltered a secret pining for an irretrievable past. Catalans undergoing fits of *rauxa* had always dreamed of an idyllic countryside retreat. In Monturiol's case, his countryside was the colorful and ragged coast of northern Catalonia, where he had spent so much of his youth, not to mention time in exile. Possibly, too, it was his father the cooper who somehow suggested to the future inventor that a well-wrought and hermetically sealed container offered the best chance for tranquillity in the face of life's infinite capacity to spring leaks. Just as Cerdà's anti-Barcelona looked very much like the idyllic country manor to which he was born, so the submarine utopia began to look like a shimmering reflection of the perfection the young Narcís had glimpsed in his summers on the shores of the Cap de Creus.

Narcís was in love, in a manner of speaking, with his submarine. All the ideals that had given his life meaning—his love for humanity, his love of knowledge, his love of the land, his love of life—fused like the brushstrokes of a painting in his vision of underwater navigation. But his was no ordinary love. According to the poets, there is a kind of love that is a yearning for the unattainable, a love that is not so much unrequited as unrequitable. That is the kind of love Monturiol had for his submarine.

There is always something otherworldly about utopias. The very word *utopia* can mean both a *good* (*eu-*) *place* (*topos*) and *no* (*u-*) *place*. When he was in London, writing his *Voyage to Icaria*, Cabet suggested that utopia lay on an undiscovered continent on the other side of the world. When he was in France, utopia lay in Texas. If it wasn't Texas, it was Illinois. And so it is with the longing to explore the ocean deep. There is always something otherworldly about the submarine passion. Of the many things that Thales—usually listed as the first philosopher in Western history—might have meant when he said, "All is water," one is surely this: that the source of all things—the primordial soup of creation, the reservoir of humankind's darkest fears and brightest hopes—is the great mother ocean. The desire to penetrate its surface is the impossible yearning for metaphysical certainty in the face of life's chaos, for a union with the cosmos, for a perfect love.

Monturiol's passion had this moment of otherworldliness about it. More than a response to a specific technological challenge, the submarine was for him the answer to all the questions in life for which there are no answers. Even as he began the voyage that would one day take him deep into the muddy waters of the harbor of Barcelona, there remained about his project a lingering sense of unreality, a vague conviction of its inherent impossibility, of something lurking out there, just beyond the field of view, that could not only never be retrieved but perhaps never even properly conceived.

The strange brew of sense and passion—of *seny* and *rauxa*—that drove Monturiol on his impossible quest was neither idiosyncratic nor accidental. Rather, it was inherent in the kind of project on which he had embarked. Monturiol's submarine was a project of *pure technology*. He knew *what* he wanted to build, but he could not know exactly *why* until he actually built it—until he could go under the surface and see what was down there. The real argument Monturiol made for the submarine's utility was really just a statement of hope. Humankind has already reaped enormous riches and a bounty of knowledge from the sea, despite having only scratched the surface, he said. How much more, then—even we know not what—could be expected, once humankind had the whole of the sea at its disposal?

Some inventions respond to specific needs and have a predictable utility. But other, grander inventions anticipate unknown and unknowable needs. They aim to change the paradigm within which human action takes place. That is, they aim to change the world. Monturiol's submarine would be such an invention. It would represent an act of *radical progress*. And that is why his imagination produced the speculative fantasies of a boatlike fish and the strange visions of an underwater utopia. He was attempting to conceive a world that did not yet exist, a world that for him was inherently unknowable, that could be nothing other than a set of ideal possibilities and extrapolations from the world that he could know. For us, living as we do in the age of the submarine, the arrival point of his project seems obvious; for him, it could only be filtered through a dream. The moment of creation is always that way: in retrospect, readily knowable; at the time, perfectly mysterious.

History does not follow a predictable path. As the philosopher Karl Popper has argued, we cannot foresee the consequences of progress because we cannot as a matter of principle know what future knowledge will consist of and what effects it may have. The desire to build a radically new technology requires a leap of faith, a belief in the beneficence of an action whose consequences cannot be entirely anticipated. Possibly, it requires a mystical moment—an inspiration, a vision, and a secret belief in some unattainable utopia. Monturiol, in any case, would never have become the submariner we know today had he not lived the first half of his life as a utopian revolutionary. Nor would he have pursued his submarine dream with such unbounded passion had it not embodied his unattainable ideals of personal and social perfection. Progress sometimes depends on the unreasonable individual and the unreasonable dream—a dream that can change the world, even if, according to the same logic of unpredictability, it inevitably mutates into something other than what it once was as it navigates through the currents and shoals of the material world.

Part II

The Fine Art of Underwater Navigation

A portrait of the inventor in his prime

Thirteen

The State of the Art

Some technologies are invented at a single point in time by an identifiable individual: for example, the telephone in 1876 by Alexander Graham Bell. Others accumulate slowly, gathering bits and pieces from scattered places and times into overlapping fragments, such that the questions about who and when tend to excite some controversy and cannot be answered without many definitions and qualifications. For example, the submarine.

In the era before Monturiol, a colorful crew of inventors descended into the watery world. Sadly, not all of them returned. The world's early submariners were a brilliant, daring, and often foolhardy bunch. They are fascinating in their own right. Together they manifest the profound features of the submarine passion. They deserve special attention here because their work reveals, by comparison and contrast, the nature and rank of Monturiol's ambition and achievement.

Like most such histories, the history of the art of underwater navigation begins with the ancient Greeks. Aristotle, true to form, was the first to go on record on the topic. In a work cited by Monturiol, the great philosopher describes how a diver may supply himself with air by submerging inside a weighted container with its mouth pointing downward. A diving bell, as such a device is known, is something like an upside-down bathtub. As long as you keep it upside down, it traps the air you go down with, allowing you to breathe. A more sophisticated version might have a glass porthole, allowing you to view the wonders of the deep. It is not likely that Aristotle himself got wet in a diving bell, nor is it altogether clear whether he was describing an actual practice or—as he so often did—speculating on a possible one.

On a break from world conquest, Alexander the Great—certainly Aristotle's most wayward pupil—allegedly descended into Athens harbor with one or two friends in a glass globe or a wooden diving bell suspended by a crane, depending on which of the many versions of the story you believe. He/they returned from the briny with somewhat implausible tales about sea monsters and underwater goddesses. Their findings were memorialized in a number of vase paintings and other imaginative works of art. As in most such matters, the thrill-seeking Greeks approached the watery world with a certain spirit of playfulness. They did not expect to change the order of things; they did expect to see interesting sights and enjoy themselves.

The Middle Ages were a dark period in the history of underwater navigation. Thankfully for future historians, the Renaissance witnessed a rebirth of interest in the subject. In fifteenth-century Venice, one Roberto Valtino reportedly created a hand-propelled wooden submarine, although evidence on the matter is about as murky as the water in the canals. Leonardo da Vinci (1452–1519) extended his universal genius to the subaquatic arts. During the gloomy phase of his life in which he occupied himself with weapons of mass destruction, he claimed to have designed both a scubalike apparatus and a military submarine. Judging from the diagrams, the scuba gear would not have worked; human lungs aren't strong enough to suck in air from the surface when they're surrounded by water at the pressures that obtain a few meters below the surface. As for the submarine, Leonardo refused to divulge his findings "on account of the evil nature of men who practice assassination at the bottom of the sea."

Leonardo was the first to go on record with a statement of the long-standing widely shared prejudice that submarine warfare is a particularly ignoble form of human conflict—a point of view evidently still in favor through the late nineteenth century, when a British parliamentarian opposed the development of the military submarine as "unfair, underhanded, and damned un-English."

Nonetheless, it was an Englishman, William Bourne (1535–1583), who provided the first published account of the theory of submarine construction. He devoted a chapter to the subject in his book *Inventions and Devices*. Though a "poore gunner" in the Royal Navy, of modest birth, and self-admittedly "alltogether ignorante" in matters of science, Bourne became a successful popularizer of science and technology—the Carl Sagan of his day. His book offers a lucid discussion of the most fundamental principle of submarine construction: the control of buoyancy. However, it seems that Bourne never applied his theoretical knowledge to the actual construction of a submarine.

Forty years after Bourne's book was published, Cornelius Drebbel (1572–1633), an eccentric Dutchman in the sometime employ of King James I, finally put the theory to use in building what is often considered to be the world's first submarine—assuming that one means a craft capable of propelling itself for a time just under the surface of the water. Drebbel began his professional life as an alchemist in Holland and then became the English king's official inventor—ranking proudly in court alongside the king's dancer and jester.

Although descriptions of Drebbel's subaquatic craft leave much to the imagination, we can safely conclude that the device involved lots of wood, leather, iron bands, and animal grease. According to one source, it looked something like a covered rowboat. In any case, in 1623 Drebbel and crew apparently "rowed" the craft for several miles under the surface of the River Thames. A doubtful report asserts that they reached depths of up to four meters.

Drebbel also claimed to have discovered the "quintessence" of air that sustains life, although if he did so he guarded this secret closely. It may be that he borrowed the discovery from a Polish writer named Michael Sendivogius, who in 1604 described how he was able to produce the "elixir" of life by heating saltpeter. In most histories of science, official credit for the discovery of oxygen usually goes to Joseph Priestley (1733–1804) in 1774, and credit for the theory of just what oxygen is and does goes to Antoine Lavoisier (1743–1794), the brilliant French chemist whose career was sadly cut short by the guillotine. Whether Drebbel used his "quintessence" aboard his submarine is not clear; reports suggest that instead he used a pair of tubes to the surface to refresh the air in the vessel.

King James, in any case, was impressed with Drebbel's submarine show, and he hired the inventor to develop underwater explosives for use against the villainous French. Fortunately for the French, Drebbel's inventions got soggy and didn't succeed in blowing up anything. After King James's death, Drebbel's standing in court foundered and he ended his days in obscurity as a brewer and innkeeper.

Drebbel clearly achieved *something* in the field of submarine development, even if it was never certain exactly *what*—yet there was always an air of magic about his work. Like the alchemy he studied in his youth, the art of submarine navigation for him was a bewitching brew of science, superstition, and showmanship—an underwater disappearing act of sorts.

In the seventeenth and eighteenth centuries, the submarine passion continued to bubble beneath the surface of Western thought. The brilliant German philosopher and mathematician Gottfried Wilhelm Leibniz (1646–1716), also fond of alchemical stews, talked of reviving Drebbel's schemes for underwater travel. At the time, Leibniz also had an idea for an air-powered horseless carriage. Neither of his ideas, it seems, left the safety of his mind. A number of other inventors of the time, however, did construct actual diving bells of various sorts. Perhaps the most successful was Sir Edmund Halley (of the comet), who in 1692 sent a few friends down 18 meters for ninety minutes. He thoughtfully supplied the crew with refreshment air brought down in weighted barrels.

Less successful was John Day, an obsessive Englishman from East Anglia who provides a cautionary example of the perils of the submarine life. "He was a man very illiterate . . . his temper was gloomy, reserved, and peevish, his disposition penurious . . . and unshaken in his resolution," wrote his reluctant accomplice, Dr. H. D. Falck. Day epitomized the misanthropic current that often courses through the submarine world. Fear and loathing of humanity can lead humans to do strange things. Some individuals would rather submerge themselves in the depths than face another day with their fellows.

In 1772, Day managed to spend four hours under 10 meters of water in something like a sealed barrel—all by himself, safe from the exertions of the noisome crowd. Emboldened by his success, he bought a pre-owned fifty-ton sloop, painted it bright red, and carefully sealed all the windows and hatches. One summer day in 1774, he gathered some biscuits, a candle, and a clock, and set his sights on 100 meters for twenty-four hours. At first, despite carrying thirty tons of stone, the bark wouldn't sink. He called for more stones, which some helpers considerately supplied. "She was sunk at 2 o'clock in the afternoon of June 20th," writes the sardonic Dr. Falck, "and Mr. Day with her into perpetual night." Although no trace of Mr. Day's bright red underwater sloop was ever found, the explanation for the disaster is clear enough. At anything approaching 100 meters, Mr. Day's watertight contraption would have been crushed about as fast as a cardboard box hit by speeding juggernauts from every side.

The first American submarine was the work of David Bushnell (1742–1826), a Connecticut native and Yale graduate. At around the time that the American War of Independence was due to start, Bushnell got the idea that underwater craft could be used to launch torpedoes against the mighty British fleet and thus bring the tyrannous King George III to his knees. *Launch* is probably not the right word; Bushnell thought of his explosive weapon as something you haul over to the enemy ship and screw onto its bottom. George Washington—military leader of a nascent country that had almost no naval power to speak of—figured it was worth a try. Bushnell built a one-man sub, the *Turtle*, so named because it looked like two turtle shells, sandwiched together, standing up.

The *Turtle* came with two hand pumps and a valve to let in the surrounding seawater. In order to descend, the pilot would admit water through the valve. Water would accumulate at the bottom on the inside, adding weight, and the craft would sink. To ascend, the pilot would vigorously pump the water out by hand. This would reduce the craft's weight and allow it to float back up. Thus, the pilot had control of the *Turtle*'s buoyancy at his fingertips. Bushnell added a hand-turned propeller to move the craft through the water and a hand-turned screw-on torpedo. A pair of brass tubes supplied air for breathing. The tubes included float valves, which closed as the craft descended out of reach of the surface.

In September 1776, an army sergeant named Ezra Lee piloted Bushnell's *Turtle* in the world's first submarine attack. Under cover of darkness, two rowboats hauled the *Turtle* across the Hudson River and into position near a fleet of British warships lying at anchor. With the tide at his back, Lee guided the craft along the surface toward H.M.S. *Eagle*, the sixty-four-gun flagship of the fleet. As he neared his hapless target, Ezra slipped underwater and thumped into the bottom of the warship. Unfortunately, or so the story goes, his screw-on torpedo was foiled by the copper bottom on the British ship. Meanwhile, aboard the *Eagle*, the suspicious banging noises seem to have alerted the crew to the possibility of foul play. The pilot of the *Turtle* beat a hasty retreat and made a narrow escape. (Revisionist historians now claim that the story can't be right because the *Eagle* didn't have a copper bottom at the time. The new theory is that Ezra was undone by the narcotic effect of breathing his own fumes for too long while handling all those pumps and propellers. Or maybe he got the wrong ship.) Two other attacks were attempted during the war, but without success. Then the *Turtle* was lost while being transported on a surface ship that sank.

Perhaps the most worthy of Monturiol's predecessors was Robert Fulton (1765–1815), the American inventor who won immortal fame for his steamboat. Like Monturiol, Fulton earned spending money in his pre-glory days by painting portraits. At the age of thirty-two he discovered what he took to be his true calling in life: to build a craft capable of navigating underwater. The steam-powered surface ship on which he later made his name was for him second

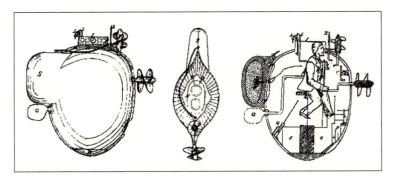

The Turtle

best, an alternative foisted on a world not ready to take the plunge with a work of genius.

The submarine fitted in nicely with Fulton's plans for a new world order. He was an ardent pacifist and believer in free trade, and he maintained that the submarine was "the most peaceful and least bloody weapon" and "a curious machine for mending the system of politics." Specifically, the submarine would improve the human condition by blowing the Royal Navy out of the water, thus guaranteeing "the liberty of the seas" and "perpetual peace" among nations—and also ridding the world of the perfidious English aristocracy. Or so he told the French in 1797, when he approached Napoleon's government with a plan to build a submarine.

As the French fleet was then locked in mortal combat with the mighty Royal Navy, it seemed a propitious proposal. Fulton received some initial support and built a craft he called the *Nautilus*. It had a single interior cavity of approximately six cubic meters, it carried a sail for surface power and hand-turned propellers for underwater locomotion, and it was designed to run just under the surface of the water, at least long enough to sneak up on enemy ships and screw nasty things onto their bottoms. In the summer of 1800, Fulton successfully tested the *Nautilus* in dives as deep as five meters. He managed to stay underwater for one hour and two minutes. Later, he attained eight meters (the limit for his craft, he estimated).

A professor in Paris named Guyton-Morveau, in a review of

Fulton's work, suggested that underwater stays could be extended by developing a system to cleanse the interior atmosphere of carbon dioxide and/or supply fresh oxygen. Fulton, ever the pragmatist, plumped instead for the much simpler solution of bringing down bottles of compressed air. In that way he was able to increase the maximum underwater stay to about four hours.

In a demonstration of the awesome power of underwater explosives, Fulton arranged to sink a scrap boat lying at anchor in a French harbor. Napoleon was not impressed. When Fulton proved unable to arrange the sinking of a real British ship, the French dismissed the American inventor. He promptly showed up in London, where he attempted to persuade the British to allow him to sink a French ship. Fulton was manifestly not the kind of man to let his pacifist principles stand in the way of a darn good invention. The prime minister, William Pitt the Younger, reportedly showed some interest, but the admirals were not keen on the idea of promoting such an ungentlemanly form of naval warfare—especially one that, in the hands of other nations, might undermine their command of the seas. At a dead end in the Old World, the inventor returned to America, where he drew up some improved submarine designs and peddled them to the U.S. government—this time, of course, with the presumed intention of sinking both the British *and* the French fleets. Backing for the project was not forthcoming, however, so Fulton eventually scuttled his submarine ambitions, built America's first commercial steamboat, and died rich in 1815.

Carrying on the tradition of the American submarine after Fulton was Loder Philips (1825–1869), a Chicago shoemaker who dreamed of striking it rich on sunken treasure in the Great Lakes. In 1845, at the age of twenty, Philips launched his first submarine. It collapsed without ceremony on its first outing as soon as it reached six meters of water. His next boat, launched in 1851, cost $241 in borrowed money and was apparently sturdy enough to allow him to take the whole family on an underwater tour of Lake Michigan. He dangled his submarine before the U.S. Navy, but the U.S. Navy didn't bite. The reply he received is illustrative of the incomprehension that so often met the world's first submariners: "The boats used by the Navy go *on* not *under* the water," sniffed one official. Later, when Philips attempted a dive for some sunken treasure, his boat sprang a leak and he made a narrow (and very wet) escape.

Determined to cash in on his expertise somehow, Philips tried to turn submarining into a consumer business. He built a new boat and reportedly sold it to an adventurous Easterner who came into his shop one day with a pet dog. The Easterner and his dog were never heard from again. Bizarre rumors circulated among the locals about the event. Some years later, a salvage crew discovered a wooden contraption resting on the muddy bottom of Lake Michigan. Inside, they found the bones of a man and his dog.

Meanwhile, during the first half of the nineteenth century, France made several contributions to the underwater cause, although none that would merit more than a footnote in the history of submarines. One invention that deserves mention chiefly on account of its controversial role later in Monturiol's story is the diving bell developed by Payerne in 1844. Like most such contraptions, Payerne's device had an open bottom, allowing direct access to the water. His chief innovation was to add a source of compressed air, which was released in the interior as the bell descended, thus keeping the high-pressure water of the deep from pushing into the interior through the open bottom. Payerne tested the craft successfully in the River Seine. Later he took it to the muddy bottom of the port of Cherbourg. He presented his vessel at an exposition in Paris. He also made plans to install a steam engine, but he couldn't figure out how to supply the engine with a flow of fresh air while underwater, so his plans for a motor remained stalled at the drawing stage.

Monturiol's most immediate predecessor and contemporary— and one with whom he was later to share a brief, indirect, and unpleasant experience—was Wilhelm Bauer (1822–1875), a Prussian army corporal who launched his first submarine in 1850. At the time, Germany was dealing with its Danish problem. The Germans believed that the northern province of Schleswig-Holstein was rightfully theirs, but the Danes didn't see it that way, so the

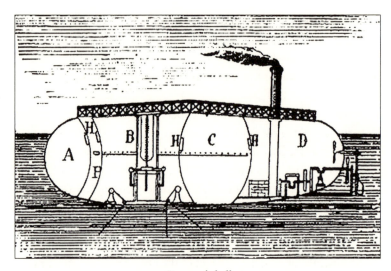

Payerne's bell

Danish navy set in place a blockade of Germany's northern ports. Bauer built a metal-hulled craft, intending to sneak up on the Danish ships and plant explosives on their keels. For propulsion, it relied on men walking on a treadmill connected to a propeller. Bauer christened it with a menacing name: *Brandtaucher*, or Fiery Diver. The name alone was unpleasant enough, it seems, to persuade the unruly Danes to move their fleet farther out to sea while they waited to see what might come of the affair.

In February 1851, Bauer and two comrades treadmilled their way out into a deeper part of the harbor and attempted a dive in 18 meters of water. The *Fiery Diver*'s nose suddenly pitched downward, and the craft glided straight to the bottom, where it got stuck in the mud and sprang a leak. Bauer and crew must surely have been in dread of the kind of hideous death reserved exclusively for the submariners of the world. With incredible cool, however, Bauer persuaded his crew to wait for six hours while the water seeping into the interior equalized the pressure on the exterior of the craft. One source says the persuasion took the form of a crowbar applied to the skeptical crew members' heads. Once the pressure was equal-

The Brandtaucher *(top)*
The underwater concert (bottom)

ized, in any case, Bauer and his mates opened the hatch and escaped, riding in a bubble of air all the way to the surface.

At this point, the German authorities understandably decided they had seen enough of the Prussian and his leaky inventions. Bauer hustled off to England, where he arrived in time for the Crimean War. He persuaded the Royal Navy to fund the construction of a submarine with an open bottom—a diving bell, that is. It was to be propelled by men walking along the bottom of the sea. On a test dive, unhappily, a number of British sailors remained at the bottom of the sea when the bell returned to the surface, and the Royal Navy swiftly relieved the inventor of his duties. Bauer then pushed his wares on both the United States, which turned him down, and Russia—Britain's enemy in Crimea—which accepted.

In 1855, Bauer built a submarine with another menacing name, *Sea Devil*, and took it on a number of successful dives in the Russian naval base at Kronstadt. The limited evidence on the experience suggests that Bauer's vessel was a "bipolar" device: It either floated on the surface or rested on the bottom, spending very little time in between. In one memorable dive, he took down an orchestra, whose rendition of the Russian national anthem was clearly audible to sailors on the docks. In another still more memorable dive, alas, the submarine refused to give up its perch on the muddy floor of the Baltic Sea. Bauer and crew were forced to make an emergency exit, also involving crowbars and a big bubble of air.

No longer in good grace with the Russians, Bauer shopped his troubled submarine project in France. The French had just ended a war, however, and declined the offer. Having apparently exhausted the supply of large warlike nations who might have backed his work, Bauer retired from the submarine business and died, poor and obscure, in 1875. Over sixty years later, when their U-boats were prowling the oceans, the Nazis resurrected Bauer and named him a hero of the German people.

The American submarine returned with a vengeance during the American Civil War. Although the submarines in question surfaced several years after Monturiol achieved his first subaquatic successes and then overlapped with his work for a time, they deserve mention here both because of their pioneering position in the history of the military submarine and because, as we shall see, they later played a role in the Spaniard's own project.

When the Civil War began in April 1861, the Union inherited essentially all the U.S. naval assets and immediately put in place a total blockade of southern ports. The Confederate states were willing to consider any measures, however desperate, to lift the blockade.

In late 1861, an adventurous sugar broker from Mobile, Alabama, named Horace L. Hunley began construction of a submarine craft in New Orleans, in the hope of puncturing the Union blockade by underwater means. Fabricated from an old, six-meter-long boiler, the *Pioneer* was intended to slip under an enemy ship with an explosive torpedo in tow. In March 1862, Hunley completed the construction of the vessel, and the Confederacy granted him a charter to work as a privateer—meaning he could undertake missions against the enemy at his own risk and expense, with a view to earning prize money. In April of 1862, however, a Union fleet captured the port of New Orleans, and Hunley scuttled the *Pioneer* rather than let her fall into enemy hands. Determined to continue with his project, he found another old boiler and built a second *Pioneer*. Before it had a chance to wreak havoc on Union shipping, however, the second *Pioneer* sank as it was being towed in a rough sea.

The Union made a brief foray into the submarine field also, mainly to make sure that it stayed competitive with the Confederacy. In April 1862, the Union fleet acquired a craft called the *Alligator* from a French inventor. The *Alligator* was about 15 meters long and relied on self-feathering oars for underwater propulsion. On its first dive, the crew reportedly panicked after breathing foul air inside the claustrophobic cabin. The navy found a hardier crew and organized a submarine performance for President Lincoln, who reportedly took a shine to the whole submarine idea. Shortly after the show, however, in April 1863, the *Alligator* sank as it was being towed in choppy weather, and the French inventor vanished mysteriously. Later, the Union began construction of a comparable submarine, the bizarrely named *Intelligent Whale*, but did not finish in time for it to see action.

The year 1863 found the rebel Hunley back in the submarine business again, this time with a craft that eventually took on its builder's name: the C.S.S. *H. L. Hunley*. The soon-to-be *Hunley*, too, was made from a recycled boiler, in this case elongated with an

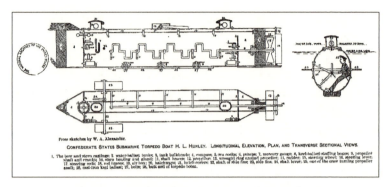

CONFEDERATE STATES SUBMARINE TORPEDO BOAT H. L. HUNLEY. LONGITUDINAL ELEVATION, PLAN, AND TRANSVERSE SECTIONAL VIEWS.

The C.S.S. Hunley: *diagrams prepared around 1902*
by William A. Alexander

extra strip of metal on the sides in order to create an oval cross section. It carried a crew of nine men, with one to pilot the vessel and eight to crank the propeller shaft. For buoyancy control, the *Hunley* sported two ballast tanks, one fore and one aft, both open to the interior of the craft, with taps to admit water and hand pumps to expel it. Two horizontal stabilizers mounted on swivels were used to drive the craft under the water and then back up to the surface. The submarine's life-support system, such as it was, consisted of four 2.5-centimeter tubes to the surface. The inventor scrapped the tow-along torpedo after discovering that sometimes the torpedo would drift faster than the sub could run, exposing the vessel to the embarrassing possibility of a self-inflicted wound from behind. Instead, he installed a spar-torpedo out front, for ramming into the bottoms of enemy ships. In August of 1863, the *Hunley* and its inventor reported for duty in Charleston harbor.

The *Hunley* sank for the first time on August 29, 1863, while still at its dock. The culprit was a passing steamer, whose wake sent water into the submarine's open hatch. Five men drowned in the incident. Several days later, the Confederates hauled the sub out of the water, removed the stiff and bloated corpses (which required the grisly application of hacksaws), and refitted the craft for battle.

The C.S.S. Hunley *refitted*

The *Hunley* sank for the second time on the morning of October 15, 1863. Ten minutes after leaving dock, the forward ballast tank overflowed, pitching the craft nose-first into the sandy bottom of the harbor 17 meters below. All hands perished, including Hunley himself. Several days later, the Confederates once again retrieved the errant sub and grimly hacked away the mess inside. The *Hunley* now came to be known variously as "the peripatetic coffin" and "the murdering machine." "It is more dangerous to those who use it than the enemy," the commanding general of the Confederates in Charleston lamented. And yet, among the fiery populace of rebellious South Carolina, there was no shortage of volunteers to take the place of the lost crew.

The somewhat exasperated officials of the Confederate navy authorized the refitted submarine to attempt another attack, with the proviso that the craft should run awash—that is, just on the surface—rather than underwater, for they had little confidence in its ability to return to the surface should it submerge. On February 17, 1864, the *Hunley* and its unquestionably courageous—not to say foolhardy—crew set out for their rendezvous with destiny. The lookout on the Union sloop *Housatonic* later said that the enemy craft looked "like a porpoise coming up to the surface to blow," which explains why he failed to raise the alarm sooner. The *Hunley* nudged up against the Union ship, speared it with the barbed torpedo, and started to back away. The charge went off with a great thud, ripping a hole in the stern of the Union ship. The *Housatonic* settled slowly in shallow water. Five of its crew drowned, while the rest climbed the rigging to safety.

The *Hunley* and its crew never returned from their date with fate. For more than a century, war buffs speculated about what had happened to the submarine after its successful attack on the *Housatonic*. Then in 1995 a salvage team located the wreck, and in December 2001 the submarine was dredged up from the bottom. Although the exact cause of the sinking is still a mystery, what is clear is that, as it withdrew from the scene of battle, the *Hunley* took on water and plunged uncontrollably, taking nine lives with it to the bottom of Charleston Bay. Such was the price paid by the crew of the first submarine in history to draw enemy blood.

Beginning in 1857 and then continuing throughout his project, Monturiol made a determined effort to understand the achievements and failures of his predecessors and contemporaries. With characteristic thoroughness and diligence, he ransacked the libraries of Girona and Barcelona, interviewed professors at the universities, and wrote inquiring letters to reputed experts. He wanted to learn what he could from previous subaquatic experience and to establish what challenges remained unanswered in the field. Although the information available to him was incomplete and often secondhand, he was able to form a reasonably accurate picture of humankind's major accomplishments hitherto in the exploration of the deep.

Monturiol learned of the theories of Bourne through the work of Marin Mersenne (1558–1648), a French priest who gathered up the Englishman's ideas and sold them as his own. Monturiol's written discussions of Bushnell, Bauer, and Payerne make clear that he was familiar with their work. Possibly he knew of the misguided Loder Philips, for the latter received notice in a journal that covered Monturiol's own exploits. He could only learn of the *Hunley* and its brethren after the events, of course—as indeed he would.

One of Monturiol's chief secondary sources was a French naval captain, Jacques-Philippe de Montgéry (1781–1839). After commanding various French warships in battle, Montgéry achieved fame as a military technologist and purveyor of outlandish ideas. He published dozens of articles on various imaginary inventions, most notably a *"Notice sur la navigation et sous-marines."* He also wrote about Fulton's life and produced an extensive critique of the *Nautilus*. Montgéry himself favored a submarine with rocket-firing capabilities—he was an expert in rocketry as well. Monturiol took particular interest in Montgéry's comments on the unheeded suggestions of Professor Guyton-Morveau to Fulton concerning the maintenance of the interior atmosphere of the submarine.

The most curious thing about the French captain, though, was that he was a utopian socialist and an intimate of the founder of the movement, Henri de Saint-Simon, who at the time was collecting as many men of science as he could to support his project for the creation of a new society based on the religion of science. A frequent visitor to Saint-Simon's cluttered Paris apartment, Montgéry did his bit for the cause by entertaining "strange ideas about floating mines and submarine warfare." When in 1838 Montgéry suffered an "attack of madness," it was Saint-Simon's estranged disciple, Auguste Comte, who came to see him at the insane asylum and made the appropriate arrangements concerning the captain's working-class mistress. Comte's succor, sadly, was of no avail, and Montgéry died unhappy in the following year.

One principal lesson of the early history of underwater navigation is that there was no single inventor of the submarine (in the broadest sense of the word). Many individuals made many efforts in the field with varying degrees of success, and they did so largely independently of one another. At least up until Monturiol's day, there was no unified body of knowledge about subaquatic technology, no tradition of collaboration and competition. The only thing the early submariners shared was their unearthly desire to travel beneath the surface of the sea.

This brings up a second lesson from history: The early submariners of the world were, to put it politely, a rather unconventional crew. At the extreme, they were charlatans and crackpots. Even the saner ones were highly unorthodox thinkers. As a group they stood outside the mainstream of society, which may explain one of the most curious features—the connection between subaquatic technology and the political underground. That there should have been three utopian-pacifist submariners in the world—Fulton, Montgéry, and Monturiol—suggests that this link is more than incidental. In part, it seems that those who believed in technological fixes to social problems seized on the submarine as a tool for eliminating the evil of maritime aggression. More than that, something about the otherworldliness of the deep attracted those who wished to transfigure the world on the surface.

But the most important lesson from the history, as Monturiol himself saw, was that the submarine tradition had been decisively shaped—more precisely, *misshaped*—by military interests. The most intense periods of submarine development so far had coincided precisely with wars: the American War of Independence, the Napoleonic Wars, the Schleswig-Holstein affair, the Crimean War, and (still to come) the American Civil War. In all cases, it was the weaker naval power that resorted to underwater means of destroying surface fleets. Even pacifists like Fulton and utopians like Montgéry conceived of their submarines as delivery systems for weapons of war; Bushnell and Bauer, of course, made no bones about their warlike aims.

Submarine designers intent on making war machines responded to a distinct and restricted set of challenges. In Monturiol's later analysis:

> All of these inventors propose, not submarine navigation in the full extension of the word, but rather, basing their craft on the principle that the external pressure should be equal to the internal pressure, the most to which they have been able to aspire has been to destroy enemy boats.

He had a point—although possibly he expressed it backward. For Monturiol's militaristic predecessors, the surface of the water was a shield under which their craft could approach an enemy with stealth. They had no interest in exploring the depths; they merely wanted to get out of the light. That is why their vessels were not designed to withstand the intense pressures found deep underwater. Nor did Monturiol's predecessors have much interest in remaining submerged any longer than it would take to sneak up on an enemy ship. In sum, the military-minded submariners conceived of underwater navigation as something that would happen for brief periods just under the surface of the sea. The capabilities of their inventions were the consequence of their mission (not the reverse, as Monturiol appears to suggest).

Monturiol approached the problem of submarine development free from the constraints of military expediency. He had no war on his hands, and he was not counting on defense contracts to build his dream. In his first memorandum on underwater navigation, written in 1858, he mentions the possibility of military applications for the submarine only once, and even then only parenthetically, to say that such applications did not enter into his considerations.

As for the small number of nonmilitary devices heretofore used to take men into the deep, such as Halley's, Day's, and Payerne's contraptions, Monturiol argued that these were mainly updated versions of Aristotle's diving bell. There are two fundamental problems with the diving bell, Monturiol wrote in 1858. First, the open exposure to the pressure of the water limits the depth of immersion to whatever it is that human beings can stand. In other words, a diving bell would never make it to the bottom of the ocean. Second, the line linking the bell to the surface impedes the free movement of the craft. A diving bell could hardly be expected to roam the deep as freely and easily as a fish. "The destiny of the diving bell," he concluded, "is to work in ports and rivers. Everything else belongs to what we properly call submarine navigation, to the *Ictíneo*s of exploration."

Monturiol offered a further subtle yet penetrating criticism of his predecessors. The legacy of the early submariners was long on amusing anecdotes but short on technical specifications. They were an unforthcoming bunch—happy enough to boast of their subaquatic exploits but careful to leave their technological discoveries shrouded in the murk. This secretiveness, too, undoubtedly had its roots in the military orientation of their work. Because Monturiol conceived of the art of underwater navigation as a branch of science, he understood that it was ultimately a body of knowledge, that this body of knowledge would have to stand independently of any particular contraption, and that it would have to be studied and verified by many independent observers and practitioners. From the start of his own project, then, he was determined to put his accumulated knowledge on a secure foundation and share it with the public as soon as possible.

Monturiol had a clear idea of what a submarine should do: It should be able to descend to any depth in the ocean, move about at will, interact with the environment in a variety of useful ways, and be able to remain down there *indefinitely*. This, in essence, is what distinguishes him from everyone who came before. None of the early submariners—not Bushnell, not Fulton, not Bauer—had dared imagine, let alone build, a craft that would answer to such a comprehensive conception. (Nor, for that matter, would Hunley even attempt such a project, when his turn came.) No one had built a craft that could reliably descend below the first few meters of surface water (and return!), no one had built a craft capable of propelling itself at a safe velocity underwater, no one had built a craft capable of interacting with the environment (except perhaps to blow things up), and no one had even thought to develop a means to sustain human life indefinitely while out of contact with the earth's atmosphere.

"The problem of underwater navigation, in all fundamental respects, remains to be solved," Monturiol wrote in 1858. All things considered, he was right. Despite some outstanding efforts, his predecessors populate a kind of prehistory of the submarine. Monturiol's ambition was nothing less than to create the world's first true submarine. His achievement would herald the dawn of the submarine age.

Fourteen

The Adventure Begins

Friendship, said Aristotle, "stimulates men to noble actions, for with friends men are more able both to think and to act." Such was the case with Monturiol as he set off in pursuit of his submarine dream. Despite recent political setbacks, the unemployed utopians of Catalonia still held in high esteem the last surviving member of the progressive triumvirate, and they seem to have had little difficulty in grasping the transcendental significance of his underwater vision. As word of Monturiol's unearthly idea spread among the wandering tribe of ex-Icarians, expressions of encouragement and support echoed across the land.

Martí Carlé, the old friend with whom Monturiol first shared his subaquatic vision, took it upon himself to launch a fundraising crusade on behalf of Monturiol and his submarine. Astonishingly, it worked. Twenty of Monturiol's friends and acquaintances promised hard cash for the project. Some were moderately wealthy residents of his home state, the Alt Empordà. Others, like Carlé himself and the old Fraternity brother Francesc Sunyer i Capdevila, were rich mainly in enthusiasm. Most were members of the class of skilled artisans, the petite bourgeoisie. Their number included a baker, a cobbler, a blacksmith, a tinsmith, several shopkeepers, a doctor, and a medical student.

Emboldened by the show of affirmation from his friends, Monturiol cast aside his paintbrushes along with any hope for a stable career and threw himself wholeheartedly into organizing

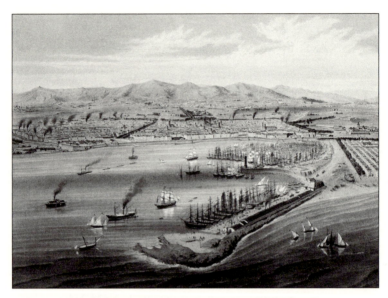

The harbor of Barcelona: view from a balloon, 1856.
The construction of the Ictíneo *took place in the area*
in the foreground of this illustration, near the tip
of the peninsula of the Barceloneta.

the submarine venture. On October 23, 1857, he and his twenty backers signed the founding charter of the association in whose name he would build his cherished *Ictíneo*. Together, the twenty anted up 2,000 duros for the project. Monturiol's enthusiasm was infectious; even the notary who officiated the signing ceremonies chipped in 50 duros. Under the terms of the agreement, Monturiol would receive a salary of 30 reales a day and would be entitled to one-third of any profits realized from the venture.*

Monturiol and family moved back to Barcelona. They found lodgings on a street that ran along the wall that separated the city

---

*The monetary system in Spain at the time was complex and fragmentary, with various currencies competing for attention. In simple terms: four reales equaled one peseta; five pesetas equaled one duro. Cerdà's meticulously tabulated statistics on working-class life in Barcelona give us some idea of the value of money at the time. Lunch for one including soup, stew, bread, and a cup of wine cost

from the port—in the building, ominously enough, where Miguel Cervantes, the author of *Don Quixote*, was said to have died. Nonplussed by the apparent historical jinx, Monturiol nevertheless settled down to work. The new apartment was just a five-minute walk to the office—that is, the shipyard where he would build his dream machine.

Nuevo Vulcano was one of the largest and proudest corporations in the new capitalist economy of Barcelona. It launched the city's first steamship in 1836, and its shipyards dominated the entire final segment of the peninsula that stretches out from the city and includes the neighborhood of the Barceloneta. It was one of a select new breed of joint-stock Catalan corporations.

Traditionally, Catalan enterprises were family owned and controlled, on the model of a giant country ranch staffed with nephews, nieces, in-laws, and grandchildren. As the economy grew, however, the capital requirements in some industries outstripped the financial (and reproductive) capacity of individual families. Leading members of the bourgeoisie of Barcelona therefore pooled their resources and created new banks, which in turn organized the funding of new, publicly held corporations. It was a decisive step in the creation of a modern, sophisticated, and unrepentantly capitalist economy. The world of Nuevo Vulcano, in other words, was about as far from utopian communism as human experience would allow.

But Monturiol was thinking only of his submarine. He needed a shipyard in order to build the vessel, and Nuevo Vulcano was the only firm whose facilities suited his unusual demands. The logic of the dream drove him into the arms of the hulking sweetheart of

---

1.65 reales. A pair of shoes cost 16 reales, and a handsome pair of workman's trousers could be had for 24 reales. Wages for the typical factory worker were 8 reales per day, or approximately 2,500 reales per year. Thus, the capital of 2,000 duros raised in the first round of funding for the submarine was equivalent to lunch for 25,000 or sixteen times the annual wages of a factory worker. The total spent by Monturiol on the submarine project over its entire course—approximately 100,000 duros—was a magnificent sum by any standard. It would have bought several frigates for the navy, 160 kilograms of gold, or 125,000 pairs of shoes.

the establishment. It was not the last time that his submarine ambition would lead him to embrace the status quo. He could not have known then the extent to which such entanglements might compromise the purity of his utopian vision.

As if to make the juxtaposition complete, the team Monturiol assembled to help him perform the work in the capitalist shipyard looked suspiciously like a band of communist revolutionaries—which, in fact, is what they once were. At his side was his inseparable friend, Martí Carlé. Josep Oliu, Monturiol's partner in the notebook business and the patron of many a revolutionary periodical, was also involved, as was Francesc Sunyer i Capdevila, Monturiol's amanuensis for subversive publications dictated from abroad. To oversee the construction of the sub, Monturiol relied on a native of Barceloneta, Josep Missé. A master craftsman, Missé usually made boats for fishermen.

On every working day, Monturiol clambered through the cranes and saws of the shipyard to inspect and supervise the construction of his dream machine. He was a bit of a nuisance. Aside from demanding perfection in every detail, as was his wont, he also insisted on maintaining agreeable and even joyful working conditions for the men in the yard. True to his utopian creed, he was sure that all conflicts—whether about rest breaks or sick leave—could be resolved if everyone believed in the common cause and showed some brotherly love.

As the submarine grew, so did its appetite for money. Monturiol campaigned for more shareholders and for more money from existing shareholders. Some of these were admirers willing to subsidize their friend's noble dreams. Most, however, were simply open-minded investors, surely amused by the inventor's enthusiasm but also hoping that their capital would someday generate a return. In any case, the money trickled in, eventually amounting to the stupendous total of 20,000 duros for the first submarine, or ten times the initial capitalization of the submarine association. Monturiol fed the money to his creation, which gradually assumed its marvelous shape.

Fifteen

How to Build a Submarine,
Part I

Obsession originally meant "the act of an evil spirit in possessing or ruling a person." In the modern lexicon it describes "an idea, an emotion, or a desire that cannot be got rid of through reason." To outside observers, Monturiol showed all the signs of obsession. While his two daughters—now ten and three years old—scampered around the family tenement, the inventor labored monomaniacally on his diagrams. While Emilia fried up paellas, he experimented with toxic chemical concoctions. When friends came to visit, the conversation inevitably circled around the finer points of the art of underwater navigation. Even his last remaining portrait clients received some unusual lectures from their artist. According to the common mind, Monturiol seemed to have come down with a case of submarine fever.

But then, the common mind often fails to distinguish between mere obsession and the work of genius. The demon that apparently ruled Monturiol was in fact a vision of the future of underwater navigation far grander than any of his contemporaries could comprehend. Even as he sat down to design the first *Ictíneo*, Monturiol knew it was to be merely an experimental craft—just a way to get his feet wet. He fully expected to build a second vessel on the basis of the lessons learned from the first, and then a third, and so on, until the submarine became as much an unthinking feature of common life as the horse and buggy. And then, once the oceans became the backyard ponds of the human race, the inventor

Model of Ictíneo I

would lift his sights to the art of aerial navigation—and who knows what else? Monturiol's global ambition demanded from him the kind of concentration of purpose and action that might easily be mistaken for obsession.

The scientific spirit with which Monturiol approached his task was exemplary. Rather than simply toss an egg-shaped contraption into the water, as so many of his predecessors had done, he began with a search for first principles. He became a master in the fields of oceanography, meteorology, biology, chemistry, physics, and engineering, such as they existed at the time. He conducted his own experiments in order to test the hypotheses about hydrodynamics, respiration, and so forth that would underpin the science of submarine construction. He intended to build his new discipline on as firm a foundation as possible.

The immediate technological challenges he faced were several: A vessel able to operate safely under the sea must be able to withstand the intense pressures of the deep, it must be able to control its depth and stability in the water, it must be able to propel itself, and it must be able to maintain a life-sustaining atmosphere inside. Through careful study and land-based experimentation, he developed provisional answers to all these challenges. The result of his labors was the world's first comprehensive statement of the nature of the art of underwater navigation and a blueprint for a vessel that responded to the most fundamental issues of submarine engineering.

Science sometimes seems impersonal, and there can be little doubt that in the pursuit of his dream Monturiol raised his thought to a plane of universality, to the kind of abstract truths about the workings of the physical world that seem far removed from daily experience. It can be no other way; the point of science is in fact to establish truths independent of the individual. But that is the point of art as well. And just as the artist nonetheless leaves in a work of art the traces of a personal struggle, so the scientist carries even into the most rarefied heights of abstraction a personal and irremediable idiosyncrasy. Monturiol helped establish a universal science; even so, his work bore the particular inimitable stamp of the character of the man who created it.

Monturiol's first step was to frame his goals in terms of measurable quantities. Since he maintained that the ultimate aim of underwater navigation is to take humankind not just under the surface of the water but rather to the deepest reaches of the world's oceans, he reviewed the data available at the time from depth soundings. He concluded that the very bottom of the oceans lay at 8,000 meters. (Actually, the deepest trenches are at about 11,000 meters, while the average depth of the oceans is around 3,000 to 4,000 meters.) Even if he failed to reach the bottom in his first attempts, he said, it was essential to develop a technological approach that would in principle lead toward this ultimate goal.

He also believed that a true submarine would be capable of moving both on and below the surface in a completely autonomous way—and not just over short distances or with the benefit of favorable tides. Any craft unable to outrun underwater currents might easily be dashed upon a subaquatic reef or dragged off into dangerous waters. An indefatigable researcher, he made an extensive survey of all that was known about ocean currents. In his day, much was documented about currents on the surface; little was known about the lower reaches. As he correctly predicted, there are indeed currents that shift the water about deep within an ocean—although, sheltered from the wind and the waves, they tend to be slower than those on the surface. He concluded, perhaps optimistically, that a submarine would have to be able to attain a speed of 3 knots to be considered safe for general use. (The submarines of the First World War, by way of comparison, achieved speeds of 5 to 9 knots underwater.)

A true submarine, according to Monturiol's thinking, would also enable human beings to interact with the environment of the deep "just as if they were in their own natural element" on dry land. Mostly, he wanted to be able to see and to touch. So a true submarine would have windows, exterior lights, and mechanical devices for gathering objects from the sea and the seafloor.

Finally, a true submarine would be capable of sustaining human life while out of contact with the earth's atmosphere—not for just a few hours but *indefinitely*. The problem of maintaining breathable air inside a submarine was not an incidental concern for Monturiol but, rather, a central challenge. The appalling safety record of the world's first submariners particularly horrified him. Safety was not a bonus for the erstwhile utopian communist; it was of the essence. In fact, according to his understanding, the art of underwater navigation was neither a branch of military science nor a form of transportation technology but rather one instance of the art of sustaining human life in inhospitable environments. That is why he provisionally described his tract on submarines as an *Essay on the Art of Exploring Spaces Inhospitable for Sustaining Human Life*. Understood in this way, the art of underwater navigation has its closest cousin in space travel.

If he was going to get anywhere near the bottom of the ocean, Monturiol understood, he would have to devise a means for withstanding the enormous pressure found deep underwater. The atmosphere on the surface of the earth presses in on everything that it envelops with a force equivalent to roughly 1 kilogram per square centimeter (or 14 pounds per square inch). Water at the surface of the ocean presses in on any enclosed space with the same pressure as that of the surrounding atmosphere. As one descends into the water, however, the weight of the water overhead pushes down with additional force upon everything in its grasp. A square centimeter at 10 meters under the surface supports a thin column of water overhead that would fill a one-liter jug and weighs one kilogram. This one kilogram comes on top of (or rather, underneath) the one kilogram of pressure applied by the atmosphere. At 10 meters underwater, then, the water pressure is double that on the surface. At 20 meters, it is triple. The relationship continues on down in a linear way, so that at 50 meters, for example, the water pressure is six times the surface pressure.

Imagine a watertight cube, one meter long on each side—a small and cramped space, to be sure, though somewhat larger than that enjoyed by the average worker in the bedrooms of nineteenth-century Barcelona—filled with air at the surface pressure of 1 kg/cm^2. Just under the surface of the water, the water presses in on the outside of the cube with an approximately equivalent 1 kg/cm^2. Since the air inside is able to meet this one kilogram of pressure with an equal and opposite one, everything is fine. However, 100 meters underwater, you've got 10 kilograms of water hammering in on every square centimeter up against the same puny one kilogram pushing out from the inside. The difference—9 kilograms—spread out over the square meter on each side, works out to 90 tonnes. At 100 meters under the surface, your little cubicle will have the equivalent of a 90-tonne weight crushing in on it from each of its six sides. At 8,000 meters, that figure rises to a pulverizing 7,990 tonnes. The implication: Think carefully before you dive.

As he contemplated this pressing problem, Monturiol hit upon an ingenious way to break it up. He decided to divide his submarine into two worlds: that is, he would give his submarine two hulls. The outside hull would be surrounded on both sides by water at the prevailing pressure of its environment. Only the inside hull would experience the difference in pressure between the water outside and the life-sustaining atmosphere inside. In this way, the outside hull could be built without concern for the added stress of deep-water pressure. It could be styled in a hydrodynamic way for more efficient movement through the water. It could also be used to house the ballast tanks and other devices that would have to interact with the surrounding water at the prevailing water pressure. Most usefully, it would absorb any blows from the outside that might otherwise threaten the integrity of the sealed interior cabin. Monturiol thus concentrated the matter of pressure resistance on the sheltered interior hull of his craft.

The shape that most efficiently withstands outside pressure is, as Monturiol knew, a sphere. A sphere distributes outside pressure evenly across its entire surface and so is sturdier than, say, a cube. However, a sphere would not make the best use of space in a fishlike sub, so he opted for the next best basic shape: an ellipsoid—that is, a sphere stretched out lengthwise and then squished a little on the sides.

From engineering manuals of the time, Monturiol derived the equation that relates the dimensions of a cylinder to the amount of pressure it can withstand. The maximum pressure, naturally, depends on the type of material used. It is also proportional to the square of the thickness of the material and inversely proportional to the product of the length and diameter of the cylinder. In mathematical symbols:

$$P = A \ (T^2/LD)$$

where P is the maximum pressure, A is a constant for each kind of material, T is the thickness of the material, L is the length of the cylinder, and D is the diameter.

In considering materials for the interior hull, Monturiol realized that a solid metal cylinder would have the greatest capacity for resisting underwater pressure (metals have much higher A's than other materials). Unfortunately, metal was not on the menu. It would have been far too expensive for Monturiol and his financially strapped association. He opted instead for materials that were readily available in Barcelona—and perhaps familiar from his childhood as the son of a cooper—wood from olive trees sheathed in copper. He designed a cylindrical barrel of olivewood staves with supporting rings of oak. He then enveloped the barrel in a skin of copper 2 millimeters thick, in order to make it watertight. This he held in place with iron studs. Applying the received equation, he figured his chamber could withstand pressures found at about 500 meters underwater. (The full 8,000 meters of the oceans, he lamented, would have to wait. He did, however, take the time to calculate how thick a sphere made of oak would have to be to achieve a depth of 8,000 meters: 1.22 meters, or so he claimed.)

Despite the 500-meter tolerance, Monturiol rated the maximum safe depth of his sub at 50 meters. Since the entire purpose of his enterprise was to sustain life in the inhospitable environment underwater, he was not going to risk his crew on the odd equation drawn from the engineering sources of his day.

Monturiol's design called for an interior chamber with a total volume of about 7 cubic meters. The cabin was approximately 4 meters long, 2 meters high at the highest point, and 1 meter wide: large enough to stand up and turn around in, assuming you kept your elbows close to your sides. It could fit a crew of up to six, provided they were all on friendly terms. Monturiol enclosed this chamber in an exterior hull that measured 7 meters long, stood 2.5 meters high, and displaced something over 10 tonnes of water.

The double-hull concept was a pathbreaking innovation in submarine technology. None of Monturiol's predecessors had used it. Fulton conceived of something like it in diagrams he drew late in life but did not apply it in the only submarine he built. Had Bauer come up with the idea, very likely his submarines would have survived their crash landings on the bottom of the sea and his reputation would not have been so thoroughly soaked. The double hull would eventually become the basis for the design of virtually all submarines to the present day. John P. Holland, an American submariner of Irish descent, would experiment with the concept in 1875, and the French inventor Maxime Laubeuf would do the same in 1899. The double hull would finally establish itself as the indisputable standard in 1905, when the German navy adopted it for their U-boats. By then, the world had forgotten that Monturiol achieved the breakthrough first, in 1858.

Once he had a design that would allow his vessel to survive the pressure of the deep, Monturiol needed a way to get down there and—more important—to get back up. That is, he required a system for depth control. The key to depth control, he understood, was the ability to manipulate the craft's buoyancy.

Buoyancy is one of those concepts that just about anybody who has led a normal childhood—with regular baths, ice cubes in drinks, summers on the beach, and so on—understands intuitively. When facing the prospect of slipping into water that may be many thousands of meters deep and thus capable of crushing your olivewood-and-copper barrel like a paper cup under a truck, however, you will want to be very explicit about your concepts. Here's the simple rule: A thing is buoyant (i.e., it floats) if and only if the weight of the volume of water it displaces is greater than its own weight. If the thing weighs more than the water it displaces, it sinks. So, a beach ball floats because it weighs a lot less than an equal volume of water. (Imagine trying to toss around a beach ball full of water.) A stone sinks because it weighs more than an equal-sized blob of water.

Positive buoyancy is a fancy way of describing anything that, at its present position, is about to float. That is, it weighs less than the water it is displacing. If you have positive buoyancy while underwater, you will experience an upward tug. *Negative buoyancy* is the opposite. It means you're about to sink. *Neutral buoyancy* is the holy grail of submariners and scuba divers alike. It means that you weigh exactly as much as the water you are displacing. If you are at neutral buoyancy 10 meters down, you may rest indefinitely at 10 meters, neither rising nor sinking, until someone messes with your buoyancy. In sum, controlling your depth is chiefly a matter of controlling your buoyancy; and controlling your buoyancy is a matter of controlling either your weight or your volume.

A couple of subtle matters complicate the otherwise serene science of buoyancy control. For one thing, not all water is the same. Salt water is denser than fresh water (so things float more easily in salt water), and cold water is denser than hot water (things sink in the heat). Another and more disturbing fact: Any submarine craft that is not made of kryptonite will contract in size somewhat as it descends into the pressure of the deep. Because its volume will

Cutaway of model of Ictíneo I, *showing how the interior chamber fits inside the exterior hull*

shrink—even if imperceptibly—its buoyancy will decrease. This produces a dangerous runaway effect as a sub descends: The negative buoyancy becomes still more negative, and the sub will sink all the way to the very bottom unless something is done about the matter pronto. Monturiol estimated that his olivewood-and-copper barrel would contract approximately 0.01 percent in volume for every meter it descended.

Monturiol's solution to the problem of depth control is the same as that applied in submarines to this day. The easiest way to add weight to a submarine and thus decrease its buoyancy is to have it ingest some of the surrounding water. The way to restore the craft's positive buoyancy is to expel that same water. Monturiol's double-hull design created a natural location for accommodating this extra water: the space between the two hulls. His design called for four *bladders,* or ballast tanks, on the sides of his craft: two fore and two aft, just within the exterior hull. He added valves that could be turned from inside the living chamber of the sub to allow water into the bladders and installed pumps to force the water out.

The only complication with this arrangement was that, in deep water, a pump used to expel water must generate enough pressure to overcome the countervailing pressure of the water on the outside of the sub; otherwise, the tanks will not empty. Hand pumps work well enough in shallow water. In order to empty the tanks rapidly in deeper water, Monturiol foresaw that he would require something stronger than a hand-driven pump. However, he realized with chagrin, the alternatives to hand pumps—such as a source of compressed air—would be costly to install. In order to save money, he installed two hand-turned propellers on the upper side of his first submarine. The idea was to let water into the ballast tanks at the surface until its buoyancy was only just slightly above zero. Then the props would take over, driving the sub down and pulling it back up near the surface, where the hand pumps could empty the tanks.

For safety's sake, a sub should have a backup means to restore positive buoyancy in an emergency. The solution Monturiol chose was to place large detachable weights on the outside of the sub. In the event of a leak, say, or the malfunction of its ballast tanks, the weights could be released, allowing the craft to increase its buoyancy immediately. Never one to take chances with his crew, Monturiol installed two sets of these weights.

In order to control buoyancy, of course, it is vital to have accurate readings of a submarine's depth. Monturiol arranged for the purchase of a very precise water-pressure gauge made in Paris. By measuring the pressure of the surrounding water, he could know his depth at all times with considerable precision.

A further problem that arises as a sub descends is that of maintaining the stability and orientation of the submarine platform itself. It's not so easy to keep a submarine on an even keel. Upon entering the water for the first time, many a feckless submarine has capriciously pitched its nose straight down or lolled to one side. Bauer's first submarine suffered just such an expected loss of orientation, which is what caused it to slam nose-first into the muddy bottom of the sea.

The orientation of a submarine in the water is a function of the relative positioning of its center of gravity and its center of buoyancy. Gravity pulls down on a submarine, as on any other solid object, as though it were a string attached to a single point: the center of gravity. The force of buoyancy, conversely, pulls upward as though attached to a single point: the center of buoyancy. Imagine a metal rod with a balloon attached to one end and

The pressure gauge used in the Ictíneo

a rock to the other. The center of gravity will be located some-where near the rock, the center of buoyancy near or in the bal-loon. Left to drift in the water, this bizarre device will obviously orient itself with the balloon pointing up and the rock pointing down. So, with a submarine, the center of buoyancy must rest directly *above* the center of gravity in the desired orientation of the craft. To complicate matters further, the centers of gravity and buoyancy in a submarine may well shift about as it goes about its business: as water enters and exits the ballast tanks, as fuel is consumed, as crew members wander back and forth in the cabin, and so on. (It was just such a shift, presumably, that caused Bauer's *Fiery Diver* to pitch forward and careen toward the bot-tom of the sea.)

The solution, as Monturiol grasped, was to devise a system that allowed the crew to move the center of gravity underneath the center of buoyancy in order to adjust the craft's orientation. His plans thus called for a large movable weight to run along metal tracks on the interior of the submarine's living chamber. By mov-ing the weight forward or backward, the crew could shift the craft's center of gravity and so achieve their desired orientation.

Like all his predecessors, Monturiol would have to rely on human muscles to power his craft. He fantasized about steam engines and other inanimate sources of power, but the money was not there. He consoled himself with the thought that a human-powered sub-marine would at least be more socially conscious, for it would pro-mote solidarity among the crew.

His design called for an aft screw to be cranked from inside the submarine's living chamber. He spent some time thinking through its design. Because he wanted the screw to lie flush with the flat-tened stern of the craft when not in motion, he preferred a screw with two arms. In order to get extra thrust from each turn of the screw, he reasoned that a second blade on each arm would help. In the event, he produced two screws, one twin-bladed, one single-bladed. After some speed tests, he concluded that the twin-blade was indeed better.

With his customary thoroughness, he also wanted to quantify the relationship between human muscle power and submarine velocity. After setting some guinea humans to work cranking pumps, he determined that a "vigorous" man could sustain an hourly output of 6 to 8 "kilogrametros." Allowing for friction, he reduced this to 5 "kilogrametros." He figured that he would need at least four men, generating twenty of these mysterious energy units, to pull his submarine through the water at the minimum safe speed.

If circumstances forced a rather mundane solution to the power problem, at least Monturiol had room for innovation in the exterior streamlining of the submarine. Submarines before Monturiol were generally unprepossessing creatures. Most looked like surface ships with sealed decks. They were designed mainly with a view to creating usable interior space, rather than with an eye on their external presentation or the efficiency of underwater locomotion. Monturiol believed it was important to give the submarine a hydrodynamic exterior, both to reduce resistance and to improve stability as it moved through the water.

After some thought on the matter, Monturiol came to the conclusion that nature had solved the problem for him in designing the standard fish. So he built his submarine to look like a fish. It had a round nose, a cylindrical body slightly elongated on the vertical axis, fins for external stabilization, and a rudder at the end in the shape of a tail. Monturiol's submarines stand out for the aesthetic quality of their smooth and gently curved exteriors. Compared with the ungainly creations of his predecessors, they look uniquely sleek and elegant. Nothing less would have been expected, perhaps, in a city that has always been obsessed with physical design.

As it happens, Monturiol's intuition was largely correct. Natural selection has favored underwater creatures whose hydrodynamic shape allows them to move through the water with a minimum expenditure of energy. When land-going mammals entered the sea many millions of years ago, for example, they rapidly shed obtrusive body parts and became the streamlined whales and dolphins we know. The architects of today's nuclear submarines learned the

The screw of the Ictíneo: *detail from model of second* Ictíneo
in the port of Barcelona

lesson and settled on something very Monturiolesque—an approximately spherical nose followed by a cylindrical body that tapers into a tail—as the most efficient body design for underwater navigation. The submarines that plied the waters during two world wars, in contrast, generally had awkward shapes intended more to connote the dignity of an ordinary surface ship than to maximize underwater speed and stability.

In several of his tracts on submarine design, Monturiol includes a description of the fate that befalls a bird locked in an airtight glass cage. For the first 60 minutes the bird is fine. One notices beads of condensation on the glass. At 90 minutes, the bird is breathing with its beak open. At 100 minutes the beak is wide open. At 104 minutes the bird starts looking pretty agitated. At 108 minutes the bird is on the point of death, and at 111 minutes the bird starts shaking violently. Just when you think he is about to sacrifice a hapless avian for science, Monturiol thankfully describes what happens when you let fresh air back into the cage. At 120 minutes the bird is stabilized but still unhappy. At 135 minutes the bird is back to breathing with its beak shut. And at 145 minutes the bird is fresh as it ever was, chirping gaily and ready to fly off to freedom.

The French chemist Antoine Lavoisier established that the earth's atmosphere consists of about 20 percent oxygen. Almost all of the rest is nitrogen, an inert gas. Our bodies need the oxygen to fuel the slow burn of chemicals that powers our muscles, keeps the heart beating, and warms the blood. When oxygen runs low—say, below 14 percent of the air—our muscles cease to function properly, the heart beats rapidly to stir the tepid blood, and the brain begins to go soft (metaphorically speaking). If the oxygen runs out, we die within minutes.

It gets worse. With every breath, our lungs not only consume oxygen, they also expel carbon dioxide. In the small concentrations found in the earth's atmosphere—less than 0.1 percent—carbon dioxide is harmless. Increase the concentration to, say, 5 percent, and it starts to cause ill effects. Increase it further, to 8 percent, and it becomes toxic; it disturbs the brain and addles the liver. Dally too long in a carbon-dioxidized chamber, and you can die. It's double trouble for anyone who is thinking about locking himself in an airtight cylinder under the sea: If the lack of oxygen doesn't get you, the carbon dioxide poisoning will.

To further add to the discomfort of submariners, breathing in confined spaces tends to result in increased temperature and increased humidity. It can also lead to the spread of microbes (*ani-malillos*, Monturiol called them). And then there is the matter of undesirable bodily emanations—"I mean those gases, the products of digestion and in particular of bad digestion," as Monturiol politely phrased it. Although submariners could put up with just about anything for a few hours, he added, on longer trips those gases could prove to be something of a problem. It wasn't just a case of a typically Catalan obsession with scatological matters. If his aim was ultimately to keep people down there indefinitely, he would eventually have to deal with these noisome issues.

Monturiol's first concern was to quantify the amount of oxygen required and the amount of carbon dioxide generated by an average submariner. Research from leading French and Spanish chemists of the time suggested alarmingly that the 7 cubic meters of his proposed vessel would be able to sustain a crew of five for a mere quarter of an hour. Monturiol did some calculations of his own and concluded that this estimate was low. In order to be sure, of course, the best he could do was to run a controlled experiment of his own. While his olivewood-and-copper chamber still rested on dry land, he hermetically sealed himself and four comrades inside and recorded changes in temperature and air pressure, as well as in their own well-being and moods.

After 1 hour everything was fine. The temperature increased by 2.5 degrees C, he noted in his log. The air pressure also increased slightly, as a consequence of the humidity in the chamber. At 75 minutes the candle went out. By 120 minutes the temperature had increased by 5 degrees. The crew complained of serious difficulty in breathing. Their mouths remained open. They began to feel dizzy and weak. It felt almost like being really, really hungry, Monturiol observed. At 150 minutes, they couldn't stand it anymore. After staggering out of the chamber, everyone speedily recovered the full vigor of life, or so Monturiol maintained—although headaches in some cases lasted for six hours or more. He conducted further experiments to determine to what extent strenuous exercise—turning propellers, for example—would reduce the available time in the sealed chamber. On the basis of these, he estimated that the maximum permissible time for underwater navigation under full steam—that is, full muscle power—would have to be reduced by about 15 percent, to about two hours.

Monturiol's aim, of course, was to be able to remain in the airtight chamber of his sub *indefinitely*. His intuition was to study the gills of fish. He wanted to understand how fish extract the oxygen dissolved in water and expel waste gases, thinking that his *Ictíneo* might someday be able to swim through the water extracting the quintessence of life from the sea just like a fish. After further thought on the matter, however, he decided that oxygen probably remains concentrated near the surface of the ocean. That's why most fish remain there, he reasoned. A deep-diving submarine would therefore have to take down its own source of oxygen anyway.

The carbon dioxide problem proved to be the easiest to crack. Monturiol drew inspiration from shellfish and coral. These and similar fauna of the deep build their bony houses by extracting the carbon dioxide dissolved in seawater and mixing it with calcium to produce calcium carbonate ($CaCO_3$): the hard white stuff otherwise known as calcite. Construction workers at least since Roman times have exploited the same chemical process. They begin by heating old seashells ($CaCO_3$) to burn off the carbon dioxide (CO_2), leaving behind calcium oxide (CaO), also known as lime. Lime mixed with water—slaked lime, or calcium hydroxide ($Ca(OH)_2$)—forms an alkaline solution that reacts with carbon dioxide to produce calcium carbonate all over again, just as the coral do—which makes it an ideal ingredient in mortar. In the language of chemical symbols, the coral-forming reaction is:

$$Ca(OH)_2 + CO_2 \rightarrow CaCO_3 \downarrow + H_2O$$

Monturiol designed a device to pump used air through a container full of slaked lime, i.e., a solution of calcium hydroxide. Any carbon dioxide would react with the calcium hydroxide and drop down to the bottom of the container in the form of solid calcium carbonate, leaving behind carbon dioxide–free air. Using his estimates for the amount of carbon dioxide generated by the average submariner per hour, Monturiol calculated the appropriate volume throughput and the amount of calcium hydroxide solution required to sustain his crew. As a matter of fact, with his usual concern for safety, he designed a system capable of cleansing about five times the amount of carbon dioxide he estimated his crew would generate. "Submariners of the future," he wrote in 1858, "need have little or no concern that they will have clean air to breathe at the bottom of the sea."

Monturiol next searched for a means to produce oxygen and came up with the following:

$$\text{heat}$$
$$2\,K_2Cr_2O_7 + 10\,H_2SO_4 \rightarrow 4\,KHSO_4 + 2\,Cr(SO_4)_3 + 8\,H_2O + 3\,O_2$$

That is, potassium dichromate—a red crystalline solid—mixed with sulfuric acid over a flame produces some sulfates, water, and, more to the point, oxygen gas. The process has a major drawback: sulfuric acid is nasty stuff, and heating it inside a tiny submarine chamber is not a good idea. Monturiol had to content himself with producing the oxygen onshore and then taking it along in bottles. For the long term, he insisted, this just wouldn't do. He was determined to make his submarine absolutely self-sufficient. But he would have to leave the problem for further research.

The problem of the increase in temperature from breathing in a confined space, Monturiol reasoned, would take care of itself. The frigid water of the deep would naturally cool the interior of the submarine to an agreeable temperature. As for the increase in humidity, *animalillos*, and those gases—he simply held his nose for the moment and awaited the opportunity for further investigation.

✦   ✦   ✦

The purpose of underwater navigation for Monturiol consisted largely in just seeing what was down there. Whereas more militaristic inventors invested in things like periscopes, Monturiol put his money into portholes—massive, circular slabs of glass, 10 centimeters thick and 20 centimeters in diameter on the outside, tapering to 12 centimeters on the inside. They had a conic-section shape so that outside water pressure would wedge them into place in the hull, sealing any possible leaks. He installed them on the sides, on the top, and on the nose. The glass was of such a quality, he boasted, that it allowed 90 percent of the light to pass through. This still left the problem that there simply isn't much light at all deep underwater. But that problem, too, would have to await further research on underwater illumination techniques.

Monturiol also needed a source of light inside the sub. Here his technological achievement was pretty basic. He used a candle. It ate up some precious oxygen, but they did need to see. As the level of oxygen in the chamber decreased, he commented, the candle flame took on a deep red color and grew dim.

Anyone faced with the challenges of underwater navigation— as defined by Monturiol—would have had to meet those challenges at least in part in about the same way that he did. Yet no one would have built the same submarine. Even within the confines of

The eyes of the Ictíneo

his specific technological challenge, Monturiol's character and aspirations imprinted themselves on his creation.

Explorers generally fall into two groups: the solitary individualists who want to do it all on their own (usually as a way of dealing with their internal demons) and the gregarious leaders of people who want to bring everybody along for the ride. Bushnell and Day, for example, went solo into the deep. Monturiol did not even imagine the possibility of a single-seater submarine. For him, the whole experience was about social solidarity, the creation of a brotherhood of submariners.

Monturiol's idiosyncrasy also manifested itself in his safety program. Of course, any submarine designer must be concerned about safety. But Monturiol's concern went far beyond the ordinary. He would not have been the kind of explorer who could climb Mount Everest or reach the South Pole, lose a few of his fellows, and still come back feeling that he had achieved his mission. His true mission was to preserve human life in an inhospitable environment. His overriding concern for safety was engineered into his submarine throughout: in the double-hull design, the double-backup weight system, and the extra air-cleansing capacity, for example.

Monturiol's luxurious way with portholes also says a lot about him. Other submariners would have been content with a single window or perhaps none at all. For Monturiol, this would have been unthinkable. For him the submarine experience was a visual one. As he so clearly declared in his inspirational poem, he dived into the mysterious sea because he longed "to view perchance its depths, its forests of coral."

Ultimately, where the character of the inventor really manifested itself was in the very shape of his submarine. The graceful curves and organic shape of the *Ictíneo* were not entirely dictated by science. Rather, they traced the outline of Monturiol's peculiar vision—a vision of a whole new form of life, swimming about in the new world under the waves, independent and self-sufficient. Just like a fish.

Sixteen

The Ride of the Ictíneo

By November of 1858, Monturiol felt confident enough about the progress of the work to organize a meeting of the shareholders of his submarine association. At the meeting, he read to his comrades a memorandum in which he summarized the findings of his research and outlined the design of the submarine then under construction. It is a document of controlled euphoria. Methodical in its treatment of the science, measured in its claims for the experimental craft, and cautious in its warnings of potential dangers, his words nonetheless manifest the inventor's overwhelming conviction that the conquest of the watery realm was near.

He cast himself in an epic battle between science and superstition, a battle from which he would emerge either bathed in glory or dead by drowning, or so he was convinced. Like an aquatic Prometheus, he intended to bring the fire of knowledge into the eternal blackness of the sea. Not in a mood to stint on melodrama, he conjured frightful images of underwater "monsters without name" and "vicious whirlpools that devour everything they encounter." But the most worrisome prospect, as his listeners sensed, was the very idea of sealing oneself inside a 7-cubic-meter hull darker and tighter than any coffin. He warned his fellow travelers that the enterprise could well be "the tomb of the first explorers." Yet he assured his anxious comrades that he, at least, was eager "to sacrifice everything" for the sake of under-

The Ictíneo *prior to launch*

water navigation. As in his days as a young revolutionary, Monturiol was strangely attracted to the prospect of martyrdom.

The inventor also did not stint on his customary self-deprecation. If he dared call the matter of underwater navigation to the attention of the public, he said in conclusion, it was only because he wished to attract to such a worthy project "other men, more intelligent than I." The shareholders, whether more intelligent than he or not, were swept up in the tidal force of Monturiol's rhetoric. They offered vows of support and even some additional funds. A week later, still riding high, Monturiol penned his lyrical poem on fiery cares and toilsome cause (page 11).

Work continued on the fishlike craft through the winter of 1858–59. In April, Monturiol sent a letter to the port authorities of Barcelona, seeking a permit to launch the *Ictíneo*. By June it was ready.

On the morning of June 28, 1859, the *Ictíneo* stood poised on its dockside ramp, its polished olivewood skin shimmering in the morning sun, its spoutlike hatch and bulbous portholes on each side giving it the look of a bug-eyed whale on dry land, gazing eagerly toward the life-giving sea. At around 9 a.m., this artificial leviathan slid down its guide rails and splashed into the water.

Unfortunately, it slammed into some hidden pilings on the way down, and an unscripted crunching sound rent the air. Distressed, Monturiol inspected the stricken vessel. Several portholes were cracked and the exterior hull and ballast tanks were damaged. Full repair, he could see, would exhaust the funds available to his submarine association. With some chagrin, he decided that the submarine could still function without the full repair, provided it was limited to dives of 20 meters. He and his team began to effect minor repairs. They tested the ship's systems in the dock.

Soon enough, the *Ictíneo* was ready to leave her berth. In the mid-morning hours of a dazzling summer day, family and friends paced anxiously along the waterfront of Barceloneta. Monturiol, Emilia, their daughters Anita, twelve, and Adelaida, five, a gaggle of revolutionary shipbuilders, and many of Barcelona's finest utopians gathered to witness the *Ictíneo*'s first sally into the deep. Monturiol and two comrades—Josep Oliu, his old business partner, and Josep Missé, the shipbuilder—nodded to each other silently, clambered aboard the *Ictíneo,* and sealed the hatch behind them. The tiny ship swayed in the water like a wobbly barrel as the crew adjusted their positions unseen inside the tiny pressure chamber.

Then the aft propeller began to churn the water, and the craft eased away from its berth. When it reached a point a few dozen meters from the dock, the *Ictíneo* stopped, released a frothy fury of bubbles, and slowly slipped beneath the dark, still surface of the water, which closed over the last traces of the ship and her crew. Silence rippled across the harbor and overtook the expectant onlookers. Swirling along the dockside, without doubt, were quiet thoughts of all the things that could possibly go wrong in such a brazen venture, of just how serious that last-minute damage was, of whether the force of hope and will could sustain life at a distance, of wishing one had only said this or done that. Twenty minutes passed.

Suddenly, the surface bubbled and broke, and the shiny brown spine of the *Ictíneo* arose from the muddy green water. The craft bobbed lugubriously for a few moments; then the hatch creaked open. Monturiol hauled his head and shoulders out and raised his arms in triumph. Whoops of exhilaration and relief washed over the docks. To Monturiol's family and friends and Barcelona's finest utopians, his return from the underworld was nothing short of a miracle.

On the inside of the submarine, the experience was eerie. To describe it after his own first voyage, the erstwhile revolutionary and current shareholder Francesc Sunyer i Capdevila was moved to write a poem, which he dedicated to Monturiol.

In the body of your monster
I descended to your mysterious world,
My breast full of courage,
Because there were you, firm, serene,
Because there was your profound wisdom.
. . . .
And at one point, in one moment,
The complicated machine moving,
The propeller slowly turning,
The air escaping hissing,
The leviathan sinks into its element.

And that light diffuse
That floods the shrinking space
Emanates still more confusion
And so abounds in shadows
That it radiates profound obscurity.

Monturiol described the experience of neutral buoyancy in a prose poem:

The silence that accompanies the dives; the gradual absence of sunlight; the great mass of water, which sight pierces with difficulty; the pallor that light gives to the faces; the lessening of movement in the *Ictíneo*; the fish that pass before the portholes—all this contributes to the excitement of the imaginative faculties, and reveals itself in the shortened breath and the utterances of the crew. . . . On reaching a certain depth, and depending on the state of the water, there are times when nothing can be seen outside by natural light, when one *sees* nothing but the *obscurity* of the deep; all noise and movement stops; it seems as though nature is dead, and the *Ictíneo* is a tomb.

The submarine feeling, for Monturiol, was transcendental, a near-death experience. It took him, he said, to the "other side." The conquest of the deep, it seems, was an exploration of a state of mind as much as it was a journey to the bottom of the sea. From the moment he conceived of the *Ictíneo* on the shores of the Cap de Creus, Monturiol imagined discovering a place of utter tranquillity, a safe harbor from life's storms. Now, he thought, he had found it.

A Taoist might have described the neutral buoyancy he achieved as a state of suspension, an action without effort, like the ideal of Tao, in which one leans neither forward nor backward but, rather, immerses oneself in the flux of becoming. A Buddhist might have said that, in locating the pure nothingness of the deep, he had successfully emptied his mind of all phenomenal apperception and thus attained the kind of nirvana that results from transcendental meditation. A Schopenhauerian philosopher might have said that he had ripped aside the illusory veil of the World as Representation and uncovered the more fundamental, inchoate World of Will (a reality that is otherwise accessible only through good sex or classical music). A Heideggerian might have intoned, perhaps more clunkily, that Monturiol had encountered *das Nichts*. And a Christian theologian might have identified the inventor's artificial death-and-resurrection as an act representative of just the kind of sacrifice generally required of those who would save the human race.

On the other hand, as a Nietzschean philosopher might have fairly pointed out, the deathlike otherworld Monturiol discovered remained at bottom another projection of life in this world. When the submariner descended into the darkness in his artificial casket, he encountered a *colorful* vision of obscurity and a *vivid* simulacrum of death. Beneath the merely apparent surface of experience, he found—still more appearances. What his prose poem

The three argonauts, Ictíneo's first crew.
From left to right: the shipbuilder Josep Missé, Narcís Monturiol,
and Josep Oliu, Monturiol's old business partner.

revealed in truth was his passionate talent for imagining the unimaginable, his vibrant longing for transcendence. It was this same life force that had impelled him to his career as a utopian revolutionary and would continue to drive him forward mercilessly through the tumultuous years ahead.

During the rest of the summer of 1859, Monturiol and his crew tested the *Ictíneo* in more than twenty dives. In increments of 5 meters, they took the craft down to 20 meters, Monturiol's self-imposed limit. The double-hull design, brutally tested in the botched launch, lived up to its advertising and successfully resisted the pressure at 20 meters. In order to test the depth-control system, Monturiol attempted both slow and rapid descents and ascents. The combination of ballast tanks and vertical propellers proved effective and reliable. He also tested the compression of the submarine as it descended and confirmed that the interior chamber contracted, as predicted, approximately 0.01 percent in volume for every meter of descent.

Next, he gathered data on the livability of the interior cabin. He found that, relying just on the air already inside, a crew of four could remain submerged in reasonable comfort for two hours. Using bottled oxygen and the carbon dioxide purifier, they were able to extend this on at least one occasion to over four hours. Monturiol was convinced that the craft was capable of considerably longer descents. However, the high cost of the chemicals involved in generating oxygen prohibited further experimentation. Such was the eagerness of captain and crew to explore the deep, Monturiol later recounted, that for the most part they simply went down with the air that was in the chamber and held out as long as they could stand it.

Monturiol put the craft through various obstacle courses in order to test maneuverability and handling. The *Ictíneo* proved to be fairly sporty, able to turn quickly and maintain an even keel. In tests for flat-out speed, however, the results were disappointing. The maximum speed verified over a long distance was 1,671 meters per hour, or about 1 knot. There was some evidence that the craft could do better than that over short distances, with bursts of perhaps 2 knots. But the fact remained that four men heaving at a propeller would not be able to pull a 10-tonne submarine through the water at 3 knots, the minimum safe speed for true underwater navigation. The problem of subaquatic locomotion, Monturiol noted with dismay, would require considerably more attention.

As the summer wore on, the *Ictíneo* performed so reliably that the dives became almost routine. The low bobbing profile of the submarine became a fixture in Barcelona harbor. Monturiol even permitted himself a certain amount of jocularity.

Francesc Sunyer recorded some of the inventor's antics in his poem on his own first dive. As the submarine descended into darkness, Monturiol noticed that Sunyer was getting agitated. The inventor put his hand on his nervous passenger's wrist and counted

out an impossibly high pulse rate. Then he surreptitiously maneuvered the vessel to an abrupt halt. He suddenly clenched Sunyer's
arm and exclaimed, "What a horrible misadventure! We have been
trapped in the mud!" The hapless Sunyer's pulse rate shot to
uncountable levels, while his heart "froze with fright." As he stared
pleadingly at his captain, he dimly perceived that light began to fil-
ter through the portholes. The *Ictíneo* was floating up to the surface. As the sun's rays spread across Monturiol's face, Sunyer made
out his mischievous smile and laughed sheepishly with relief.

After a thorough run of test dives, Monturiol was satisfied that
his submarine had met and even exceeded expectations.

> The *Ictíneo* descends and ascends, moves and turns on the
> surface and in the depths of the ocean. Man lives as well in the
> *Ictíneo* as in the open atmosphere. Underwater navigation, then,
> is a fact.

He was pretty sure he had invented the tool that would allow
humankind to conquer the watery realm:

> After the successful trials of my first *Ictíneo*, which is no more
> than an experimental prototype . . . it is no exaggeration to
> assert that, henceforth, man can dominate the entirety of the
> solid crust of our globe, for he has in his hands the means to
> transport himself to any depth in the Ocean.

Although the *Ictíneo*'s adventures had thus far been conducted
without fanfare, word of mouth soon brought forth the curious of
Barcelona. Groups of Sunday strollers ambled by the dock to view
the strange new fish boat. On days when Monturiol and his crew
performed trials, small crowds watched in delight as the mysterious craft dashed out its trail of bubbles in the harbor. By the end of
the summer, the *Ictíneo* was like a debutante preening herself in
anticipation of her official presentation to society. Monturiol felt
the time had come to introduce his creation to the world.

Seventeen

The Greatest Show on Earth

For most of its history, Barcelona had turned its back on the sea. The bustling port wore little but scruffy workman's overalls. It had all the charm of a necessary but messy biological function in the city's economic organism. As if to leave no doubt about the position of the water with respect to the body politic, the city discharged its bowels into the harbor through the pair of underground rivers that bounded the medieval district. One of these rivers was called the Merdança, the other the Cagallel—two of the many ways to say, in Catalan, Stream of Shit. Only the Barceloneta, with its smells of fried fish and fresh laundry, publicly acknowledged the city's vital links with the watery world.

On September 23, 1859, notwithstanding its customary diffidence about the sea, the city of Barcelona put on its finest clothes and came down to the port. Factory workers, industrialists, children, and homemakers wearing their Sunday best streamed through the city's restraining walls under the bright morning sun and collected along the waterfront, where they clogged every inch of the wharves and docks. A boisterous fleet of fishing boats and launches dappled the muddy green water with speckles of color and noise. A huge steamship idled in the center of the harbor, its rails occupied by the entire city government, the port authorities, representatives of the press, and many other persons of privilege and worth.

At the end of an old pier bobbed the object of the city's interest. For the event, the *Ictíneo* sported tall poles at either end, intended to allow spectators to chart its depth and movement underwater. Flying above the submarine's berth, for the first time, was the official flag of Monturiol's submarine association. It was the inspired work of his wife, Emilia: On a background of Spain's national colors was a bright red tree of coral under waves of ocean blue, all beneath a shining yellow star—presumably either the submarine's headlight or the star of underwater enlightenment. The motto inscribed in large dark letters read PLUS INTRA PLUS EXTRA— loosely translated: The deeper the better. The submarine association also made available to the public a photograph of the *Ictíneo* just prior to its launch (page 156) and a group portrait of Monturiol, Missé, and Oliu, the three argonauts who had earlier piloted the *Ictíneo* on its first, historic voyage beneath the waves (page 160).

At 9:30 a.m., Monturiol and four trusty crewmates funneled themselves down the hatch. The *Ictíneo* pulled away from the pier, released its signature trail of bubbles, and, to the collective gasp of the crowd, slipped gurgling beneath the surface of the sea. The two depth poles attached to its ends withdrew silently into the water and then vanished. The submarine descended to 10 meters, where it remained for twelve minutes. It then rose and descended three times, in the space of six minutes, each time showing first the poles and then no more than the spine of its back, like a fish just breaching the surface. Still underwater, it turned to the south, toward the hulking cliff of Montjuic, and charged forward at full throttle— about one knot. After covering 500 meters, it turned round and steamed back to the north, in the direction of the Ciutadella. Along the way, it descended and ascended to various depths and performed pirouettes and other elegant maneuvers. At 11:48 a.m., after two hours and eighteen minutes without contact with the atmosphere, the *Ictíneo* surfaced near its starting point. The hatch opened, the intrepid captain came out to salute the multitudes, and the city of Barcelona erupted into a joyous celebration that lasted well into the night. The submarine was a splash hit.

A new door seemed to open in the port of Barcelona on that day, a door to the world beneath the oceans. The incredulity and

The submarine flag

amazement at Monturiol's feat would be hard to overestimate. It was, as far as those present were concerned, no less an achievement than landing a man on the moon—and bringing him back still breathing. For the celebrated inventor, it was public proof that the principles of reason could build a safe and perfect home for humankind—underwater and, maybe one day, on land as well. The next day's newspaper exulted, "The problem of underwater navigation has been completely solved."

"The enthusiasm was universal and profound," wrote another commentator. "Monturiol's personal friends, his political friends, and his countrymen regarded the new invention as a Glory of Humanity, of Scientific Progress, of the Nation, of Catalonia, and of the Empordà." *El Museo Universal*, a leading journal of science and culture, added, perhaps wishfully, "If this invention can be applied on a large scale, there will be no more shipwrecks."

Monturiol's spectacular submarine show marked the beginning of an unexpected future for Barcelona. The inventor found a city turned inward on itself, and he turned it outward, in the direction of the sea, toward a future of constant movement and exploration. The city's fascination with marvelous new machines, the undisguised diffidence toward central authority, and the love of a good spectacle came together in a single moment. What Monturiol offered was, in a sense, an answer to the problem of Barcelona. He provided the city with a vision of modernity and of its own place within it. He demonstrated that technology could dramatically expand the range of human experience, and that it could do so without aggravating social conflict or forsaking the virtues of the native land. He convinced Barcelona that it was at the forefront of modernity, that its harbor was the gateway to a whole new kind of civilization. The submarine was to Barcelona what the lunar landings would be to America in the twentieth century. It had no real utility beyond what it symbolized. But as a symbol, it had a tremendous effect.

It was a grand moment for Barcelona's former Icarians, and not just for Narcís Monturiol. Earlier in the year, the city government announced a competition to select a design for the Extension to be built on the empty land outside the city walls. The point of the competition was largely to stop Ildefons Cerdà, utopian urban planner and friend of Monturiol, from getting any farther with his patently communist designs. Cerdà seemed to have some support in Madrid, and the Barcelona politicians weren't happy about that. Proposals were due in early September, just as Monturiol was warming up for his submarine show.

A dozen architects and engineers submitted plans, among them Antoni Rovira i Trias, the maker of the cascading starburst design. The city elders loved the starbursts. They thought Rovira's French motto showed sophistication and taste. In late October, a month after the *Ictíneo*'s dashing debut, the city government declared the winner. To no one's great surprise, they chose Rovira. Cerdà's utopia, it seemed, would remain just a dream.

Then, suddenly, history jumped its tracks. Over in Madrid, Pascual Madoz—the former progressive governor of Barcelona—and other friends of Cerdà from his days in the Civil Engineering Corps exerted their influence to overrule the decision of the Barcelona city government. On the heels of the city's announcement, the authorities in Madrid declared that Cerdà's plan, not Rovira's, would be the official basis for the Extension of Barcelona. The city government squawked indignantly, but in the face of some further royal decrees it retreated sullenly into its coop.

Icaria wasn't going to be in Texas after all. It would be built right here at home. The rationalist-utopian creed of Étienne Cabet, as filtered through Narcís Monturiol into the ears of Ildefons Cerdà, would soon be tested on the streets of Barcelona. And while Cerdà would deploy the principles of utopia on land, Monturiol was already applying those same principles in his conquest of the deep. To Barcelona's hardy band of Icarians, it seemed that two frontiers for humankind had opened at once.

As 1859 came to a close, Monturiol was a happy man. Flush with the success of his experimental submarine, he dreamed of building another, bigger vessel, one that would remedy the shortcomings of the existing model and take him outside the harbor of Barcelona, to roam the oceans, to return one day with the glistening treasures of the deep. Old and newfound friends lavished him with praise and vows of devotion. To cap it all off, Monturiol and his wife Emilia ended the year celebrating a new addition to the family: a third healthy baby daughter, whom they named Delfina.

Eighteen

A Fish Out of Water

Just as his underwater imagination was straining for new and splendid feats, Monturiol's submarine association ran out of cash. Everything raised thus far had been invested in the olivewood-and-copper body of the *Ictíneo*. To realize his dream of building a second, superior submarine capable of deep-sea missions, Monturiol needed money. Although his estimates of the amount required varied enormously—from 100,000 to 300,000 duros "or maybe more"—it was clear in any case that he needed lots of it. The despotic logic of the dream forced the communist submarine visionary to become a professional fund-raiser.

The submarine project thus far had relied on money from private investors. In the wake of the successful debut of the *Ictíneo*, Monturiol decided to turn to the government for further support. It seemed a sensible move. The shareholders of the submarine association did not have nearly enough money to finance their hero's dream. Friends with friends in high places had whispered that some very important people had taken a keen interest in events in the harbor of Barcelona. Besides, all previous submariners of note had relied on official patronage.

Yet it would prove to be a fateful decision. The quest for government support would render his project hostage to the political processes of a truculent bureaucracy. Worse, it would force Monturiol to consider the hitherto overlooked military applications of the submarine. Ultimately, the engagement with the gov-

The Ictíneo *in action. According to a descriptive note provided by Monturiol, the engraving shows the same* Ictíneo *in five different phases of activity. Clockwise from bottom: The* Ictíneo *retrieves a lost cannon. Lower left: the submarine snips coral off the lower side of the ledge with special clippers mounted atop its bow. The coral bits fall into a net placed conveniently beneath the coral clippers. Upper left: seen head-on, the* Ictíneo *looks set to enter a mysterious cave. Upper right: the* Ictíneo *hauls the cannon to the surface. Right: The* Ictíneo *scoops up coral from the bottom. The scooper is designed to arch up around the nose of the craft, in order to drop the coral bits into a couple of open doors on the exterior hull.*

ernment would prove to be the kind of compromise with the status quo that inevitably threatens the very meaning of a utopian dream.

Nonetheless, on December 5, 1859, oblivious to the perils of bureaucratic entanglements or perhaps just desperate at the sight of his association's evaporating bank balance, Monturiol mailed his plea for funds to the minister of the navy in Madrid. While he waited for a reply from on high, Monturiol badgered his shareholders for more money. But because they were not terribly rich themselves and because they too hoped that the government would eventually foot the bill, their expressions of support generally took the form of words, not cash.

In hopes of whipping up public enthusiasm for the cause, he wrote a lengthy treatise on underwater navigation. Published in February 1860, it was, in most respects, vintage Monturiol: moving discussions of ocean currents and tides, mesmerizing depictions of undersea lucre, and detailed technical analyses of the finer points of submarine construction. The *Ictíneo*, he claimed, would soon be "more perfect" than merely biological fishes, for it would eventually be able to face the crushing pressure of the water at depths of 1,000 meters—where no ordinary fish dared to venture. He spared the reader few details of his innovative mechanical designs. Like no previous submariner (and few other inventors of any kind, for that matter), he was determined to make his dearly acquired knowledge available to the public. His pamphlet included an illustration of five potentially worthwhile applications of the submarine (page 169).

But there was one new development mirrored in the latest pamphlet. Monturiol's 1858 memorandum to his submarine association had mentioned the possibility of military applications of the submarine only once, toward the end, and then only to say, parenthetically, that such applications were not considered part of the project. The 1860 work, on the other hand, elevated the military applications to stand alongside saving the coral divers, farming the sea, and advancing the cause of science.

It was a breathtaking reversal for a man who had consecrated the first half of his life to pacifist agitation. The stress it caused at the base of Monturiol's being was evident in the herculean effort he made to convince himself that it all made sense. The submarine was a purely defensive weapon, he now argued. Its widespread adoption would stop aggression by the naval powers of the world and thus "end maritime war as we know it." Like Fulton, he maintained that the submarine would even inaugurate an era of universal peace:

> [E]verywhere immense sums are deployed for war; everywhere are vast arsenals of arms and provisions worth thou-

sands of millions of duros. . . . If these enormous efforts were directed in favor of the arts of peace, how much happier would mankind be! Ah! Now is the time that underwater navigation and aerial navigation should arrive and equalize the forces of nations and bring an end to war, enthroning democracy everywhere. If the insanity of war is real, how could universal peace not be possible!

Monturiol was clearly standing on two stools. On the one foot, he wanted to remain true to his pacifist creed. On the other foot, the principal prospective sponsor of his dream—and the man to whom his pamphlets were now really addressed—was the minister of the navy of Her Majesty the Queen of Spain. The stools were rather far apart.

The minister of the navy, in any case, seemed to have limited interest in perpetual peace. He failed to reply to Monturiol's inquiry of December 1859. In April 1860, the inventor wrote again to ask the minister to consider the burning issue of underwater navigation. This time the minister did respond to say that he would have his director of engineering look into the matter right away.

Three months passed with no news.

At Monturiol's behest, the representative to the national congress for the district of Girona paid a visit to the navy's director of engineering to pursue the submarine proposal. This was the first of many instances over the coming years that Catalan congressmen would lend a political hand to their compatriot genius. Unfortunately, in this case the personal chemistry between the politician and the bureaucrat proved to be violently combustive. As politely as he could, Monturiol's friend suggested to the director of engineering that he should assign the analysis of the submarine proposal to some "intelligent" naval engineers; he was sure "there must be some in the Spanish navy." The director of engineering took this the wrong way and retorted, "Have you come to reprimand me?" The meeting ended abruptly.

On July 9, 1860, the director of engineering sent his reply to Monturiol. In a single curt paragraph, he informed the inventor that, according to navy research, a certain Mr. Payerne in France had already built a submarine and that therefore Monturiol's work was "not so original as it appears" and not worthy of navy support.

Monturiol was outraged. Payerne's invention, he knew, was a *diving bell*. Comparing such a primitive contraption to his beloved *Ictíneo* was like comparing a scrambled egg to a soufflé. A day after receiving the letter, he fired off a furious response to the director of engineering and his boss, the minister of the navy. "Have you read my proposal?" he thundered. "I think not," he said in answer to his own question, for even a cursory reading of his essays would have made clear the fundamental difference between a diving bell and a true submarine. After counting all the ways that the submarine might help humanity, the frustrated inventor railed at the navy's director of engineering: "But you, from the depths of your office, without deigning to study my proposal, would destroy so much good for society in general, so much honor for our dear Spain." Monturiol told his friends that he feared the submarine would founder not "on the floating meadows of the ocean" but in the offices of the Ministry of the Navy. His letters to high navy officials occupied their recipients' in-boxes for some time before disappearing unmarked somewhere into their files.

Furious but unbowed, Monturiol decided to raise his sights from mere ministers to royalty. Queen Isabel II, he knew, planned to visit Barcelona in September to lay down the first stone in the ceremonial inauguration of Cerdà's Extension. So he sent Her Majesty an invitation to attend a performance of the *Ictíneo* in the harbor of Barcelona. He enclosed a leather-bound copy of his latest tract on submarines, on the cover of which he embossed the grand inscription:

> That Queen Isabel should be the monarch of the submarine world is the ardent desire of Narcís Monturiol.

But the queen seemed to be in no hurry to claim her new realm. In fact, Her Majesty was in a difficult mood. City authorities were still bickering over Cerdà's plan, which had yet to leave the safety of the planner's meticulous blueprints and make its mark on the city's streets. Officially, the squabbles concerned the detail in the treatment of the spaces at the border between the old city and its planned Extension. Under the surface, however, the debate was really about whether the city still had a chance to sabotage Cerdà's plan before it could be implemented.

Caught up in the catfight, Queen Isabel grimly patted the first stone of the Extension and then retreated to the nearby convent on the jagged heights of Montserrat for spiritual and physical renewal. She passed her regrets on to Monturiol. As a consolation, she sent in her stead General O'Donnell—ironically, the man Monturiol had accused of dictatorship only six years previously. O'Donnell was the head of the latest military government to take power in Madrid. The general preferred to be known as the Duke of Tetuan, an honorific he earned earlier in the year for his role in crushing some unarmed Moroccan villages for no other apparent purpose than to demonstrate the greater glory of Spain.

At 9 a.m. on September 28, 1860, the *Ictíneo* was introduced to society. Among the 400 guests at the invitation-only event were General O'Donnell himself, a number of his deputies, the civil governor of Catalonia, the mayor, various personages from the royal court, the dean of the local university, sundry academics, and representatives of "many distinguished families" of Barcelona. Three hundred of the VIPs rode aboard specially commissioned launches. A hundred others sat on chairs lining the waterfront. It was quite a turnout for a man who, in an earlier life, had sought the overthrow of the existing political order.

The *Ictíneo*'s performance was flawless. Its creator, too, showed considerable grace in the circumstances. As the submarine descended and ascended and pirouetted under the command of its crew, Monturiol stood by O'Donnell's side on the flagship launch and kept up a steady stream of technical explanations. The ex-dictator and the ex-revolutionary got along famously. Greatly impressed with both the inventor and his invention, the Duke of Tetuan exclaimed, perhaps with unintended prescience, "In two centuries they will call us barbarians, despite our steamships and trains." The *Ictíneo*, he added with delight, could serve perfectly as a "skewer with which to sink a ship." Monturiol, bursting with pride, responded, "And that, nonetheless, is just one and possibly the least significant application of my invention."

An elderly aristocrat at the general's side chimed in, "Spain will never lack for eggs, for we now have a chicken." Monturiol could not fail to have been pleased to hear his invention pronounced the chicken of the sea. He boldly pressed the general to help arrange a submarine show for the Queen herself before she returned to Madrid. O'Donnell enthusiastically agreed to bring up the matter at court.

In subsequent days, however, the court remained silent on the subject of underwater navigation. Frustrated, Monturiol appeared at the offices of the civil governor to inquire whether her royal highness might still wish to see the submarine. The governor bluntly replied, "Her Majesty is tired of so many things." The inventor stammered, "It's not about a festival; it's about the discovery of a new world!" The governor gave him a disdainful look and got up to leave the room, and the following day the queen departed for Madrid without deigning to lay claim to her new watery realm.

In the following months, the inventor heard little from the ruling circles. Lacking the interest of its highest member, it seems, high society was disinclined to pursue the conquest of a new world. No doubt the generals and other members of government felt they had weightier matters on their plate than Monturiol's peculiar fish boat.

Nineteen

The Struggle for Recognition

Monturiol had not yet been fully understood. For all the fanfare surrounding his first sallies into the deep, he had not yet secured comprehension of his achievement and his aspirations in the field of underwater navigation among those who mattered. He was engaged in what the philosopher Hegel would have called a struggle for recognition. The decisive break in the struggle came in November 1860, courtesy of a curious medical man and his culture club.

Earlier that same year, members of the enlightened classes of Barcelona had come together to found the Ateneu (as in ancient Athens), a very respectable sort of club with a library, a dining room, and a bar where they could go and smoke cigars, sip cognac, write their memoirs, and otherwise plot the continuation of the republican revolution by more comfortable means. What progressives failed to accomplish on the streets of Barcelona, they would attempt to achieve in the salons of the intelligentsia. A leading light of this new cultural establishment was Dr. José de Letamendi y Manjarres (1828–1897), vice president for the sciences section of the Ateneu.

Letamendi was a young man in the process of accumulating a number of feathers in his cap, in a variety of exotic colors. Trained as a seminarian and then a medical doctor, he became a professor of anatomy, composed a dozen works of music including at least one requiem mass, spoke a range of languages, ancient and mod-

Dr. José de Letamendi

ern, painted enormous pictures (as much as 24 square meters in size, mainly having to do with human body parts), and wrote hundreds of publications, from articles on the origin of man to abstruse theological pamphlets to serious textbooks on clinical medicine. Letamendi introduced Darwin's theory of natural selection to Spain, in a largely favorable account marred only by his weakness for esoteric theological banter. He saw himself as a Humboldtian—like Monturiol—though perhaps he should be classed a left-Humboldtian—unlike Monturiol—on account of the emphasis he placed on aesthetic intuition and spiritual transfiguration over and above empirical observation. He attracted public notice, if not necessarily comprehension, with his efforts to unify mathematics and medicine. He attached much importance to a formula he intuited:

$$V = f(\,I,\,C\,),$$

where V = vida, or life; I = individual energy; and C = the cosmos.

Letamendi's own life energy was cosmic in scale. His debates with his intellectual antagonists reached such a pitch that at one point he agreed to a duel—but then, thankfully, withdrew. Typical of men of culture of Barcelona, perhaps, he was knowledgeable enough to seem dangerous but idiosyncratic enough to be, in fact, harmless. When he heard of Monturiol's unearthly submarine project, the polymath Letamendi naturally had to know more. For the greater glory of the new culture club of Barcelona, he organized and chaired a commission to assess the submariner's progress and prospects.

October 21, 1861, must on the surface have been a typical autumn afternoon, when a mellow sun cuts through the crisp blue sky; but 7 meters below, the watery light flickered through the portholes, oxygen hissed periodically from pressurized bottles, carbon dioxide bubbled through a calcium hydroxide solution, silently forming a precipitate of calcite, and the air grew warm and thick as Monturiol and Dr. Letamendi debated the metaphysics of underwater navigation. Judging from the doctor's later report, the conversation was wide-ranging and highly speculative.

With a "charming rudeness very much his own," the doctor wrote, Monturiol got the ball rolling. "Listen, you, let's take advantage of our time here."

"Would it be a sin for a naturalist," the doctor replied, "to use the time to pry into the private life of sardines?" The doctor was finding life inside the *Ictíneo* just a little cramped.

"If you don't lose time, I do," Monturiol said animatedly. "I would really like to hear your opinion as an anatomist on a subject that is central to my project."

"Speak."

Monturiol expanded: the *Ictíneo* would leave his hands incomplete, he knew, but he wanted to anticipate all the secondary problems that subsequent inventors would face in perfecting the submarine. The chief deficiency of his creation, he predicted, was its motor. The *Ictíneo* would never reach its full potential until it had an engine that could move it through the water as easily and naturally as a fish. "I want to know what you think about electricity as a source of energy for submarines analogous to that of living creatures."

He was way ahead of his time. In Monturiol's day, electric motors were too rudimentary and batteries too weak to offer much hope for submariners. By the beginning of the twentieth century, however, the electric motor would become the standard form of underwater propulsion. Indeed, the main U.S. submarine construction group would operate under the name of the Electric Boat Company.

But Letamendi was unmoved. "No," he interrupted brusquely, "the living energy transmitted through the nervous system is not electricity." And besides, electricity is not a "fluid, entity, or thing" but a "mode of action." And to this apparently decisive metaphysical refutation, Letamendi added that electric motors were very expensive and inherently unstable.

Monturiol protested, and the pros and cons bounced back and forth inside the tiny chamber of the *Ictíneo* for some time. Then, eyes brightening, Monturiol described another wild idea. He said he hoped to develop a form of combustion that would not consume oxygen. Such a source of power, he said, might one day be used for underwater propulsion.

But by that time, the doctor notes, they had been underwater for four and a quarter hours, and before they could pursue such an outlandish discussion any further, "we cast off from those desolate depths in order to return to the amiable world of the rational."

The air aboard the *Ictíneo* in those days was clear enough; but the atmosphere, it seems, was more like that of the smoky cafés in the back alleys of Barcelona. The bantering friendship that Monturiol and Letamendi formed 7 meters beneath the sea survived for decades to come.

On November 9, 1860, Letamendi and his colleagues released their verdict on the *Ictíneo* in the form of a twelve-page report. It was a rave. The report hailed Monturiol as a genius "both analytically and synthetically" and compared his achievement to that of Columbus in discovering a new world—the world of the deep. The submarine's life-support system in particular attracted favorable notice. "Inside the *Ictíneo* life takes place in perfect normality," it stated—implying, of course, that speculative philosophical discussions were part of normal life. On the inventor's behalf, the Ateneu's report described the crucial distinctions between a diving bell and an exploratory submarine and between a submersible vessel and a deepwater submarine. It concluded that Monturiol was the first to solve the fundamental problems associated with building a true exploratory submarine.

The report also provided a sort of metaphysical gloss on the very meaning of the *Ictíneo*, a shiny patina of ontological rhetoric that could only have been Letamendi's work:

> The *Ictíneo* is like a true organic system. An economy of parts, a superabundance of action: herewith one of the formulae for the construction of living beings; herewith the formula that may well be named the principle of the anatomy and physiology of the *Ictíneo*. It is a fish in its exterior form; a fish in many of its interior parts; a fish in its public life; a fish in its private life.

Accustomed as we are to the idea that machines have no soul, we tend to look politely askance at anyone who would speak about the private life of a submarine. For Letamendi, however, achieving physical intimacy with new underwater technologies was a key part of his job as a scientist. For him and like-minded left-Humboldtians, the organizing principle of life was the divine center of the universe, and *progress* was progress toward a single organic entity that would span the cosmos and bind everything into a living whole. The submarine seemed like a good idea, according to this line of thought, precisely because it was a quasi-living creature, a new form of marine life; it represented one small step in the advance toward the organization of the world. Thus Dr. Letamendi had no doubt that, so far as the private life of the submarine was concerned, the fishier it got, the better.

On the heels of the Ateneu's metaphysical endorsement of the *Ictíneo* arrived yet another laudatory verdict from a pair of unusually alert naval officers. Miguel Lobo, a frigate captain who had witnessed the *Ictíneo*'s performance for General O'Donnell, gave a highly sympathetic review of Monturiol's work in November 1860. The captain was lavish:

> Fortunate is the genius who, superior to the innumerable mediocrities who populate our planet, finds a means to wrest new secrets from nature! What matters to such a genius that he must fight these same mediocrities, when he knows for sure that, sooner or later, the moment will come when the Universe must do him justice, and pass his name on to remotest posterity? Such is the case of Don Narciso Monturiol.

It was heady stuff for Don Narciso. Lobo concluded his review with an exhortation for the beleaguered inventor: *Faith and perseverance.* Clearly, he felt Monturiol's pain in facing the military-industrial complex. Lobo's superior officer, Admiral Lasso de Vega, seconded the highly favorable assessment of Monturiol's project in a separate article. It seems that not all the lights were turned off in the offices of the Spanish Admiralty.

Monturiol was jubilant. He could not help but cling to the verdicts of the Ateneu, Captain Lobo, and Admiral Lasso de Vega as though they were themselves the long-sought lucre of the deep.

The interest from the naval officers, added to General O'Donnell's earlier description of the *Ictíneo* as a skewer of war, prompted Monturiol to entertain Leonardo-like fantasies of the ultimate war machine. He set aside his plans to build an improved *Ictíneo*—a modest two or three times bigger than the first one—and instead dreamed of leapfrogging from the back of defense contracts onto a whole new plane of subaquatic being. In a manuscript of December 1860 titled *Ictíneos of War*, he drew out plans for a true monster of the seas, a 1,200-tonne submarine 36 meters long, to carry a crew of 250, powered by a steam engine on the surface and human brawn underwater, capable of descending a full kilometer below the surface. (Modern nuclear subs tend to stop at around 800 meters.) He endowed this artificial killer whale with a periscope, retractable lights, and an iron hull. In a startling anticipation of a technological development that would be another twenty years in coming, he proposed to give the hull a ribbed surface, in order to make it sturdier. And he supplied the craft with fearsome weapons: a revolving battery of four cannons mounted on top, and a "torpedo" out front intended to act something like an exploding nose. The whole package could be had, Monturiol claimed, for the bargain price of 10 million reales.

Monturiol labored hard to convince himself that he was on a mission of peace. In *Ictíneos of War* he argued that the naval powers of the world, such as Great Britain, would be unable to defend their fleets against his behemoth. Thus, "this machine would resolve the difficult problem of equalizing the maritime forces of nations, and consequently would have taken a step toward the peace and concord that should rule among civilized peoples." In fact, he was so sure that "the inevitable consequence of the *Ictíneos* will be peace in Europe" that he went out of his way to assure readers that, "in that case, the creation of this new machine will not be useless for humanity." For, he concluded, "any *Ictíneo* of war can be converted into an *Ictíneo* of scientific exploration." The inventor was going to hold on to his utopian dream and was willing to follow any path, however warlike, that might lead him to the final destination of a peaceful oceanography.

When the new year of 1861 dawned, Monturiol gathered up the fistful of glowing reports on his first *Ictíneo* and his tracts and designs for its successor and journeyed to Madrid, high on the plateau in the central part of the Iberian peninsula—possibly the point farthest removed from the sea in all of Spain—where he hoped to persuade government officials to buy a submarine.

Once in Madrid, Monturiol called on the Catalan deputies to the national congress for help. A leading deputy was none other than Pascual Madoz, the progressive politician who had served as civil governor of Barcelona at the start of the revolution of 1854. Another

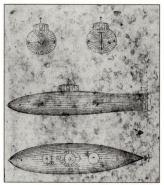

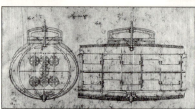
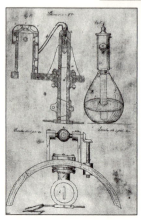
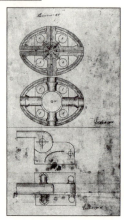

Design of the monster Ictíneo: *exterior* (top left); *interior cross sections showing gears for underwater propulsion* (middle); *exploding nose cone/torpedo* (bottom left); *battery of four cannons* (top right); *details* (bottom right).

was Estanislau Figueras i Moragas, a fellow native of Figueres and future president of the Spanish republic. The youngest deputy, Joaquím Pi i Margall—whose elder brother later became president of the republic for five weeks—befriended Monturiol and seems to have been responsible for an engraving of the inventor made at the time. Pi took his new friend out into the shimmering nightlife of Madrid, in hopes of relieving the troubled genius's mind of his underwater obsessions.

Pi later recalled with amusement his efforts at entertaining the submariner. One night as they left the opera, Pi noticed that his companion seemed dissatisfied. Monturiol explained that the singing was fine, but that the scene with the flour mill ruined the show; the stage version of the machine was so ineptly represented that it could not have served to grind even a single grain of wheat. Monturiol could sometimes be that way.

The Catalan deputies, always partial to the claims of a fellow progressive and compatriot, worked the halls of power on Monturiol's behalf. With their help, he found his way into the offices of various ministers and their assistants. Unfortunately, he did not manage to stay in those offices for more than a few minutes at a time. The bureaucrats, he complained, were "petulant" and "sanctimonious" paper pushers who put on "the false airs of experts and wise men." They didn't like him either. To the political appointees and their well-groomed assistants, as Monturiol himself guessed, the inventor seemed obsessive, pushy, and *"bruto"*—that is, impolite, lower-class, and altogether rather dirty. Madrid had its mandarins, and they tended to sour when faced with an upstart son of nobody-in-particular from the country with bizarre ideas in his head. "In this centralizing government," a bitter Monturiol wrote in a letter to his fellow shareholders, "intrigue and false merit run at full sail and with the wind at their back." His struggle for recognition from the bureaucrats engendered only mutual fear and loathing.

The frustrated inventor was ready to give up altogether on the idea of government support for the cause. But, in another unlikely twist in the submarine tale, a new savior suddenly appeared on the scene, a man three years younger and several lifetimes more

Don José Xifré i Downing

sophisticated than Monturiol—a man who, more than a man of the world, seemed to own the world, or at least a very large part of it, and knew how to put it to work for his own pleasure and amusement. It takes an individual of unusual gifts and exceptional means to save a foundering submarine project, and that is what Monturiol found in Don José Xifré i Downing.

The Retiro was Madrid's central park, a grand affair of sculptured gardens, elaborate monuments, and reflecting pools sprinkled along meandering paths through a semicultivated forest, occupying the meadows behind the Museo del Prado. On the other side of the Paseo del Prado, facing the museum and the park, sprawled the luxurious residences of Madrid's most excellent people. In a mansion that no longer exists, built in the so-called Arab style, with Moorish arches in alternating black and white stone, quasi-minarets, rampant crenellation, interior patios, fountains, and lush vegetation, lived Don José Xifré i Downing.

Don José's father, to whom he owed everything that came with a price tag, was born in Arenys de Mar, a humble village on the coast north of Barcelona. José Xifré i Casas was an earthy Catalan archetype: rough at the edges, sentimental when the need arose, and about money all the way down. He set off for Cuba in 1789, an impoverished twenty-one-year-old out to make his fortune. He went to work in a laundry shop, started dealing on the side in leather, set up shop on his own, diversified into slave-based sugar plantations, bought two cargo ships and later a whole fleet, acquired real estate in Havana, later a bank, and then settled in New York, where he played the casinos of Wall Street in style, using the skills and assets acquired in Cuba to multiply his already stupendous wealth several times over. In 1818, at fifty years of age, he paused long enough to get married.

Judith Downing was a manic socialite with depressive tendencies. She was twenty-five years her husband's junior and apparently had nothing in common with him save possibly an interest in his money. She gave birth to Joseito—Joe Jr.—in Havana in 1822. In 1829, the family moved to Paris, where mother and father continued to live as though the other did not exist. When the burning of convents created some interesting real-estate opportunities in Barcelona in 1835, Joe Sr. swooped down and snatched a choice property on the waterfront between Barceloneta and the old city, where he built the city's first luxury condominiums. Still known as the Porxos d'en Xifré, the apartment blocks boast handsome arcades decorated with reliefs of Neptune and other motifs suggestive of the sources of their builder's great wealth. Xifré decided to stay in Barcelona and occupy one of his own apartments, until he was at last able to fulfill his lifelong dream of returning to his hometown of Arenys de Mar in triumph, dispensing schools and hospitals and municipal buildings and other gifts to the village like the caring, prodigal billionaire that, deep in his own heart, at least, he imagined himself to be.

Meanwhile, Judith stayed in Paris and raised Joseito in a style to which he became very accustomed. The pair moved about together so much that the son was often mistaken for the husband.

Not lacking in vanity or material for potential psychoanalysis, the mother would recount with delight an occasion in which she was taken for her son's daughter.

Half American, half Catalan, raised in Havana and in Paris, shuttling down to Barcelona and Madrid to keep up on his Spanish and visit his distant, tough, but loving father, Don José Xifré i Downing grew up to become a man of the world. Although he was not the type to hold anything that could be described as a job, he did take over his father's portfolio, upon the latter's death in 1856, and oversaw major stakes in the Suez Canal and the trains in Catalonia. He was also a member of the national congress for most of his life, though this duty seems to have taken up precious little of his time. Mainly, Joe Jr. lived well. He converted his father's Cuban assets into his Arab-style mansion, cultivated friendships in high places, developed a reputation as a gregarious spirit, and became a world-class sybarite, with special emphasis on cigars and other tobacco products. He set up his principal residence in Madrid, but he lavished his time generously on Barcelona, Paris, and New York, usually in the company of other members of the steamship set.

When he learned of Monturiol's dazzling submarine, Xifré fell in love with the idea. He immediately grasped the potential advantages a submarine might offer to Cuba. As Joseito knew too well, the Americans coveted the bountiful isle of his birth, and as their naval power expanded to match their presumption, they were increasingly likely to take it. If Spain—more precisely, if Cuba—had a fleet of submarines, perhaps it could keep the Americans and others at bay. But more than strategic calculus attracted Xifré to the project. He saw something remarkable in Monturiol, a nobility of character, possibly a hint of genius. Later in life, Monturiol would always remember Xifré fondly and say that he had never failed him as a friend.

Xifré may not have had regular employment, but he did know all the right people, including ministers of government—possibly he had one or two in his pocket—and he was on familiar terms with the royal family. A few choice words whispered in a few well-bred ears accomplished what all Monturiol's letters and treatises had failed to do. Thanks to the intervention of Xifré, the minister of the navy along with the minister of commerce consented to attend a formal trial run of the *Ictíneo*. If the results proved satisfactory, the ministers let it be known, they would sponsor Monturiol's submarine activities.

The test was scheduled for May 7, 1861, in Alicante, a major naval port about 500 kilometers to the south of Barcelona. Now that the bigwigs were involved, the Spanish navy hustled into action. A hulking transport ship pulled up near the *Ictíneo's* berth in the far corner of Barcelona harbor. Under Monturiol's fretful supervision, the sailors winched the submarine out of the water, swung it, dripping, over the deck of the transport, and lashed it down with blocks and tackles. The navy ship and its fishlike passenger made an odd sight as they headed out of the port on the way to Alicante. Monturiol set off by coach, anxious but hopeful. At last, his subsea creation would present itself for judgment before the powers of the land.

Twenty

The Blind Trial

May 7, 1861, was a blustery day in Alicante, and the cold sea boiled into an angry white spray. Monturiol was feeling out of sorts. It wasn't just that he was nervous on his big day. The trouble was existential. "Whenever I must pass through one of those decisive events that mark out an epoch in one's life," he later wrote, Hamlet-like, "I feel a weight that oppresses me, an anxiety that does not let me rest. I would almost rather that the event, for all that it matters to me, should not take place."

The moody inventor gathered his crew and sailed out in a small boat past the breakwater to observe the state of the seas. According to his measurements, the waves were 1.5 meters high and 6 meters apart. Shouting over the breakers, he asked the crew if they were prepared to brave the weather in the *Ictíneo*. Without hesitation, they responded with hearty aye-ayes. Josep Oliu, the designated captain for the trial, added that he knew from experience that the waters would be calmer 10 meters down. Satisfied with the crew's morale, Monturiol directed them to return to shore.

Once on land, he set off alone for the train station, where he paced the platform for some time. The train arrived late. Out of a special government railcar stepped the minister of the navy and the minister of commerce, surrounded by a buzzing cloud of deputies and assistants. Monturiol batted his way through the sycophantic swirl and approached the minister of the navy. Before he could introduce himself, he overheard the minister saying to one of his assistants that he thought the sea was so bad that he was sure the trial would be canceled.

"Where is Monturiol?" the minister bellowed, with the kind of gruff pomposity that afflicts those whose needs are met too readily and for all the wrong reasons. Monturiol, already facing the minister, introduced himself and assured him that the *Ictíneo* would indeed sail that day. In fact, as a submarine, Monturiol added, the *Ictíneo* could take to the sea even in conditions that might prevent surface ships from sailing.

"Very well, then, let's get on with it," the minister huffed.

The ministers and their entourages exited the station and swarmed into the waiting carriages. After they had loaded themselves up, it became clear that there was no room for Monturiol in any of the carriages. No one offered him a ride. Awkwardly, he stuck his head in the navy minister's window and asked where they were going and whether he should follow. The minister told him they were going to have lunch at the restaurant of the local inn and he might as well join them. The carriages left in a cloud of dust, while Monturiol followed on foot.

At the restaurant a sullen silence lay thickly over the tables. "I have never attended a colder gathering," Monturiol later wrote. Conversations took place only between those sitting next to each other, and no one spoke to Monturiol. "I felt like a victim of the plague, from whom everyone flees." After the grim meal, the representatives of government returned to their carriages. Once again, there was room for everybody save the inventor of the day. As the port was some distance from the restaurant, Monturiol decided to humiliate himself by asking straight out for a ride. The minister grudgingly permitted him to hang on to the running board. "The minister is worth little," Monturiol later said, "but worth even less are the many who pushed their way to occupy seats as near as possible to him at the table, in the carriage, and on the boat."

In the harbor of Alicante, a school of eighty pleasure craft and fishing boats darted around the *Ictíneo*. Official launches roared in from the docks and shooed away the curious. The government party collected around the submarine. Aboard the flagship launch with the minister of the navy, Monturiol set about explaining the fundamental principles of underwater navigation. The representatives of the government listened for a few minutes and then demanded to see the submarine perform its tricks. At that moment, the *Ictíneo*, as Monturiol explained, was moving along the surface in an area full of ships' lines and anchors. Only when the submarine cleared these obstacles would it be safe for the craft to submerge. The minister's helpers grumbled about the delay, "like the public attending a spectacle, who feel themselves cheated."

Soon enough, though, the *Ictíneo* passed the obstacle course and then disappeared beneath the waves. Under the experienced command of Oliu, the submarine calmly went about its routine. In order to demonstrate that the submarine could follow directions faithfully, Oliu set off on a straight-line underwater run of 2 kilometers, surfacing from time to time to show that the vessel remained true to its course. The high seas clearly had little effect on the *Ictíneo*'s ability to perform its tasks. The same was not true, however, of the representatives of the government. One by one, they gave way to seasickness. Amid the sprawled and regurgitating mass of government officials, only Monturiol remained standing, offering his continuing discourse on the art of underwater navigation to the howling wind and crashing whitecaps. Half an hour into the show, with the *Ictíneo* still hewing obliviously to its 2-kilometer course, the minister decided he had seen enough and ordered his launch to pull up alongside a larger transport ship. All hands boarded the larger ship.

During the transfer between boats, one of the minister's aides whispered to Monturiol that he had overheard the minister say that the submarine had "no useful applications." The news, though distressing, hardly came as a surprise. The minister's body language had already told Monturiol everything he needed to know.

When the minister and his acolytes reboarded the launch in order to return to the shore, it became apparent that there was no longer room on board for Monturiol. The minister curtly suggested that Monturiol take another launch and meet them later at the restaurant.

Monturiol commandeered a launch and caught up with the *Ictíneo*, which, still blissfully unaware of developments among the official observation party, was approaching the end of its 2-kilometer dash. He signaled the crew to return to port.

Back on the quay, Monturiol greeted Oliu and crew with a strained smile. Hiding behind a white lie, he told them that the test had gone extremely well and explained that the contented observers had retired to formulate their verdict. "I know from experience how depressing it is to return from a test without finding the people for whom it was performed," Monturiol later confided to a friend. He made his way to the restaurant, alone and glum.

Twenty-five people gathered around the innkeeper's tables. After an awkward silence, one government official presented Monturiol with a series of polite questions. Then another of the navy minister's assistants, a particularly officious individual, attacked Monturiol directly. He suggested that there were no useful applications of the submarine and that, furthermore, building a larger submarine would be impossible owing to all sorts of technical complications. The inventor answered in response that there were many potential uses for the submarine and that the principles of submarine construction were not dependent on size. The official, clearly intent on showing off his superior knowledge, returned the bizarre assertion that children require more oxygen than adults. Monturiol, who was by this time a world expert on respiration, pointed out that this was not just irrelevant but silly. As the quibbles mounted, the navy minister dozed off.

Monturiol woke the minister by asking him pointedly what he should do with the *Ictíneo*. Brushing off his sleep, the minister muttered that one of his assistants would arrange transport for the *Ictíneo* back to Barcelona. With a yawn, he announced that it was time to return to Madrid. Monturiol asked what he should do. Should he accompany the minister to Madrid, for example?

"Very well, you may come back to Madrid," the minister replied.

The train stopped at a small town along the way for dinner. The minister and his retinue ate in silence. Back on board, Monturiol stared out of the window as the train plowed through the night to Madrid.

Meanwhile in Alicante, the *Ictíneo* and its crew awaited transportation to Barcelona. They took advantage of the delay to cruise the local waters, offering rides to the curious. On one such excursion, they suddenly found themselves in a thick forest of undersea algae. The green vines wrapped themselves round the craft. Fearing that the vegetation would entwine the screw and trap them at the bottom, the crew stopped cranking the shaft and rapidly pumped the water out of the ballast tanks, raising the *Ictíneo* to a shallower depth. Then the crew moved the vessel forward again through the water, just skimming the tops of vines. Gazing through the portholes, they marveled at the subaquatic forest below.

In Madrid, Monturiol faced a tougher challenge in tangling with the vines of the military-industrial complex. Every day or two, he attempted to visit the minister of the navy in his offices, but each time he was turned away with one excuse or another. Exasperated, on May 16 he fired off an indignant letter to the press. "I have done my duty" for the cause of underwater navigation, he declared. "Now it is up to others to do theirs." The cold shoulder the navy had shown him in Alicante gave him little reason to expect that the establishment would ever live up to its "duty." He retreated to Barcelona in a black mood, doubting the goodwill of Her Majesty's government, doubting his future prospects, doubting justice itself—doubting everything, it seems, but the fundamental truth of the art of underwater navigation.

Twenty-one

Barcelona Dreaming

Barcelona in the middle years of the nineteenth century was a city of poets. In 1859, the same year that Monturiol offered his underwater art to the public, the city organized the first of its annual poetry competitions, the Jocs Florals. These Floral Games purportedly revived a tradition of contests among troubadors in the princely courts of medieval Catalonia. First prize was a perfect red rose. By the early 1860s, hundreds of local versifiers gathered every year to bewitch one another with heartfelt odes on the glories of their native land.

The literary spectacles were in fact part of the flexing of identity by a newly empowered city—and in particular by its muscular middle classes. As the Catalan economy surged ahead, its leaders demanded to be reminded just who they were and why fate had destined them for so much earthly success. The poets seemed to have the answers, so they achieved immortal fame, at least for a time. No decent social function was complete without the celebrated rhymesters. The Jocs Florals, according to one reviewer, became the spinal column of the Catalan *renaixença*—the rebirth of Catalan literature that took place in the final third of the nineteenth century.

As for the poetry itself, it was a case of *rauxa* in its dreamiest form. The favorite topics were the glistening mountains of Catalonia whose peaks touch the heavens, the torrents of springtime that gush sparkling through the meadows, and the heroic deeds of noble princes who in all likelihood never existed in the first place.

The language—Catalan de rigueur—often took archaic forms that not everyone could understand. Barcelona's rebirth turned on the theory that there had been a previous life, and so its poetasters labored hard to imagine the past as it should have been. In its all-too-Catalan way, Barcelona was walking backward into the future, its misty gaze fixed permanently on an irretrievable past.

Between the lines there was a separatist message. But it was a soft-core form of separatism, more inclined to assert moral superiority over Madrid than to seek independence. Catalan separatism was always essentially a bourgeois affair, removed from the struggles of the working classes, secretly aware that financial security was probably best served by maintaining the union with the principal market for Catalonia's manufactured products—namely, the rest of Spain.

In his origins and his character, Monturiol was as Catalan as the rocky soil of the Alt Empordà. In his politics, however, he showed little interest in Catalan separatism. Instead, like most progressives, he was an internationalist. He fought for all humankind, not just a provincial bourgeoisie. If anything, he favored Spain over Catalonia, simply because Spain was a bigger part of the human world. His appeals for help with his submarine project alluded often to the "glory of Spain" and the "glory of Humanity" but never to the glory of the not-yet-independent state of Catalonia. Although he harbored grave doubts about the nature and value of the nation-state itself, those doubts did not extend to the question of his own national identity.

Monturiol's submarine, on the other hand, had yet to establish its national identity. It was a loose signifier on the ship of state. Then, one day, it rolled into the field of view of the poets of Barcelona, who were stunned by what they saw. In what must count as a prime example of the kind of rich juxtaposition to be found only in paradoxical cities like Barcelona, a whole provinceful of hindsighted poets suddenly wheeled themselves around in service of a global-minded inventor and his futuristic technology.

Events are singular; interpretations are multiple. For Monturiol, the trial at Alicante was an unmitigated disaster. For the poets and opinion makers of Catalonia, on the other hand, Alicante was a resounding triumph. No one took note of the navy minister's harsh judgment of the *Ictíneo*, for indeed no official judgment had been promulgated and no offensive body language had been recorded. The mere fact that so many navy officials had taken the trouble to arrange for the submarine test was, for the Catalans, proof positive of official recognition of the genius of its native son. When the test pilot Oliu and his crew arrived in Barcelona, furthermore, they had only jubilant tales to tell of a test passed with flying colors under demanding conditions. Alicante (in the interpretation favored by the poetical mind) was the spark thrown on the highly combustible material left over from the first test runs of the *Ictíneo* and the glowing reports of the Ateneu and Captain Lobo and Admiral Lasso de Vega. Soon all of Catalonia was aflame with passion for the submarine—which perhaps goes to show that in the course of human affairs it is the interpretations that decide events and not the reverse.

Twenty-two

The Submarine Roast

At three o'clock in the afternoon of June 10, 1861, Barcelona's best and brightest gathered in the Hotel Vilaseca, at the top of the Passeig de Gracia, for a lunch in honor of Catalonia's native submarine genius. Two hundred guests attended, among them the mayor of Barcelona, the Catalan representatives to the national congress, the regional governor, ward politicians of all stripes, and many other dignitaries, perhaps the most dignified of whom was the recently appointed captain general of Catalonia, General Domingo Dulce y Garay—the same General Dulce who seven years previously had entered Barcelona in the heat of revolution and authorized the demolition of the city's medieval walls. Naturally, José de Letamendi and his enthusiastic brethren from the Ateneu were there, as was Don José Xifré i Downing, Monturiol's millionaire-playboy friend. Also present were some of the leading actors of Barcelona's cultural stage, such as Victor Balaguer, the city's most well-known historian and writer, who was even then dreaming up names for all the new streets in Cerdà's Extension; Josep Anselm Clavé, the singing socialist; a posse of famous poets and poetesses; and the journalist and author Antonio Altadill—a shareholder in Monturiol's submarine enterprise, a popular playwright and novelist, and a fixture in café society as ubiquitous as cups and saucers. It was he who took the initiative in organizing the lunch in honor of Monturiol. Making quite a splash was Monturiol's own fourteen-year-old daughter, "the beautiful Doña Anita," as the next day's newspaper gushed. (She must have been the first, if not the only, young woman ever whose debut took place at a submarine gala.)

From the patio an orchestra serenaded the lunch crowd with renditions of Clavé's tunes and other rousing works. Inside, guests sat at two long tables in parallel, joined at the end by a third, the head table. In front of the head table, garlanded with tasteful floral arrangements, stood a proud wooden model of the *Ictíneo*. The setting was typical of those in which much of nineteenth-century scientific progress took place. In the era before national science foundations and corporate-sponsored university institutes, science was a rather more personal affair. It advanced through a combination of public spectacles and face-to-face encounters.

As guests tucked into the traditional Catalan fare of fish, sausages, and rice, General Dulce arose from his seat at the head table next to Monturiol to offer a toast. Dulce was a small, hard man in his fifties, compact and leathery on the outside, at the peak of his authority and self-assurance. He was a military hero from the civil war with considerable combat experience and scars to show for it. In 1841, while guarding the Royal Palace, he had personally foiled a plot to kidnap the infant Queen Isabel II. Yet, according to the tortuous logic of nineteenth-century Spanish politics, he was also among the most liberal and progressive political figures of his time. Aside from authorizing the demolition of Barcelona's walls, he also sanctioned the growth of new political and economic freedoms in Catalonia. His popularity in the region was such that when it eventually came time for him to leave his post, Catalans from all levels of society gathered for a special festival to offer him a warm farewell. The general and the submariner soon formed a lasting friendship.

Dulce first toasted the queen, as one does, praising Her Majesty as the monarch of a new world of science and progress. (Of course, by this time it was common knowledge that Isabel was the monarch of a fairly old world of sexual license and weird spirituality.) Dulce then turned to Monturiol and raised his glass—in honor, he said, of a man whose industriousness and ingenuity amply represented the native talents of Catalonia. After a chorus

General Domingo Dulce y Garay—engraving, 1861

of "Hear! Hear!"s, many of the other dignitaries present followed suit, offering generous toasts of their own. The mayor, the president of the Ateneu, the congressmen, and a number of others vied with each other to heap beautiful words on Monturiol and his marvelous machine. Victor Balaguer made explicit the regionalist orientation of many of those in attendance. "Onward!" he cried. "Have no fear!" Then, somewhat implausibly: "For no Catalan ever gets scared or turns back!" The *Ictíneo* had apparently uncovered a whole new world of Catalan sentiment.

Around dessert time, the poets took the floor. It is safe to say that never in the history of submarines have an inventor and his vessel inspired so much verse, and such ebullient verse at that. Antonio Altadill, the organizer of the event, kicked off the poetry slam from his seat on the other side of Monturiol. Altadill was the kind of man for whom the double espresso was invented. He had sunken cheeks, bright burning eyes, and dark untamed hair. According to his contemporary Conrad Roure, "Antonio was physically so fragile that, despite his small stature and slim build, the ethereality of his reduced body was still too much for his weak muscles to support and he walked with a stoop, his legs bowed and his step vacillating." He was also so prolific a writer that the critics called his brother—a well-respected writer in his own right—"the lazy one" for having produced only half a dozen books.

Altadill's 1860 novel, *Barcelona and Its Mysteries*, was on its way to becoming Barcelona's best-selling novel of the decade. In the novel, Diego Rocafort, a humble carpet weaver, rises to glory and saves Barcelona from its oppressors, even though he must sacrifice everything himself. Now Altadill raised his fragile frame to toast the real Diego Rocafort, the man who would liberate humankind from the fetters of the earth's atmosphere, the good submariner himself, Narcís Monturiol. His poem set the tone for the evening's literary contributors:

> *You it was, Monturiol, you the chosen one.*
> *Genius called you, and at its potent voice*
> *You lifted up your head*
> *And, in raising it from the humble earth,*
> *Stardust sprinkled your brow.*

Next, María Josefa Massanés de Gonzalez, a poet very much in demand in Barcelonan society, grabbed Monturiol with her eyes and exhorted him with passion:

> *Onward, Monturiol, onward!*
> *For Nature offers you freely*
> *The goblet of her secrets*
> *That other mortals in vain*
> *From her hand would wrest.*

Monturiol's friend and fellow native of Figueres Damás Calvet, an engineer with a sparkling sideline in poetry, took to the floor to assure Monturiol that he would one day be King of the Oceans:

Antonio Altadill y Teixidor

And so does your genius dominate
The unfathomable depths of the sea;
Where none have dared to penetrate,
You, mocking the elements, descend.

Barcelona's finest utopians chimed in with verses of their own. Ex-revolutionary and crew member Sunyer i Capdevila read a poetical account of his first marvelous voyage beneath the sea (page 158). F. J. Orellana—the fellow Cabetian who by now had achieved considerable prominence as a left-leaning journalist and essayist—found some rhyming comparisons between his comrade's achievements and those of Columbus. To be compared with Columbus, by the way, was about as much as any Catalan could hope for in life. Catalans in the nineteenth century were convinced—on the basis of little more than patriotic intuition—

that Columbus was one of their own. Furthermore, in their eyes, Columbus had not only discovered a New World, he had discovered Cuba, the miraculous source of much of their present wealth.

Possibly the brightest star of the evening was Monturiol's musical friend Josep Anselm Clavé. Although his choirs were banned for a time in the early 1850s, Clavé had by now staged a dazzling comeback. In 1860 he held the first in an annual series of grand choral festivals. These soon became massive civic events, attended by vast audiences. By the early 1860s, there were 2,000 singers in over fifty choral societies all over Catalonia. Thanks to Clavé, too, the musical horizons of these singing Catalans were broadening; he led Spain in importing Afro-Caribbean rhythms from Cuba, and he was also, by way of extreme juxtaposition, the first to introduce the Wagnerian phenomenon to Catalonia.

In his poem, Clavé put the whole submarine affair in its political context. He reminded his listeners of the persecution suffered in the recent past by Monturiol, himself, and other utopians at the hands of repressive governments. Acutely aware of Monturiol's ongoing difficulties in finding support for his work in Madrid, Clavé proposed a lyrical solution:

> *If you find not the favor of the governors*
> *Take courage nonetheless*
> *For the people will lend you a big helping hand.*

Clavé also put his finger bluntly on what many surely suspected was the geopolitical source of Monturiol's troubles:

> *Had you been born in foreign land*
> *So would you now be more* GRAND.
> *But ay! Narcís, your eyes first opened in Spain,*
> *A nation that, alas, makes such a sorry state.*

With his trademark combination of self-deprecation and self-assurance, Monturiol rose to address the adoring lunch crowd. He read from some prepared notes, yet, as the next day's newspaper

Josep Anselm Clavé in his prime

commented, his speech was "as opportune as if it had been composed in the heat of the moment." He described the ambition and purpose of his project and, without bitterness, related the story of his many troubled encounters with officialdom. He explained why he needed support either from government or from other sources, hinting strongly that the time had come for these "other sources" to step forward. The audience received his words with a foot-stomping fit of *rauxa*.

The party did the trick. The enthusiasm of the luncheoners spilled out of their pockets. Over dessert wine and coffee, they voted unanimously to form a commission to oversee a public fund-raising drive on behalf of the second *Ictíneo*. The chairman of the new commission would be General Dulce himself; Xifré and Altadill would be the committee's mover and shaker, respectively. The people's submarine was just a few tens of thousands of duros away.

Rather: the *Catalan* people's submarine. For somewhere on the road to financial independence, the question of the *Ictíneo*'s national identity had been resolved. This was the message that ran between the lines of all that poetry of underwater navigation: The *Ictíneo* is the spawn of Catalonia. A watchful observer might have tallied the costs as well as the benefits of this sudden provincial adoption. For example, the Catalanization of the submarine involved a certain sacrifice in the global aspirations of the utopian dream. It also risked alienating the very large part of the world that had no stake in Catalonia's pride. Most worrisome, perhaps, all the great Catalan poems were about martyrs: heroes of the past who had sacrificed everything in the futile effort to transform Catalonia into an independent state.

But Monturiol was not thinking along those lines. He had been swept up in the *rauxa* too. After two years of brutal treatment at the hands of the central government in Madrid, he felt only relief and exhilaration in the embrace of his fellow Catalans. All that mattered to him was that he had taken a giant step in the direction of the true submarine.

It was eight o'clock in the evening by the time the lunch finally came to an end. In the warm summer twilight, when the Barcelona sun paints the sky in dusty oranges and reds, Monturiol, Emilia, and the beautiful Doña Anita strolled down the Passeig de Gracia toward home, basking in the conviction that, together with the *Ictíneo*, they were about to make their entrance onto the brightly lit stage of world history.

Twenty-three

The People's Submarine

Monturiol's appearance on the stage of Catalan mythopoesis, in any case, had only just begun. As a second act to the Barcelona lunch, the highly caffeinated Altadill organized a victory tour through Catalonia. On June 14, the city of Girona hosted a grand luncheon in the inventor's honor, complete with local dignitaries and exuberant poets. On June 16, Monturiol and his submarine entourage made their triumphant entrance into the inventor's hometown of Figueres.

As he approached Figueres in a public carriage, city officials rode out to greet Monturiol and offer him a private carriage with the convertible top down. Tailgate partiers and bystanders lined the road into town, eager to be among the first to salute the returning hero. When Monturiol's cabriolet crossed the city limits, an orchestra and choral group dressed in sailors' costumes filed out in front and erupted into songs of local pride. Up ahead in another carriage four young virgins strewed flower petals along the prodigal son's path and recited poems about submariners and ancient heroes. As the procession wound through the streets, women on balconies tossed flowers and blew kisses. (His friend Martí Carlé, who had done much of the advance work for the Figueres celebrations, later teased Monturiol with: "You must still be cute.") In the central town square, a delegation emerged from city hall to recognize the inventor officially as a Favored Son. This meant his portrait—his *full-body* portrait, they assured him—would hang in the city council's chamber. Estanislau Figueras, the local deputy to the national congress, rushed to embrace Monturiol, while the local poet laureate rendered homage to the hero of the day.

Carlé, highly aware of his friend's emotional fragility, had forwarded Monturiol a copy of the poet laureate's lines, "for I fear that if it catches you unprepared it will overwhelm you." It was no use. As the verses reverberated across the Figueres main square, the impossibly sensitive Monturiol collapsed into a pool of sobs, crushed under the weight of all the great expectations heaped upon him. Carlé, hoping to prevent so much good news from sending his hero into a metaphysical funk, tried joking with Monturiol. "What else do you want, my boy?" he wrote in a note. "You threw yourself into the arcane world of science, but now it is the party that pays. You'll find enough silence and isolation in Neptune's abysses." After regaining self-control, Monturiol wiped away the tears and thanked his well-wishers.

That evening the town held a ball in honor of the inventor. The poets of the evening cajoled their hero into dancing at least some of the night away. When it was over, Monturiol retired to his mother's house. If he had been hoping for a restful sleep, however, he was disappointed. A few minutes later an orchestra pulled up under his window and serenaded the hero of the people. The next morning, and for several days thereafter, the party continued. There were more banquets, more poems, and more dancing—traditional Catalan dances called *sardanes*, in which a large group of alternating sexes forms a circle, holding hands up high, kicking and twisting in intricate patterns to chirpy horn music. At one benefit concert, a choir of sixty boys sang a "Hymn to Monturiol." A theater company put on a show called, touchingly, *Narcisito*.

Several times Monturiol gave the same speech, in which he humbly thanked his countrymen for revealing to him the importance of his work, the transcendental historical significance of which even he had not fully grasped, and modestly avowed that despite the poets' encomiums, he was not in fact a genius, that he lacked the faith in himself and the knowledge of things that characterize genius, that whereas a genius might be able to guarantee success in his enterprise, he, poor little Monturiol, could only offer his best efforts.

Never before had Figueres produced such a celebration in honor of one man, said Monturiol's first biographer and fellow Figuerenc, Puig Pujadas. According to a local paper of the time, the townspeople came "to celebrate a triumph that unites all parties, a triumph that cost neither tears nor blood, the triumph of science." The overwhelming reception for Monturiol was the moral equivalent of a ticker-tape parade for astronauts. It was a moment of *rauxa*, of Dionysian rapture, an apotheosis of sorts, that brought Monturiol to heights of glory from which he glimpsed the destiny of subaquatic humankind, all the while oblivious to the fact that the higher he rose the harder he would fall and that no failure haunts one so much as a destiny unrealized.

When Figueres at last released its Favored Son from its loving embrace, Monturiol went to Cadaqués, to the place where the submarine adventure began. There on the rocky shores, the lifelong friendships that germinated during years of exile blossomed into bouquets of flowers, intimate embraces, quiet celebrations, and companionship on long walks by the sea.

Toward the end of June, the public subscription effort for Monturiol's project took wing. In Barcelona, interested parties discussed earnestly how best to price the offering of shares. *Seny* took over from *rauxa*, as the Catalans turned their thoughts to hard cash. They spoke of raising the magnificent sum of half a million duros, divided into tiny shares available to the small investor. (Shares were eventually priced at a very reasonable 25 reales, or about the price of a pair of workman's trousers.) In Figueres, the city council authorized the use of all post offices and public buildings for the collection of funds. In Cadaqués, one of Monturiol's friends, a vintner named Lito, talked of selling his vineyard in order to help the *Ictíneo*. (Monturiol dissuaded him from such a rash move.) The submarine would be a project of, by, and for the people.

With his head still spinning from the poetry and the dancing

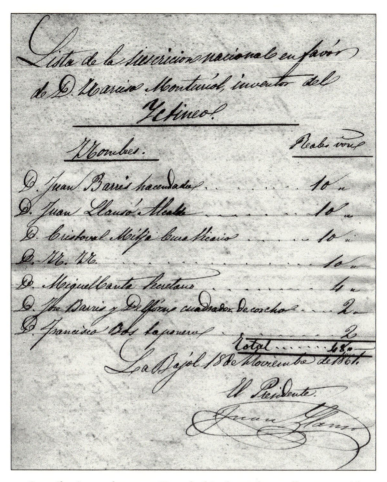

Contributing to the cause. Here the big shots of a small town outside
Figueres cobble 48 reales together for the submarine venture.
The mayor, the local priest, a farmer, and a person who wished
to remain anonymous each gave ten reales. The town secretary was
good for four. A cork cutter and his colleague each chipped in two.

on his victory tour, Monturiol began to fantasize once again about gargantuan underwater machines. He still had his drawings for the 1,200-tonne leviathan in his pocket. In his notes, however, he sketched out calculations for an incredible 5,000-tonne vessel, 111 meters long. (The largest submarines of the Second World War

were about this size.) He also created an imaginary School for Submariners, complete with departments of Respiration, Buoyancy
Control, Propulsion, and so forth, to train the many specialists
who would be required to man his proposed vessel. Vessels,
rather—for in the massive, socially conscious shipyards of his
mind, he had already manufactured a fleet of thirty such monsters,
accompanied by a hundred or so minisubs, to satisfy the most
pressing industrial and scientific needs of the time as well as to
provide for the coastal defense of Spain and Cuba. The inventor
still dreamed of leapfrogging into a whole new plane of subaquatic
being. It was as if, after launching a first satellite in low orbit
around the earth, the pioneers of space travel had suddenly
decided to plan the colonization of Mars.

On July 12, 1861, the government of Spain crashed the submarine
party. A Royal Decree tumbled out of Madrid with uncommon celer-
ity, announcing that Monturiol would be entitled to receive any and
all support required for the construction of a new *Ictíneo* from the
naval shipyard of his choice. It was, on the surface, everything that he
had asked for: a blank check to build his dream. The public at large
certainly took it as the crowning glory of his achievements and an
appropriate response to their own show of admiration and support.

The immediate effect of the Royal Decree, however, was to
quash the public fund-raising effort. Potential contributors sensi-
bly concluded that with the submarine receiving the protection of
the government, sacrifices from their own purses were no longer
required. In a letter of August 24, 1861, to his prospective chief engineer, Joan Monjo, Monturiol lamented that his association had no
money, for since the issuance of the Royal Decree, "the subscription
effort has died." The submariner and his friends harbored a sneak-
ing suspicion that the government's motive was precisely to quell
the public ardor for the project, a submarine passion that perhaps
carried one too many overtones of intellectual independence and
regionalist aspirations. In any case, Monturiol's project, which had
been just about to take off as a private venture, was suddenly
dependent again on the whims of government officials.

Monturiol decided to take the government at its word. In October 1861 he journeyed to Madrid, in hopes of securing the support promised in the Royal Decree of July 12. Typically, he dropped the plans for an *Ictíneo II* and opted to present his designs for leap-frogging into a new state of aqueous being. The admirals were stunned and perplexed. They had thought of the submarine project as a harmless frill, to be paid for out of the office petty cash. They were in no mood for leapfrogging anything. To be fair to the admirals, Monturiol's proposal was, in fiscal terms, grossly unrealistic. The Spanish government finances in the 1860s were in disarray, and the gargantuan submarine project would have added an appreciable percentage to the already oversized national debt.

Monturiol reconciled himself to the budgetary reality and agreed to pursue his original plans for the more tadpole-like second *Ictíneo*. Throughout the autumn and winter of 1861 and 1862, he called on government ministries in order to secure the promised support. The Catalan deputies to congress, as before, rallied to his side. Pascual Madoz put his shoulder up against the doors of the Spanish bureaucracy. But the government's offices remained firmly shut. The bill for so much Catalan support for the submarine was coming due. By early 1862, Monturiol understood that the Royal Decree issued six months previously had no real backing in the government. It had, in fact, been a ruse.

Monturiol returned to Barcelona and advised his submarine associates that he did not expect the government to live up to the commitment it had made in the Royal Decree. Madoz and his fellow deputies wrote to ask whether they should retrieve the various documents Monturiol had provided to the Ministry of the Navy in connection with his application for support. He sent back a letter laced with bitter sarcasm: "May the documents remain eternally in the Ministry as testament to the wisdom and patriotism of the current government."

In January of 1862 came the terrible news that the first *Ictíneo* was no more. While idling innocently in its berth in the port of Barcelona, it fell victim to a hit-and-run attack by an irresponsible freighter. Although the submarine had served its scientific purpose, after more than fifty dives, and Monturiol's mind was now fully concentrated on the yet-to-be-built second submarine, its loss was a devastating blow for the inventor. It was like losing a home—or, worse, losing a longtime friend.

At the urging of his fellow submarine enthusiasts, Monturiol moved to reopen the public subscription for the construction of the new *Ictíneo*. In a letter to the press dated April 2, 1862, he wrote:

> Ah! If the people of Spain should accept the responsibility that the government has declined, with what enthusiasm would I launch this enterprise that would have received the approbation of my compatriots, from whom it would have received a moral force and positive impetus!

Monturiol's most ardent fans stepped up to the challenge. Xifré and Madoz spearheaded a campaign to raise funds privately from wealthy individuals in Madrid. From base camp in Xifré's luxurious mansion, the pair made dozens of forays into high society, dramatizing the importance of the submarine mission for the benefit of select audiences.

While he waited to see whether the public would support his underwater dream, Monturiol learned of efforts in other countries to develop the submarine. From an article in an English magazine, he discovered that the Americans were beginning to experiment with underwater craft for use in the Civil War, which had just been declared. He also heard from contacts in Madrid that the Russian ambassador had sought to acquire information about the *Ictíneo* through underhand means. Although they had fired Bauer for making leaky submarines, the Russians still believed in the future of underwater navigation. Monturiol was shocked but perhaps not a little flattered that his *Ictíneo* should receive such clandestine attention. His competitive instincts were stirred, but his sense of frustration at the delays in getting support also increased.

Monturiol and Joan Tutau, a fellow revolutionary submariner, traveled to London and Paris over the summer of 1862 in order to take in some technology expositions. Their goal was to survey cutting-edge technology in a variety of fields and to assess the level of competition in the submarine world in particular. More impressive than the World Expo in London for Monturiol was the sight of English industrial civilization. The shipyards at Woolwich in particular bewitched him. He gazed in awe and horror at the immense field of cranes and docks, all deployed for the sake of building machines of war. Now more than ever, he wrote to his friends in Spain, must we concentrate on developing the art of underwater navigation, an art that will equalize the forces of nations, bringing an end to war, and ensure the spread of democracy and the triumph of a universal peace. The inventor still cherished the idea of a peaceful submarine.

The English demonstrated curiosity about Monturiol's activities as well. The journal *Twice a Week* learned of the visit of the Spanish inventor and published a favorable review of his project.

In Madrid, the dogged efforts of Xifré and Madoz were starting to pay off. By the time Monturiol returned from London, the Madrid team had rounded up a stunning 20,000 duros for the submarine project. Queen Isabel II provided 4,000 duros. Xifré himself was another major contributor.

In late 1862 the chairman of the submarine association's subscription drive, General Dulce, received a new assignment: He was to become captain general of the island of Cuba. Altadill and other friends of Monturiol arranged a going-away party for the general in Madrid. At the event, members of the submarine association awarded Dulce with a fancy certificate, saying, "We, as Catalans, as Spaniards . . . are doubly grateful to you, for we owe you a debt for your powerful and effective support of our invention." Many Cubans, too, had reason to be grateful. Once in Cuba, Dulce initiated a series of liberal reforms, including new laws to curtail slavery, which improved living conditions for many on the island.

Dulce's appointment was good for Cuba, but it was a godsend for the cause of underwater navigation. In early 1863, Altadill followed Dulce out to the Caribbean with presentation notes and several submarine treatises in his suitcase. Xifré footed the travel and entertainment expenses. With the general's blessing, Altadill published the treatises and set off on a road show through Cuba's major theaters, attracting the public with the great promise of underwater navigation.

Cuba's businessmen understood the defensive potential of submarines instinctively. Their wealth depended on the free flow of international trade in sugar, rum, coffee, tobacco, and other forms of Caribbean lucre. The Spanish navy was all that stood between them and ruin—or, worse, between them and the Americans, who had looked on Cuba with covetous eyes since the days of their own War of Independence. Given the parlous state of the Spanish navy at the time, the businessmen of Cuba cannot have slept soundly at night.

Furthermore, Cuba was in truth a province of Catalonia, economically speaking, even if it was administered politically by Madrid. Catalonia's manufactured goods monopolized the island's markets. Catalan capital funded much of its native industry. Catalan merchants did not hesitate to traffic in the slaves who constituted the backbone of the island's plantation economy. Not surprisingly, then, the men who made their fortunes in Cuba—men like Xifré Sr.—were mostly Catalans. At the same time, to balance the score perhaps, the men who brought to Cuba the republican theories and progressive ideals that would eventually incite the islanders to rise up against their colonial rulers were also often of Catalan origin.

With the enthusiastic support of Dulce, the former captain general of Catalonia now military ruler of Cuba, the submarine dream captured the hearts and minds of the islanders. After four months in the Caribbean, Altadill returned to Barcelona in triumph, bearing with him 20,000 duros in cash and at least as much again in future commitments. The utopian inventor and his progressive friends somehow were able to overlook the fact that the money had been made from the sweat of slaves.

The motives of the donors were mixed. Some, inspired by the same vision of cosmic progress as Monturiol, were moved by a kind of scientific philanthropy. Certainly Dulce and Xifré saw a link between the progress of science and the strength of liberal democratic institutions. Others responded to a patriotic impulse. They believed that the submarine would represent a boon to Spain, Catalonia, or Cuba—which were increasingly different concepts. The supporters of Spain saw the submarine as a way to beat the English, the Catalanists saw it as a way to assert superiority over Spain, and the Cubans saw it as a way to eliminate anybody who would take away their island and their way of life. Many contributors, however, undoubtedly took Altadill and Monturiol at their word when they insisted that the submarine was a lucrative investment.

Like any good venture capitalist, Monturiol had a knack for stacking fat numbers on top of thin facts. Assume coral sells at 8 duros a pound, that a submarine can haul in an average of 50 pounds of coral a day for 200 days a year, that running costs are 18,000 a year for maintenance and crew, he said. Do the sums, and you will see that there is a potential profit of 62,000 duros a year! Now, imagine that the submarine brings in as much as 300 pounds of coral a day—a perfectly reasonable assumption—instead of 50! And suppose that the submarine develops sidelines in underwater farming and deep-sea fishing! In fact, if all the cards turn up in the right order, you could get your money back within weeks of the first dive, and everything after that would be pure gravy. Altadill used these numbers shamelessly to lure prospective investors—but then it seems likely that he believed in the giddy calculus himself, for he invested heavily too.

Monturiol's prestige in Barcelona continued to climb, reaching a new peak when he was named vice president of Ateneu's sciences section in 1863. From his newly exalted position, he opened up another front in the cultural revolution in which he was engaged. Together with Altadill and his fellow revolutionary submariner Sunyer i Capdevila, he edited a *Democratic Almanac* on behalf of the Ateneu that later earned the double distinction of being both denounced by the Catholic Church and banned by the Spanish government. The *Almanac* and similar publications served an important purpose: They convinced the intelligentsia of Barcelona that the republican cause was alive and well despite its enforced absence from national political life.

At around the same time, Monturiol's friend and master in the art of portrait painting, Ramón Martí i Alsina, painted the image of the submarine visionary. Martí, by the way, put his money where his friendship was. A share certificate now in the possession of the Museu Marítim bears the impecunious artist's name.

By the end of 1863, after riding a roller coaster of recognition and rejection, his hopes for government support raised, dashed, revived, and dashed again, Monturiol had finally amassed enough money to take the next step in his submarine project. Along the way, he had found some unlikely friends: a progressive military ruler, a millionaire playboy, a theologically disturbed medical doctor, and a caffeine-driven pulp novelist. It was a strange set of bedfellows for an ex-utopian communist. Even stranger was the extent to which the monomaniacal pursuit of his dream drove Monturiol to collaborate with the forces of a very pre-utopian status quo. He had set up shop in the central shipyards of Barcelona's rabidly capitalist economy; he had sought the benediction of the queen of a society he had once called corrupt; he had embraced the bourgeois poetasters of a Catalan separatism he had previously rejected as provincial; he had accepted wealth expropriated from the slaves of Cuba; and he had offered his scientific invention as a savage weapon of war to a general he had previously labeled a dictator—all for the sake of the art of underwater navigation.

Had he been another inventor—or anybody else, for that matter—one might well have doubted the depth of his convictions. But Monturiol was Monturiol: a true believer to the end. Everything he did was, indeed, for the sake of his submarine, a submarine that might one day save the world. As the money flowed into the coffers, the incorrigible utopian showed only relief at the opportunity to turn his thoughts from the madding crowd at last and devote his energies once again to the fine art of underwater navigation.

Twenty-four

The New God of Movement

Riding the same roller coaster of hope and despair was Barcelona's other Icarian pioneer, Ildefons Cerdà. Back in the first weeks of May 1861, when Monturiol's submarine project entered its darkest hour and he issued his plaintive lament to the press, Cerdà, too, published an anguished call for help with his own post-utopian project. The Extension of Barcelona still existed mainly in his own mind. In the first three years of its existence, in fact, the Eixample hosted the construction of a mere twenty houses, scattered haphazardly over the lightly marked blocks. Hostile property owners and uncomprehending city authorities forestalled any advance on the project.

In his pamphlet "A Few Words about the Extension, Addressed to the Public of Barcelona," Cerdà renewed his plea for support for the plan that had, at least officially, already been adopted. Most importantly, he offered some groundbreaking proposals on the management of the relationship between the public sector and private property owners in Barcelona (and, by extension, in any comparable exercise of urban development). In essence, Cerdà outlined an innovative system in which the private sector would assume responsibility for financing infrastructure development, while the public sector would guarantee the integrity of the conceptual framework that would ensure the private property developments an appropriate return on their investments.

But the politics of urban planning were ugly. In 1862, both

Cerdà and his rival Rovira were elected to a committee to oversee key aspects of the development of the Extension. When each learned of the other's presence, both quit the committee. The wind blew freely over the flat fields around Barcelona.

In 1863, just as Monturiol's project resumed a propitious trajectory, things also took a turn for the better for Cerdà's urban plan. Cerdà accepted a seat on the city council, and from this new position of relative authority he began to have a direct influence on the implementation of his plan. He immersed himself in the details of negotiating the transfer of the crazy quilt of landholdings in the territory of the Extension and organized teams to lay down the lines for new streets across the vacant lots outside the city limits.

Falling victim to Cerdà's renewed assault on the city was his already weakened family life. Fed up with his monomaniacal focus on urban planning, his wife Clothilde ran off to Madrid in the company of their three daughters, a lover, and a fourth, illegitimate, daughter (who nonetheless bore the name of Cerdà).

Cerdà barely paused to take notice of his crumbling domestic life. Instead, he took time to reconceive the basis of modern human society. He began, true to form, by refining the details of his master plan for Barcelona. In the latest draft, he installed an additional series of railroad lines that cut through the heart of the Eixample and then looped together around the old city to reach the port, whence they connected with the long-distance lines linking Barcelona to the outside world. He rearranged the houses on the blocks between which the trains ran so that their backs would show to the tracks. He specified that the tracks should run in trenches, so that trains could pass under the cross streets.

Cerdà's concern with railroads was very much of the moment. At the time, Barcelona was experiencing the thrills of a bubble economy. Its stock market was surging to new heights on the back of its railroad shares. While Barcelona's poets labored over fusty verses about a mythical past, its businessmen scrambled to catch up with the future—a future, they were certain, that would be crisscrossed by train tracks.

Cerdà's approach to the railroad craze reflected his trademark combination of *seny* and *rauxa*. On the one hand, his technical specifications for the layout of the tracks were as detailed and pragmatic as anything else in his *seny*-ish plan. On the other hand, his visions of a locomotive future were as exalted as those of the most *rauxa*-ish utopian. "Railroads and electric telegraphs will harmonize language, weights, measures, and currency," he wrote. "They will destroy ancient hatreds between nations and secure the supremacy of universal peace, sweeping away class antagonism. . . . They will give rise to the harmony needed between the different classes within society." Cabet maintained only that the trains would haul in democracy; in Cerdà's future world, the trains *were* a democracy of sorts. Decades before the invention of the modern automobile, he planned his city around the vision of a locomotive that "might penetrate into a town, circulate through every neighborhood, cut through every street block, approach every house, and even enter the houses!" The ability to move around quickly within the city was more than a gesture toward economic efficiency; it was a question of personal liberty.

Supporting Cerdà's post-utopian proposal was a radically new conception of the nature of urban life. According to Cerdà's new way of thinking, the city was no longer primarily a place in space with an identifiable center. Instead, it was movement. The city was simply a name for a vast and complex network of connections, a network that flourished to the extent that the number and efficiency of its interconnections increased. Thus, in place of the old ceremonial plazas, he now offered railroad tracks. The only facsimile of the old center in the new Barcelona would be the train stations. And the most important train station would be the one located near the port, where the trains would meet the ships that linked Barcelona with the rest of the world.

Cerdà's ideas about networks would have made any information-age sociologist proud. In the century before the hi-tech seers forecast a world without frontiers, Cerdà wrote, "Everything in this century is aimed at the disappearance of boundaries, everything tends toward general fusion, everything favors peace." Cerdà's

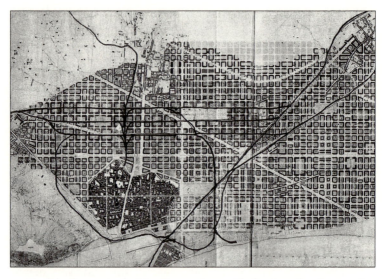

Cerdà's plan revised, 1863. Comparison with the 1859 plan (page 92)
shows that the blocks above the midsection have been rearranged
to allow for three parallel railroad tracks. In addition, lines
connecting the port with the rail network have been added.

utopian ideals—like those of many an Internet guru—were not far
below the surface.

The year 1863 found Cerdà worshiping at the shrine of a new
god: the god that elides boundaries, harmonizes tones, fuses all
things—in short, the god of movement. Cerdà's earlier work had
the same inspiration, to be sure; but now its divine source lay
revealed. Although there are any number of factors that might
have precipitated Cerdà's shift to a subtly new frame of reference—and no telling which was truly decisive—it seems much
more than a coincidence that, at the very moment of this
epiphany, the city of Barcelona had already universally recognized
one individual as the official boundary breaker, the great fuser of
new elements, the inventor of the most outlandish form of movement known to humankind: Narcís Monturiol. Monturiol's
strange dreams once again stood at the beginning of a most
unlikely chain of events.

As the year came to a close, Cerdà and his crew started work on the foundations of the Gran Via, longest avenue of his plan—and the longest in any continental European city. While Cerdà was laying down the grid of a new Barcelona, Monturiol was laying the keel for his new submarine.

Twenty-five

How to Build a Submarine,
Part II

As the money poured in, Monturiol redoubled his efforts to build a superior submarine, the *Ictíneo II*. The first submarine had been an experimental craft, intended to test his theories about underwater navigation. In his design for the *Ictíneo II,* he sought both to remedy defects in his previous submarine and to add new capabilities. The second craft, he insisted, was going to be the real thing, an oceangoing vessel capable of retrieving treasure and scientific knowledge from the deep.

The work once again took place at the Nuevo Vulcano shipyards. Joining the old crew of revolutionary shipbuilders were two critical additions.

Joan Monjo i Pons, a highly capable naval architect, took over as chief engineer on the project. One year older than Monturiol, Monjo hailed from the island of Mallorca. Monjo's past was one of hard work and even harder luck. At the age of eight, he lost his father, and then he lost the rest of his childhood to work. As a young man he sailed for Cuba to make his fortune but came back five years later empty-handed. He wrote the premier textbook on naval architecture of his time, a work that filled two volumes and won an award as a "work of public utility" from the Barcelona government, but he failed to make any money on it and was forced to take on more work. "I could not enjoy my youth, I have always been a slave to work and to economy, and yet my luck has always been adverse," he complained.

Model of Ictíneo II

His past made Monjo into an unusually disciplined and driven man. It also left him with a thin skin—easily pricked by unintended slights, apt to swell and blister with an unspoken sense of injustice—and a phobia for uncertainty and lack of clarity. "I cannot live in ambiguous circumstances," he said, identifying a character attribute that was perhaps not ideal for managing a utopian submarine project.

Yet, underneath the thorny exterior, Monjo remained an idealist. He immediately understood that the submarine represented the greatest challenge facing naval architecture of the time. "Monturiol cried out for me, I dropped everything, and I followed him." Mesmerized by an engineering ideal and its heroic sponsor, Monjo volunteered to work for minimum wage—less than minimum wage, in fact—and he also invested his own small savings in the venture.

Monjo's skills would prove to be of decisive help in converting Monturiol's designs to physical reality. It was Monjo who kept the detailed records of the construction of the *Ictíneo II* and drew the blueprints we have today.

The other important addition to the team was Josep Pascual i Deop, a whiz kid from Barcelona's newest school of engineering. Although he was only twenty years old, he soon proved his worth as a submarine mechanic and would eventually assume responsibility for the vessel's propulsion and life-support systems. Monturiol treated the young engineer like a favorite son. Josep idolized the inventor and took more than a passing interest in his daughter, the beautiful Doña Anita. She, in turn, visited her father in the shipyard more than was strictly required by filial piety.

As work progressed in the submarine yard, the social conditions in the workshop did not always live up to Monturiol's communist ideals. At times, the stress of performing the complex engineering work distorted personal relations among the ship's builders. Chief engineer Monjo, in particular, seemed to get on everybody's nerves. On one occasion, a number of comrades protested to Monturiol that Monjo was being autocratic. Monjo told the inventor, in private, that some of the workers just could not follow orders. Ever the utopian, Monturiol urged his chief to treat the workers with "extreme consideration and benevolence" and suggested that the problems would go away if only he would be "more kind." Naturally, Monjo got even more annoyed. Meanwhile, as everyone could see, the youthful Josep Pascual i Deop was becoming Monturiol's favorite, his right-hand man and youthful heir apparent. This irritated Monjo even more. In the end, however, Monjo seems to have taken Monturiol's advice. He took long Sunday strolls with his politically rambunctious crew, and eventually the rifts were healed.

The design for the *Ictíneo II* called for a substantially larger craft than the *Ictíneo I*. It would be 17 meters long to the latter's 7 meters, displace 72 tonnes of water as opposed to 10, and have an interior chamber with 29 cubic meters of space, compared with the 7 cubic meters of the first submarine. It would carry a crew of twenty submariners, compared to the four or five of the first *Ictíneo*.

In Monturiol's view, size mattered. A larger submarine would be able to gather more coral and carry more powerful armaments. A larger crew meant more power for propulsion. The inventor hoped his twenty-man team would be able to drive the submarine at the minimum acceptable velocity of 3 knots. The increase in crew size further offered an opportunity for specialization: individuals could master distinct functions, such as depth control, the gathering of coral, and the operation of life-support systems. Above all, Monturiol believed, a larger submarine would be a safer submarine. It would be better able to hold its own against those unnameable

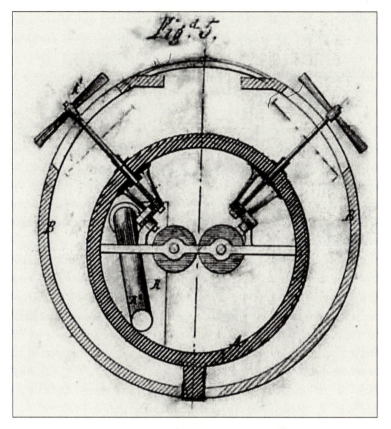

Cross section with maneuvering propellers

monsters and voracious whirlpools, not to mention the irresponsible freighters. With more room for improved life-support systems, the larger submarine would further his mission of sustaining human life in an inhospitable environment.

The *Ictíneo II* would make use of the same double-hull design that had proved its worth in the first submarine. The increased size of the submarine, of course, meant that the walls of the interior pressurized chamber would have to be sturdier. For the newly enlarged interior chamber, Monturiol prescribed olivewood walls 10 centimeters thick, reinforced with rings of oak and sheathed in 2 millimeters of copper. In order to ensure that the copper coating was hermetic, Monturiol made use of advanced welding techniques that were very unusual in Spain at the time. He estimated that the chamber could withstand the water pressure at 500 meters but, once again, set a limit of 50 meters for safety's sake.

The propulsion system of the second submarine was essentially the same as that of the first, but larger. The power train connected to the aft propeller now had space for twenty cranking men, facing each other in two rows of ten. In order to improve the maneuverability of the new submarine, Monturiol added two small, outward-facing propellers to the aft of the vessel. These would allow the pilot to turn the craft in the water even when it was not moving forward.

The *Ictíneo I* used ballast tanks only to achieve neutral buoyancy and relied on hand-turned propellers to pull itself up and down in the water. In the second submarine, Monturiol was determined to achieve total buoyancy control. He wanted to be able to descend by admitting enough water into the ballast tanks to create negative buoyancy and then ascend by expelling the water to reestablish positive buoyancy. The complication lay in the second half of the equation. He had to find a way to empty the ballast tanks of water even when in the intense pressures of the deep.

His first step was to divide the problem. He created two sets of ballast tanks. The first and by far the larger set were the so-called "flotation bladders." These could carry up to 8 cubic meters (or tonnes) of water. When filled to the brim, they would bring the submarine to something just above neutral buoyancy at the surface. They would be filled and emptied only on the surface and so did not require any special pumping mechanism.

Real depth control would depend on the second set of ballast tanks, the so-called "natatory bladders." These carried only about one-tenth as much water as the flotation bladders. On the surface, once the flotation bladders were full, the natatory bladders would be filled with enough additional water to tip the submarine over into negative buoyancy. As the craft descended, the increasing water pressure would compress the hull, thereby decreasing its volume and making its buoyancy still more negative. Once the sub reached the desired cruising depth, the natatory bladders would be emptied of enough water to reestablish neutral buoyancy. Owing to the compression of the hull, the greater the depth reached, the emptier the natatory bladders needed to be. In order to ascend, the tanks would be emptied further, thus reestablishing positive buoyancy.

Monturiol decided on the size of the natatory tanks by estimating how much volume the submarine would shed at its maximum rated depth and then putting double that volume (for safety's sake) into the natatory tanks as compensation. In a formula:

volume of natatory tanks = 0.01 percent compression per meter × 50-meter maximum × 72-cubic meter total volume × safety factor of 2 = 0.72 cubic meters

The remaining problem, then, was how to empty the small natatory tanks at great depths. Monturiol figured that a tank of compressed gas could be used to expel water from the tanks, provided the pressure of the gas exceeded that of the surrounding water by a safe margin. So he set to work creating a reliable source of compressed gas.

The system he devised made use of controlled combustion to generate high-pressure gas in a confined space. He found that a mix of coal, nitrate soda, and manganese oxide, when ignited, would combust slowly and generate excess gas; about a kilogram would generate 150 liters of gas in the space of twenty minutes. By containing the reaction within a small sealed tank, the resulting gas would be highly compressed. Monturiol recommended that the gas tanks remain at a pressure double that of the deepest water in which the craft would be expected to go. In that way, the crew would always have, within a large margin of safety, the capability to expel water from the natatory tanks and thus achieve positive buoyancy.

In order to make underwater operations easier, he complemented the compressed gas tanks with mechanical pumps that

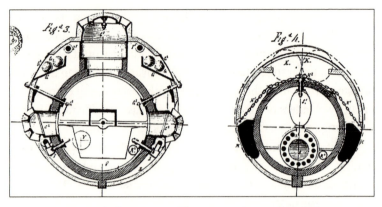

Emergency ballast system. The cross section on the left shows
two pairs of lead balls that would serve as the first set
of emergency ballast weights. In the cross section on the right,
the black smudges represent the second set of emergency ballast weights,
to be released by action of the chain.

could inject water under pressure into the tanks. By adding water
at high pressure, he could return the gas to its required pressure
after use without going through further combustion.

As always, the comfort and safety of the crew were foremost in
the inventor's mind. Just in case the bladder system failed, Monturiol installed two sets of emergency ballast, to be dropped in the
event of an emergency ascension.

In order to meet his objective of being able to remain underwater indefinitely, Monturiol still needed a way to replenish oxygen.
In his earlier experiments, he had failed to find a reaction that
could be performed in the confines of the submarine to generate
oxygen. Now, he concocted hundreds of chemical stews in search
of the elixir of life. His notebooks of the time read like the cookbooks of a mad alchemist. His kitchen sink must have been a hazardous site.

What the inventor sought was a recipe that did not require the
application of an open flame and was otherwise safe for use in the
hermetically sealed cabin of a submarine. The key to safety was to
use relatively friendly chemical compounds that did not threaten

to generate unwanted noxious gases along with the oxygen. The key to avoiding fire was the use of catalysts. As Monturiol knew, some chemical reactions that otherwise require heat can be initiated in the cold by means of a catalyst.

After much experimentation, Monturiol settled on a brew that answered his needs. He found that manganese dioxide catalyzes the decomposition of potassium chlorate into potassium chloride gas and oxygen gas at low temperatures. That is:

$$\overset{MnO_2}{2\ KClO_3 \rightarrow 2\ KCl + 3\ O_2}$$

Thus, submariners of the future would bring aboard a small, manageable supply of chemicals—potassium chlorate and manganese dioxide—and by mixing them in the appropriate quantities generate fresh oxygen as required.

The next challenge was to devise a method for deciding just when and how much oxygen should be produced inside the submarine cabin. Monturiol could have chosen to rely simply on the crew's sense of smell and well-being. However, such a solution seemed imprecise and even potentially risky—after all, an oxygen-starved crew might lose their senses altogether. So he devised an instrument to measure the amount of oxygen in the submarine chamber. The instrument relied on the simple fact that phosphorus, when it burns, will consume all the oxygen available within a confined space. Monturiol partially filled a tube with mercury, added some phosphorus, sealed the tube, and ignited the phosphorus. After the phosphorus consumed all the oxygen in the sealed tube, the mercury would rise to fill the emptied space. The relative amount of the rise of the mercury thus indicated the oxygen content of the air in the tube. The atmosphere normally consists of about 20 percent oxygen. Monturiol discovered that anything from 18 to 24 percent was acceptable inside the submarine chamber.

The inventor devised a comparable instrument for measuring the concentration of carbon dioxide. The principle was the same, only the device used a solution of caustic potassium, which would absorb any carbon dioxide in a sample and thus indicate the concentration. If the concentration reached 5 percent, he found, it was essential to purify the air of carbon dioxide or return to the surface.

On most trips under the waves, Monturiol confessed, he forwent such costly and complex analyses of the submarine's atmosphere. Instead, he brought along a few candles and a sealable jar. He knew how long the candle would burn when the jar was filled with ordinary air. By comparing that to the time it would burn when the jar was filled with underwater air, he would get a rough estimate of the air quality in the sub.

At this point Monturiol also gave some thought to the matter of those *animalillos*—the germs and other impurities that could foul the air of the submarine. The world's knowledge of microbiology at the time was very tiny indeed. Louis Pasteur had made his famous discovery about sour milk only a few years previously, in 1856. Monturiol cited the contemporary work of a Russian scientist who conducted an experiment to discover the source of the foul odors emanating from groups of young soldiers. The Russian scientist apparently hung a metal ball full of snow in a small room where a squadron of twenty soldiers slept. The following morning, he collected the condensation that formed on the ball. The resulting fluid reportedly smelled just like the squadron and tasted spicy and unpleasant. When examined under a microscope, this pestilent brew was found to contain millions of tiny, moving beasts— bacteria.

Monturiol figured that submariners would want to eliminate these odoriferous and foul-tasting creatures. He believed that the slaked-lime solution of his carbon dioxide purifier would probably do them in, but just in case the critters survived the alkaline solution, he also sketched the design for a separate purification chamber that would pass the submarine's air through a solution of sulfuric acid. That would get them, he figured. In the language of nineteenth-century organic chemistry:

$$H_2SO_4 + \text{animalillo} \rightarrow \textit{dead} \text{ animalillo}$$

Monturiol's investigation of the matter of "those gases," the result of "bad digestion," led to a similar conclusion. Slaked lime, sulfuric acid, and potassium are reactive absorbents, he discovered, and would soak up a range of unpleasant fumes. Although it is unclear whether he performed extensive experiments on the matter, he was confident that a good mix of absorbents would eliminate foul odors from the interiors of submarines of the future.

On the basis of his discoveries in chemistry, Monturiol designed a larger integrated version of the air-supply system for the new submarine. He connected the output valve of the oxygen generator to the intake of the carbon dioxide purifier so that any unwanted gases mixed in with the oxygen could be removed. The combined output flowed through a valve into the back end of the interior cabin. He ran an input pipe for the air purifier all the way to the front of the cabin, thus ensuring circulation of the air throughout the vessel. With the design of the integrated air-supply system, Monturiol had created the blueprint for a fairly complete solution to the problem of life support in a hermetically sealed environment. The fundamental idea was that submariners would take aboard relatively small and manageable quantities of chemicals—lime, manganese dioxide, potassium chlorate, phosphorus—along with some appropriately configured instruments, and by following a few simple instructions they would be able to purify the air inside the chamber of noxious elements and replenish the oxygen required to survive. Humankind would be able to live in the inhospitable environment of the deep, if not indefinitely, at least as long as the potassium chlorate and the other supplies held out. And if he could figure out how to mine the required minerals from the seafloor or extract them from seawater itself, the submarine and its crew would be able to remain in the watery world forever.

Monturiol splurged on portholes. The new *Ictíneo* would have a total of nineteen, each 10 centimeters thick and 20 centimeters in diameter on the outside, tapering to 12 centimeters on the inside, clustered in bulbs like the eyes of a fruit fly. These would be Monturiol's cherished windows on the underwater world.

In his voyages on the *Ictíneo I*, however, Monturiol had seen firsthand just how dark it could get under the ocean's surface. Under the best of conditions—sun high overhead, water still and clear as glass—the amount of daylight penetrating the sea diminishes considerably for every meter of depth. Under the conditions that obtained in and around the harbor of Barcelona—muddy water, silt from rivers, sand kicked up by waves, and uncounted trillions of *animalillos*—the world 30 meters down could be as dark as night. A part of Monturiol's plan, furthermore, was to take the submarine underneath submerged ledges, where he imagined that rich crops of coral sometimes grew dangling down in the shade, and possibly into undersea caves.

He needed a powerful source of underwater light. From his adventures in chemistry, he knew that when H_2 (hydrogen) and O_2 (oxygen) combine to produce H_2O (water), the reaction releases energy in the form of a bright flame. The problem, of course, is that the flame can easily become too bright. Hydrogen and oxygen form an extremely combustible mix and will explode if not monitored carefully.

Monturiol's design called for hydrogen and oxygen to be supplied through separate valves, each with a pressure gauge, into a chamber lined on one side with a parabolic mirror and on the other with glass. By carefully monitoring the admission of the two gases into the chamber, the reaction could be controlled in order to generate a steady light. Monturiol also found that he could enhance the brightness and color of the flame by adding small amounts of zirconium, magnesium, zinc oxide, and other materials to the mix. He tested such a lamp on dry land and found it could illuminate an individual so as to be recognizable at 200 meters at night in the driving rain.

In his design, he positioned a single powerful hydrogen lamp on top of the forward half of the submarine. The oxygen tube for the lamp tapped into the oxygen generator already included in his design. The hydrogen would be stored in a separate pressurized container. The lamp was mounted on a swivel, so it could be

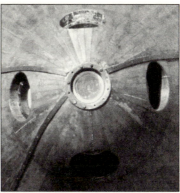

The portholes of the Ictíneo II. *Model in the Port of Barcelona*

turned in any direction to light up the wonders of the eternal darkness.

Since the principal purpose of the new *Ictíneo*, at least according to the shareholders' prospectus, was to reap a harvest of untold riches from the bottom of the sea, the submarine required implements with which to do the reaping. Monturiol included retractable pincers at the front end of the submarine. These were to be manipulated from inside to reach out and grab coral or other treasure from the seafloor and from those overhead ledges.

Monturiol also described a cylindrical storage tank to be carried underneath the *Ictíneo*. The idea was to stuff the treasure into the tank for transportation to the surface. Monturiol never drew the detail for the tank, however, so it appears it was never built. As for the pincers, they look nimble enough; the surprising thing is how small they are. They look like the vestigial paws on whales. They are more a gesture toward the possibility of manipulating objects on the outside of the submarine than implements designed to pillage the ocean floor.

The *Ictíneo II* was in every sense a more complete submarine than its predecessor. It offered dramatically improved capabilities in

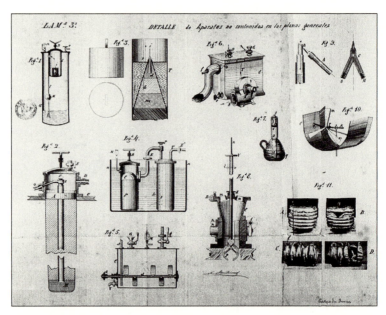

Details of Ictíneo's *mechanical systems. Figure 1: oxygen generation tank;*
Figure 2: chemical fuel rod for engine; Figure 3: detail of chemical fuel rod;
Figure 4: pressurized gas generator; Figure 5: waste gas container;
Figure 6: air-purification system; Figure 7: gas concentration
measurement device; Figure 8: coral pincer; Figure 9: hydrogen lamp;
Figure 10: water speedometer; Figure 11: results of pressure tests
on metal tanks.

depth control, maneuverability, life support, lighting, and acces-
sories. Even in its outward appearance it seemed a more purposeful craft. It had the same curvy fishlike exterior as the earlier
machine, but the proportions were different. It was longer, sleeker,
and more tubular. If the first submarine was a guppy, the second
was a barracuda.

Twenty-six

The Ictíneo *Rides Again*

Throughout 1864, Monturiol was riding a wave of psychic optimism to narcotic heights. In a letter of April 8, 1864, to his friend and benefactor General Dulce, he confided his deepest thoughts:

> This enterprise, taken to its conclusion, has an incalculable transcendence for our poor country and a powerful influence on the destiny of Humanity. This importance absorbs me completely and overwhelms me.

Indeed, the transcendental importance of his project was such, in Monturiol's own eyes, that at times, as he confessed in his bipolar way, the forces of darkness threatened to emerge right out of the sun of hope itself and submerge him in an existential mire. The very idea of underwater navigation was "of an order so superior," he said, that he was worried he might faint or regret having pursued it. But he persevered despite all, he told Dulce, because he believed he was being faithful to an ideal. It was the nearest thing he had to religion:

> To comprehend and dominate nature in all its parts is the ideal of Science, and it will be the ideal of Humanity, just as soon as humankind can break the fetters that keep it subject to the limited atmosphere on earth. This ideal I desire with the same fervor that religious people feel before their ideal of God the creator.

The Ictíneo II *prior to launch*

Monturiol wasn't just building a submarine; he was participating in the greatest—the only—project on earth: the liberation of humankind. People of the world unite, he might have said. You have nothing to lose but your chains to the earth's atmosphere!

On May 6, 1864, members of the submarine association met to reorganize themselves as a limited liability corporation under the name of La Navegación Submarina. The board of the new corporation consisted of Monturiol, the novelist Altadill, and a man named Font—one of Monturiol's fans from the Ateneu. Joan Tutau was named president. The new arrangement was intended to make raising capital easier and also to clarify the relationship between the first investors and the new investors. La Navegación Submarina was capitalized at 58,900 duros—the sum of contributions collected by Altadill and credit for the capital provided by previous contributors.

In an address to his shareholders, Monturiol did not temper the flaming emotions that roiled in his overheated mind. "I swing between doubt and hope, between enthusiasm and dejection," he declared. He contemplated out loud the possibility that he was a *loco*, that he was living a life of fantasies, like a poet in search of mermaids and underwater cities. If it turned out that he was indeed just another *loco*, he said, he would feel sorry not for himself but for all those he took along for the ride, and for the wider public that would then have cause to be skeptical of all great and worthy enterprises. For what he did not doubt was that underwater navigation was a great and worthy enterprise. As for his poor humble self, it was a matter of life or death. Either his submarine would conquer the deep, he announced dramatically, or he would remain buried with it at the bottom of the sea.

By the end of the summer of 1864, the *Ictíneo II* had assumed its final outward shape. The exterior and interior hulls were complete, although much work remained to be done on the internal machinery. On September 9, friends and family of the *Ictíneo* gathered in the shipyard for a pre-launch celebration. Victor Balaguer, by now the unofficial leader of Barcelona's cultural elite, gave the keynote address. Monturiol thanked his supporters. Throughout the ceremonies, the *Ictíneo II* remained perched on its trailer with motionless grandeur. A journalist described it in the following day's paper as a "marine monster."

On October 2, 1864, all 72 tonnes of the *Ictíneo II* slid "majestically" down a ramp and splashed into the water of the harbor of Barcelona to an "explosion of applause and *vivas,*" as the reporter from *El Ampurdanés* put it. This time great care was taken to ensure no damage was done, and the launch was free of incident. Once in the water, the 17-meter beast showed an oddly low profile next to the fishing boats and freighters moored alongside. "Our hearts trembled with a sense of profound satisfaction and pride," wrote the reporter.

The story of Monturiol's frightful encounter with the bureaucratic Other in Madrid had by now become part of local mythology—especially in his home region of the Empordà. The reporter from *El Ampurdanés* exuded sympathy:

> Yes, Monturiol, the history of your past eight years has been a continuous series of tempestuous ups and downs that would have crushed a hundred minds less powerful—we bear witness to the disappointments, frustrated hopes, the deceptions that oppressed you; and, above all, to the ceaseless plots hatched

against you by men who, blinded by their repugnant prejudice, fight with any means the science that comes from unorthodox minds. But enough: Your heart, much bigger than your head, does not deign to bear grievances.

The successful launch of the *Ictíneo II* was a vindication not just of Monturiol but of the native virtue of northern Catalonia. The submarine, the inventor's regional champion exulted, now looked upon a "smiling future" of great riches and scientific glory. The writer concluded with what must count as one of the most unusual exhortations in human history: "To the water!"

The *Ictíneo II*, however, was not quite ready to leave dock. Work continued on the inside of the submarine throughout the winter and until the spring of 1865. Led by Monjo and Pascual, builders installed the various propulsion mechanisms, the air-supply system, the lights, and so forth. In the meantime, Monturiol recruited members of the crew from the interested public. The men who powered the *Ictíneo* through the water came largely from the class of artisans: independent workers, like coopers and tailors—the same class from which Monturiol himself originated.

On May 6, 1865, Monturiol conducted a final inspection and decided that the submarine was ready for preliminary trials. On May 12 he conducted the first tests of the ship's systems while she lay in her berth. The crew took the ship underwater in order to test the buoyancy and balance-control systems. Everything checked out. On the night of May 16 they fired up the hydrogen lamp underwater. This, too, proved satisfactory.

On the morning of May 20, Monturiol and a crew of sixteen took the *Ictíneo II* for its first ride in open water. The craft churned its way out of the harbor and turned to run along the beaches stretching to the north of Barcelona. Monturiol ordered a dive, and the *Ictíneo II* descended below the surface of the waters in front of Barcelona's beaches. Every 5 meters, the inventor halted the descent and paused to ensure the integrity and balance of the boat. Step by step, they reached a depth of 30 meters, which he decided would be the limit.

The crew of the Ictíneo II

Next, Monturiol decided to see how far the submarine could advance underwater while maintaining a constant depth. In the test, the submarine covered an impressive 1.2 kilometers along the beaches while not deviating appreciably from a depth of 17 meters. Neutral buoyancy was a fact.

The new ship handled like a dream. Many years later, the engineer Pascual i Deop recalled the experience of the *Ictíneo II*'s first dives:

> I was intimately familiar with all the mechanisms of the ship and its scientific functions, and all this allowed me to envision

its behavior underwater; yet I would not have presumed that a mass like the *Ictíneo*, easily unbalanced on account of its length and its 70 cubic meters of volume, could be maneuvered with a half-turn of a simple faucet, detaining itself in the body of the sea at the will of its pilot.... Twenty-five years have passed since those remarkable tests, and yet the effect those first immersions produced on me has never faded from my memory.

Manifestly, Pascual, like Monturiol before him, felt the transcendental effect of neutral buoyancy. As much as it was a machine for underwater locomotion, the submarine was a vehicle for the exploration of consciousness. What astonished those who took the trip was the way in which this clunking coffinlike contraption, when immersed in the utter obscurity of the sea, could induce a sense of imperturbable serenity. They expected sound and fury, but they found nirvana—or at least a dark and peaceful place very like it.

The Zen-like ride of the *Ictíneo II* had its tranquilizing effect on other passengers too. For crew members not near the pressure-depth gauges, the only indication of the submarine's position in the water as it descended was the gradual subsidence of rocking motions from the waves and the diminishment of light penetrating through the portholes. It must have been something like an exercise in sensory deprivation. One day, Pascual took along four new crew members to replace others who had called in sick. After the submarine had descended to 21 meters, one of the four—blissfully unaware of the submarine's movements—awoke from a meditative slumber and asked if he could go up top and smoke a cigarette.

The sense of calm was shattered on June 16. Monturiol, Pascual, and a full complement were enjoying the ride at 23 meters, when suddenly water began to spray into the interior living chamber of the submarine. A quarter of a tonne of water—enough to fill a couple of bathtubs—sloshed into the bottom of the leaking vessel. If nothing was done, the craft would flood and sink to the bottom within minutes and take the crew with it to a watery grave. Montu-

Monturiol during construction of the Ictíneo II:
starting to get that worried look.

riol instinctively grabbed the valve for the ballast tanks and
cranked it open all the way, allowing the pressurized gas to blast
the water out from the tanks. Then he reached for the emergency
ballast lever, which would release large lead weights. Fortunately,
the rapidly evacuated ballast tanks were doing the job of lifting the
submarine, so Monturiol chose to keep the safety weights in
reserve. Once on the surface, the nervous crew pumped the water
out and then brought the ship back to the dock.

Inspection soon revealed the source of the leak. The copper
sheath enveloping the interior chamber of the submarine had been

held in place with iron studs. Whereas the copper resisted oxidation and remained watertight, the iron screws did not. During the course of previous immersions, a number of screws had rusted and, at one moment, given way under the pressure of the deep.

The remedy was straightforward: All iron fittings in the submarine would have to be replaced with copper or bronze. The crew hauled the vessel back up onto the dry dock, and from June to October the shipwrights refitted the vessel. The repair was costly and time-consuming. Ever the perfectionist, Monturiol took the time to rework a wide range of minor elements that had displeased him in one way or another during the trial runs. The process of debugging the submarine provoked great frustration on the part of the inventor. He wrote to his patron Dulce that "the *Ictíneo* lately has given me a thousand headaches."

In November 1865 the *Ictíneo* was seaworthy again. Tests resumed, this time with a focus on the life-support system. The revamped carbon dioxide purifier worked as advertised. The system kept the concentration of carbon dioxide in the cabin well below 1 percent, mostly at undetectable levels. The first attempts with the oxygen generator, on the other hand, produced mixed results. The oxygen was breathable, but it emerged from the reactions in such a vaporous form that the interior of the *Ictíneo* filled with a thick fog.

After some experimentation, Monturiol discovered that the vapor could be eliminated if the oxygen was held for a few minutes at high pressure before being released into the cabin. He devised an implement consisting of two cylinders, one inside the other, connected by a pipe. The decomposition of the potassium chlorate took place in the smaller, interior cylinder. The resulting mix of gases then passed through the pipe to the bottom of the larger airtight cylinder enclosing the first. The gases bubbled through water at the bottom of the larger cylinder in order to remove the potassium chlorate, leaving pure oxygen to fill the larger cylinder. Monturiol prescribed the quantities of reactants so as to produce enough oxygen to fill the outer cylinder at the pressure of two atmospheres. By opening a valve at the top, the crew could admit fresh oxygen into the submarine. The oxygen that came out was free of cloudy vapors and, according to Monturiol, smelled as pure as "forest air."

In the first test of the improved life-support system, the *Ictíneo* ran for five hours underwater on artificial atmosphere. Upon returning to the surface, the crew reported no significant difference between the outside atmosphere and the inside air. As a further test of the quality of the artificial atmosphere, Monturiol played a practical joke on one of his mechanics. He asked for some repairs on the interior of the submarine while at dock. After the mechanic entered the vessel, Monturiol surreptitiously sealed the hatch behind him and started up the life-support devices. The mechanic worked for two hours. As he exited into the outside air, the mechanic noticed nothing, and he was apparently incredulous when told that the submarine had been sealed all the time he had been at work and that he had been breathing "artificial air."

Later in the month, Monturiol and crew remained six hours and then a record eight hours underwater, surviving on the artificial atmosphere of the life-support system. They took along ample lunches and whiled away the time in conversation. In each case, Monturiol reported, the air in the chamber remained just as breathable as normal air. The only noticeable difference was a gradual increase in temperature and humidity on the inside of the sub. Each test ended not because the crew lacked for comfort, Monturiol said, but because they had better things to do than remain underwater indefinitely. The problem of building a chamber in which man could survive in the inhospitable environment of the deep, the inventor averred, was solved. His engineer Pascual i Deop agreed: "The *Ictíneo* had a simple and safe process for maintaining a pure atmosphere, however long it remained underwater."

In December 1865, with all systems operating smoothly, Monturiol decided to make a final attempt to attract government support for his project. He installed a cannon on the top of his *Ictíneo*.

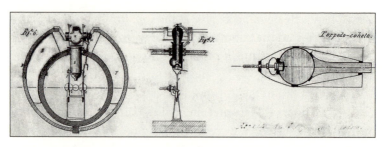

*Detail of submarine weapons. The figure on the left shows the cannon
in firing position; the figure in the middle shows the cannon
in loading position. The figure on the right is the torpedo rocket,
which was never built.*

Once again he told himself it was all part of a plan to achieve universal peace. The cannon had a bore of 10 centimeters and a length of 6 calibers and could hurl projectiles of 8 kilograms. It wasn't a huge weapon, but it was large enough to make trouble for surface ships. Monturiol devised a system for loading, aiming, and firing the cannon from the inside of the submarine when underwater. While he was at it, he also sketched out designs for a torpedo—that is, an underwater bomb—that could be propelled in the direction of an enemy ship.

On the morning of December 22, 1865, bystanders in the port of Barcelona were startled to hear a loud bang and see a geyser of water shoot up 12 meters from the surface. Moments later, the performance was repeated. The port authorities were mystified. Unbeknownst to them, the crew of the *Ictíneo* were following Monturiol's battle plan: Take the *Ictíneo* down to 20 meters, load the cannon, move the craft into position, ascend to within 90 centimeters of the surface, fire the cannon from under the water, descend to a safe depth, retreat, and then repeat the procedure. The *Ictíneo* had become a stealth weapon.

Inside the submarine, according to the crew, the cannon's bang was terrifically loud. The recoil shook some screws loose on the exterior hull. Otherwise, the new weapons system performed very well. On December 28, the *Ictíneo* sallied forth for a second show of arms. Once again, mysterious thunderclaps filled the air and strange geysers shot up from the water in the port of Barcelona. The port authorities were not amused. On the *Ictíneo*'s third armed sally into the port, they finally figured out who was responsible for the racket. A pair of officers galloped over to Monturiol's end of the shipyard, charged him with disturbing the peace of the water, and ordered an immediate cessation of all firearms activities.

Ironically, Monturiol's demonstration that the submarine could in fact become a formidable weapon of war backfired and brought down upon him the wrath of the same authorities whose interest he had sought to attract. He removed the cannon from his vessel, dropped plans for a torpedo, and gave up for good on the idea of ever receiving government support.

As the *Ictíneo II* bumbled around the port of Barcelona during the summer and autumn of 1865, it demonstrated impressive capabilities as a submarine in all respects save one: propulsion. Despite the much larger crew, the second *Ictíneo* proved only marginally faster underwater than the first. The average cruising speed was still about 1 knot, with some evidence for peak speeds of perhaps 2 knots—still short of Monturiol's minimum acceptable level of 3 knots.

Monturiol could see that he was bumping up against the limit of human muscle power. To confirm that this was the case, he conducted some interesting thought experiments. A submariner, he assumed, requires a minimum of 1 cubic meter of air space inside a submarine in order for the life-support system to work properly. For every cubic meter of interior cabin space, he estimated, a submarine requires a total volume of about 2.3 cubic meters to accommodate ballast tanks, an exterior hull, and machinery. A vessel with a volume of 2.3 cubic meters underwater will have a mass of precisely 2.3 tonnes. In a human-powered submarine, then, each individual will in effect be moving a 2.3-tonne mass through the water—or about thirty-eight times the average person's body weight. On the assumption that the submarine takes the most hydrodynamic shape possible, there is still a limit to the velocity that a human being can achieve with a 2.3-tonne mass underwater.

How to determine the velocity limit? One way was to look at the empirical data—the actual speed attained by the two *Ictíneos*—taking for granted that these submarines were at least reasonably, even if not perfectly, hydrodynamic. Another way was simply to look at a fish. A fish has a maximum velocity consistent with survival in the deep. A submarine should aspire to move about as fast as the average fish. Furthermore, a fish, he argued, is perfectly (or nearly perfectly) hydrodynamic, which is why a submarine ought to look like a fish. In the case of a fish, however, the ratio of mass moved through the water to body weight is exactly one, not thirty-eight, as in a human-powered submarine. Looking at the other side of the coin, if a man were thirty-eight times as strong as a fish—pound for pound—then he could expect to move a perfectly hydrodynamic submarine through the water as fast as an average fish. Now, Monturiol theorized that human beings were indeed mightier than fish, pound for pound. The concentration of oxygen in the atmosphere is about nineteen times greater than the concentration of oxygen in the seas, he pointed out, so a human being could be expected to generate up to nineteen times as much power as a fish. Even under such an unlikely assumption about human prepotency, however, a human-powered submarine would still have only half the power-to-mass ratio of the average fish. In sum, human muscle power would not suffice for a true submarine.

If human muscle power would not do, Monturiol determined, he would have to install an inanimate engine. That would be the only way to create a submarine capable of autonomous movement under the water—a true submarine. No one in history had yet succeeded in creating a reliable motor for underwater navigation. Monturiol now confronted what would prove to be the ultimate challenge of his art.

The challenge, unfortunately, was not just technological. In Monturiol's case, it was financial. The development of an underwater motor would cost money, lots of money, and his submarine association was flat broke once again. The many thousands of duros raised in Altadill's frantic subscription efforts had all been sunk into the sinuous olivewood and copper of the existing submarine, not to mention all those hazardous chemicals. Raising still more money before turning a profit would not be easy.

Another submariner, in view of the adverse circumstances, might have accepted the risks of a slow-moving submarine and persisted with the plan to deploy the existing vessel for commercial gain. As it stood, *Ictíneo II* was a fine machine, perfectly capable of exploring the coastal areas and harvesting coral. But it was not a *true* submarine—not as long as its feeble propulsion system left it hostage to the currents of the deep ocean. And that was just not good enough for Monturiol.

Later, the inventor would have to answer the charge that he lost an opportunity for profit by not going out immediately on the hunt for coral, even with his lumbering machine. The inventor's answer to the charge was passionate:

> And for this I received blame! They wanted that I, despite having at my disposal a powerful motor, should navigate solely with the force of human muscles; that I should take down to the depths of the sea 16 crew and a submarine, denying them the force that they would require to battle with the dangers of the deep! After having looked for 12 years for this force that could substitute with so many advantages for our arms, could I defer its application to a third *Ictíneo*, exposing myself to the risk of losing the second for lack of power?

Truth was, Monturiol was in the grips of a vision, the vision of a true submarine, capable of braving all the challenges of the deep with utter self-sufficiency and security. That was the rock upon which he stood, while all those about him succumbed to the importunities of practical necessity. He simply had to build a submarine capable of propelling itself at the minimum safe velocity, for otherwise he would not have demonstrated the inner truth of the concept of the art of underwater navigation. He had been seduced by the idea of the machine.

Twenty-seven

The Struggle Continues

In January 1866, General Joan Prim i Prats, a proper Catalan general known for his distinctly progressive political positions, decided it was time to act. Ten years of rule by a lascivious queen and her reactionary warlords were enough. From exile in Belgium, he hatched a plot to dethrone Isabel II and install a more liberal government. General Dulce slipped in from Cuba to join in the coup—against the same queen whom he had rescued from kidnappers twenty-five years earlier. Also in on the job were, among others, Pascual Madoz and Estanislau Figueras, the Catalan deputies to the national congress.

But the conspiracy was exposed. General O'Donnell, aka the Duke of Tetuan, who was the current head of government, organized a swift and brutal crackdown on the plotters. Prim was stopped at the border, Figueras and Madoz were banished from the realm, and Dulce exiled himself to the sunny beaches of the Canary Islands. O'Donnell's hand was not hard enough to please the queen, however, and she soon spurned him in favor of the notorious General Narváez, who carried out still more repressive measures. This time Narváez took on a partner in government, an unpleasant man named Gonzalo Bravo whose chief aim while in office was, he proudly declared, "to show Spain that a civilian can be dictator."

One victim of the commotion was Ildefons Cerdà, who lost his position on the city council in 1866. Although the lines of the streets of the Extension were already laid out according to his design, many of the other distinctive features of his plan—the zoning concepts and the garden spaces, for example—were under threat from avaricious developers, uncomprehending politicians, and rival architects. Disgusted with the venality of city politics, Cerdà retreated into theoretical work, while his utopian plans flew on autopilot into the waiting storm.

Monturiol landed in jail. The charges were at the very least anachronistic, not to say unjust. Over the past decade, his energies had been diverted entirely into the conquest of the watery realm, not to the overthrow of landlocked regimes. Although his sympathies still lay with the republican cause, he was not in on the plot against the queen. On the other hand, many of his friends were among the conspiritors, and he did hold suspicious beliefs, all of which added up, in the paranoid eyes of the authorities, to a serious offense.

In the dank and overflowing cells of Barcelona's prison, Monturiol bumped into his friend Josep Anselm Clavé, also found guilty mainly of knowing the wrong people and having a suspicious past. The two old Fraternity brothers embraced. Clavé's choirs were still singing, but his project for the musical liberation of the working classes was faltering. In the previous year the authorities had taken a close look at the lyrics of his songs and decided to cancel the spectacular festivals he had been holding on the fields bordering the Passeig de Gracia. Together in jail now, the two old socialists naturally sought to convert the prison population into a harmonious brotherhood of man. They led their fellow inmates in singing stirring anthems of liberty, such as "La Marseillaise" and some of Clavé's own popular hymns.

Both Monturiol and Clavé were at this time public figures in Barcelona, and within a few days their many influential friends prevailed upon a kindly judge to order their release from prison. The two heroes of the working class steadfastly refused to leave the grimy cells, however, until the authorities consented to release all their fellow inmates who had been falsely accused of political crimes.

Once out of jail, Monturiol set about campaigning for funds to develop a motor for the *Ictíneo II*. But the world was already a different place, and the powerful friends Monturiol had previously relied upon were no longer in a position to help. General Dulce languished in self-imposed exile on the arid Canary Islands. Pascual Madoz was incommunicado, and little Joe Xifré, too, was living in Paris, weakening every day from the tuberculosis that would soon carry him off.

To make matters worse, in May 1866 the Barcelona stock-market bubble burst, property prices collapsed, and the economy stumbled into a depression. The railroad boom of the past ten years had reached its destination, viz., an economic bust resulting from the squandering of national resources through overinvestment and corruption. The industrialists and small businessmen who had previously contributed to the submarine association no longer had a peseta to spare. Monturiol published another submarine treatise, this time explaining the need for a new motor, but it seemed like a futile effort. No one could afford to pay for his underwater fantasies.

A glance at chief engineer Monjo's pay stubs tells the story of La Navegación Submarina's financial predicament. Up through early 1866, Monjo's salary was as regular as the tides. Then it stopped and started, accumulating in odd amounts over random intervals, like water dripping from a tap, all the while falling farther and farther below subsistence level.

In a desperate ploy to raise funds, Monturiol dusted off the cigarette machine he had invented fourteen years earlier. With Altadill as his partner and little Joe Xifré's backing, he attempted to sell the device to a cigarette manufacturer in Cuba. Unfortunately, Altadill got greedy and set the price at an exorbitant 30,000 duros. Although the invention sparked some interest, the manufacturer decided that its cigarette girls were less expensive and chose not to invest in the new device.

Around this time, an article in the English *Mechanic's Magazine* describing the submarines developed by the Americans during the Civil War led Monturiol to believe that there might be a market for his *Ictíneo* on the other side of the Atlantic. In reviewing the efforts of the American submariners, Monturiol must have concluded that his technology was far superior to theirs. With their open ballast tanks, hand pumps, and single-hull designs, American submarines like the *Hunley* were neither intended nor able to dive more than a few meters under the surface. Monturiol's submarines, on the other hand—with their external compressed-air ballast tanks, fishlike exteriors, and double-hull design—were indisputably creatures of the deep. They had been tested down to 20 and 30 meters and were very likely capable of considerably more. Furthermore, the American submarines were notoriously unreliable. While the *Hunley*, as one chagrined Confederate noted, "would sink at a moment's notice and sometimes without it," Monturiol's submarines had already logged hundreds of hours underwater in over sixty dives without a single injury or loss of life. In addition, while the American submarines had no internal life-support capability, Monturiol's inventions carried his patented air-freshening systems. Finally, even in the field of armaments—a much more central concern for the Americans than for Monturiol—the Americans had yet to develop a submarine that could be relied upon to inflict damage on the enemy without destroying itself in the process, whereas Monturiol had tested a cannon-bearing vessel that would have been able to do just that.

In happier times, Monturiol had disdained the possibility of selling his technology to some foreign nation. Indeed, a number of the poets who celebrated his achievements in the fabulous banquets of 1861 made a point of his admirable loyalty to Spain, citing his avowal that he would rather starve than provide another people with his great invention. One chronicler of the times claimed that the French government had made an offer for the first *Ictíneo*, which the inventor grandly declined. Now, with his bank account empty once again and having just been released from a stint in a Spanish jail, Monturiol was ready to move beyond petty nationalist politics. It was time to sell his *Ictíneo* to the Americans.

On July 3, 1866, Monturiol wrote to the U.S. secretary of the navy with his proposal. "As it is very long since I am thoroughly engaged in an elaborate course of investigations and practical experiments concerning . . . Submarine Boats, I am convinced that my cooperation may be of great importance to you," he wrote, in purposeful if imperfect English. His first submarine, the inventor asserted, "solved practically the long controverted problem of submarine navigation." After describing the exploits of the original "Ichthyneus," he went on to give an update on the status of the second submarine, drawing special attention to the highly successful gun experiments. "I am so firmly confident upon the success of the decisive trials of my second experimental Ichthyneus, that I have now nearly finished the design of a submarine steamer of war," he added. Then he detailed, with notable prescience, the possible uses of the "submarine steamer" in warfare: defending the coastline, lifting blockades, attacking enemy vessels in their harbors, and even taking aim at land-based targets. Naturally, he could not forgo mention of the possible peaceful applications: pearl and coral fishing, exploration of the deep, and the "safe and perfect laying of transatlantic wires." "If in consideration of the advantages offered by my invention you believe that my services may be available to your country, to which I am bent by interesse [*sic*] and sympathy, please impart it, as soon as possible," Monturiol signed off.

But the moment had passed. The Civil War was over. "The country being now at peace," the American secretary replied to Monturiol on August 9, 1866, "the government is not pursuing the subject of submarine warfare or navigation in such a manner as to require your services." Not for another twenty years would the United States Navy acquire, from the Irish inventor John P. Holland and others, the kind of subaquatic technology on offer from Monturiol in 1866.

Meanwhile, the debts of Monturiol's submarine association were mounting. The association's chief creditor was Navegación e Industria, a new megacorporation that had subsumed the old Nuevo Vulcano shipyard operation. In October 1866, ominously, Navegación e Industria required that Monturiol sign a chit recognizing the massive debt he owed. At the same time, disgruntled shareholders in the submarine association began to make unpleasant noises. Some pestered the submariner to skip the plans for the new motor and go straight into coral diving. Others sought legal means to regain their money. As the submarine project dragged on, the celebrated inventor's personal prestige began to slip.

Fiscal salvation came suddenly and unexpectedly from a group of businessmen known informally for their footwear: the *espardenya* gang. The *espardenya* is the kind of shoe that makes a statement by saying as little as possible. With a sole made of old string bundled together and a top of simple canvas, the *espardenya* is an unpretentious no-nonsense walking shoe for unpretentious no-nonsense walking people. Up in the village of Sant Andreu, now a suburb of Barcelona, lived a group of rough-hewn, pragmatic businessmen who commuted to work in their *espardenyas*. The *espardenya* gang showed only polite interest in Monturiol's scientific ambitions. What attracted their attention was the coral. They saw gold in those red animals of the deep. In October 1866, just as the submarine dream seemed about to sink into the night for lack of funds, these businessmen pooled together 4,000 duros for his project—enough, Monturiol believed, to build the motor that would make the *Ictíneo II* into a true submarine at last.

As 1866 came to a close, Monturiol had scraped into the final stage of his project. His resilient optimism once again poked its little head above the rubble of so much adversity. Also poking its little head up at this time, by happy coincidence, was the last of Monturiol's children, a bouncing baby boy. Emilia and Narcís now presided over a brood of five: Anita, nineteen; Adelaida, twelve; Delfina, seven; Emilio, four; and a tiny bundle of hope named Joan.

Twenty-eight

Fire and Water

For most of recorded history, humankind has had only one serious alternative to human muscle power for locomotion: the muscle power of other animals. But in 1788 James Watt invented the steam engine, and the field of human locomotion moved to a whole new plane. By the mid-nineteenth century, the steam engine was transporting people over land and sea around the world.

In the 1860s, when Monturiol sat down to contemplate the issue of underwater locomotion, there were few serious competitors to the steam engine. Electric motors—which later became a mainstay of the underwater fleets of the world—were too weak, and their batteries too bulky, to be considered a realistic option. Compressed-air engines and wind-up springs were feasible, but they too were feeble and short-lived. Bold experimenters were at work on the internal combustion engine, but the fruits of their labors would not be available until later in the century. Short of inventing a whole new kind of power unit, Monturiol would have to make do with the trusty old steam engine.

But there was one burning problem. Steam engines available at the time used coal or wood fires to boil water, whose pressurized vapor in turn powered the motor. For surface propulsion, of course, the submariner could run intake and exhaust pipes to the surface and so deploy a steam engine in the ordinary way. To take an open flame underwater in the hermetically sealed cabin of a submarine, however, was obviously a bad idea; it would rapidly consume all the oxygen and release noxious fumes such as carbon monoxide. The application of the steam engine to subsurface locomotion was the ultimate challenge in the art of underwater navigation. The inventor had to find a way to fuse two elements that since ancient times stood for irreconcilable opposition: fire and water. Monturiol's was the kind of mind that thrives on adversity. The higher the barrier he faced, the greater the leap of his imagination in overcoming it. The problem of underwater locomotion elicited perhaps the finest of his technological achievements.

He began by reviewing the results of his earlier experiments in the chemistry of oxygen. While concocting his various chemical stews, he had observed that some reactions that produce oxygen also generate heat. He now realized that such a heat-producing chemical reaction, properly controlled, could be used to boil the water for the steam engine while leaving as exhaust only pure oxygen—which, far from polluting the interior cabin, would replenish the air breathed by the crew.

It was an insight that illustrates what Dr. Letamendi called the "synthetic" side of Monturiol's genius: the apparently disconnected problems of underwater locomotion and life support were united and solved in a single stroke. As a bonus, the inventor planned to drive the air-purification system and the water pumps for the ballast tanks with the new underwater engine. Thus, while propelling the craft through the water, the chemical fire in the submarine's belly would not only supply the oxygen for its lungs but also cleanse its air and power its depth-control system. The *Ictíneo* was looking more and more like the kind of organic system of which Dr. Letamendi could only dream, a living machine that could sustain itself through the complex interplay of its many parts.

In his meticulous way, Monturiol performed literally thousands of experiments in order to determine the best mix of chemicals to power his underwater steam engine and run the life-support system. The reaction had to generate heat, but not so much that it would melt its containers. He discovered and listed many possible combinations but in the end favored a brew containing 53 percent zinc, 16 percent manganese dioxide, and 31 percent potassium chlorate.

The representation of the ensuing reaction is:

$$KClO_3 + Zn \xrightarrow{MnO_2} KCl + ZnO + O_2 + heat$$

The reaction, Monturiol observed, generated heat in a controllable way and produced enough oxygen to supply the crew whose muscle power it supplanted. A further benefit of this particular cocktail, he noted, was that the ingredients were not too pricey, and one of the solid by-products, zinc oxide, had some commercial resale value. His chemical recipe carefully noted, the joyful inventor was at last ready to attempt the challenge of building an underwater motor.

In October 1866, Monturiol took the 4,000 duros he had collected from the *espardenya* gang and bought a 6-horsepower steam engine, the kind that in those days was used in the textile mills of Barcelona. He then divided the engine in two. The first engine would run on coal, like a normal steam engine, and would be used for surface movement of the *Ictíneo*. The second, smaller engine would have a separate boiler running on his special chemical cocktail, which would be fired up for underwater locomotion. Monturiol devised rodlike cylinders to house his chemical brew. At the appropriate moment, fifteen of these would be inserted into the specially designed boiler—much like uranium rods are inserted into a modern-day nuclear reactor—and the chemical reactions initiated.

On November 21, 1866, Monturiol invited twenty of his closest friends and shareholders to witness his new engine in action on the floor of his workshop. To his enormous satisfaction and to the amazement of fellow workers like Pascual and Monjo—who were still grappling with the theoretical issues in chemistry—it worked. The surface version, as was to be expected, ran normally. The underwater edition, fired up with its bizarre chemical fuel rods, cranked without interruption for three hours.

Monturiol's spirit once again burned bright. In a shareholders' meeting of December 8, 1866, he glowed with renewed enthusiasm

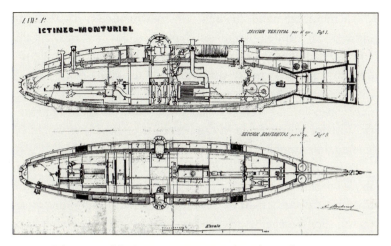

Diagrams of the Ictíneo II. Ensayo sobre el arte de navegar por debajo del agua, *Lamina #1.*

for the project. "If before I seemed beaten down," he said, "today I present myself to you with the tranquillity of one who has resolved a problem and feels in his breast the satisfaction of a duty completed." After counting all the money the association would earn once the submarine began harvesting coral, he concluded his address with lyrical grandeur: "The dawn of a beautiful day illuminates the present of the *Ictíneo*, a day that shall have no night; for the heat that warms her entrails, the flame that burns in her heart, shall never be extinguished: the *Ictíneo* has been born into immortality." Like a latter-day Prometheus, Monturiol believed that he would bequeath to humankind a fire stolen from the gods—a fire that would burn in the water.

He was getting a little ahead of himself. A fundamental engineering challenge remained. He had a working engine, and he had a working submarine, but the one was not yet inside the other. In fact, as he contemplated the matter, Monturiol could see that the new engine really called for a new submarine, one designed specifically with the new engine in mind. Since building a new submarine would undoubtedly spark a revolt among his shareholders, this was clearly not an option.

On the other hand, installing the new engine in the existing submarine presented two major challenges. The first was that the *Ictíneo II* had only one entry point: the 54-centimeter hatch on the top. The engine—a bulky contraption that filled a small shed—would somehow have to pass through this upward eye of the submarine needle. The second was that the *Ictíneo II* had no obvious way to cope with the significant amount of heat that would be generated by an onboard engine.

Throughout the first half of 1867, Monturiol and his team labored to squeeze the motor through the hatch and install it in the submarine. It was a tight fit. Fortunately, Pascual found ingenious ways to slice the engine up into small pieces and then glue it back together again. The formerly capacious interior of the *Ictíneo II* was now cluttered with the boilers and valves and cylinders of the engine, leaving space for a crew of only four or five. But it worked. In July, they fired up the engine, while the *Ictíneo* remained at its dock, and successfully managed to churn the water along the pier.

All the while, the financial pressure on Monturiol was building. The bank account was bouncing on the bottom of a sea of debt, and creditors were circling. More shareholders griped about their investments. Yet success, the immortal flame of underwater locomotion, seemed just within his grasp, only weeks away. He was in a race against money.

Just as Monturiol was preparing himself for the first voyage of the *Ictíneo II* under inanimate power, the winds of political fortune blew him off course yet again. Spain went through another cycle of rebellion and repression. General Prim launched a coup from out of town, just as in the previous year, and the authorities put it down by the usual means. Gonzalo Bravo, the "civilian dictator," organized the deportation of hundreds of liberals. On a warm night in August 1867, a dozen police appeared at Monturiol's door, ready to hustle him off to exile along with the other political undesirables. Fortunately for future submarine historians, Monturiol got wind of the impending raid and managed to flee the city before the police arrived. With four children huddling behind her and an infant son in her arms, Emilia feigned ignorance of his whereabouts, and the police went off in search of other prey. That same night, twenty-five less fortunate progressives in Barcelona were packed into a small ship and sailed off to the Philippines.

The political upheavals also resulted in an ominous economic development. In order to trim government expenses during a time of severe recession, the dictator Bravo decided to cancel the orders for the construction of a new fleet for the navy. Much of that construction was to have been performed in Barcelona, by the same shipyard involved in building Monturiol's submarine. Suddenly, times were very lean in Barceloneta.

As he fretted away the days in hiding up in the mountains around Vic, Monturiol lost precious ground in the race against money. The submarine association's debts continued to accumulate, the *Ictíneo* languished, and any chance of turning a profit receded farther into the distance. Three months passed before the political situation cooled enough for Monturiol to climb back down the mountains and resume work.

On October 22, 1867, the *Ictíneo II* left its dock for the first test run of its surface motor. It steamed out of the harbor of Barcelona into the open sea, then over to the mouth of the River Llobregat some 8 kilometers away, and back. The round-trip took less than three hours. The peak rate of progress was 4.5 knots, and the average was about 3.5 knots. It wasn't exactly blazing speed, but it was enough to meet Monturiol's requirement for surface propulsion. The advent of the true submarine was nigh.

On December 14, Monturiol took the *Ictíneo II* underwater in its berth and fired up the underwater propulsion system. The chemical rods boiled the water that fed the engine that powered the propeller and cranked the air-supply system. Although the submarine didn't go anywhere, the test demonstrated convincingly that the submarine now had the capability to move itself underwater. Monturiol believed he had discovered the solution to the problem of underwater propulsion: an inanimate power source that could both propel the submarine through the water and supply its crew with the "quintessence" of life.

Inspired by his oxygen-producing engine, Monturiol composed a prose poem:

> It is a true pleasure to find oneself hermetically sealed in a chamber wherein there is a steam engine, whose flame both supplies the *Ictíneo* with the motile force it requires and nourishes the respiration of the crew. One has to have navigated with the sole power of human muscles in order to understand what a good fortune it is to have an inanimate power source aboard the submarine. . . . No longer will one hear the sighs of a fatigued crew; and the crew, in abandoning their happy home in the earth's atmosphere, will exude greater confidence, knowing that their safety depends not on their weak and tired arms but rather on the powerful steam engine.

Once again, the submarine proved a powerful tool for the exploration of consciousness. In this case, it uncovered the place in Monturiol's imagination where the perfect world resided—a peaceful world, naturally, in which machines do all the work and humankind's only duty is to relax, breathe deeply, and enjoy the ride. If neutral buoyancy had previously taken him to a tomblike nirvana, the experience of underwater steam power, it seems, now brought him straight to utopia.

But there was a hitch. In reality, descents making use of the underwater engine were not yet entirely pleasurable. The underwater engine may have demonstrated its ability to churn the water under its dock and to refresh the imaginative faculties with oxygen that smelled like pure forest air, but the throbbing chemical furnace also rapidly heated the interior chamber to intolerable levels. After twenty minutes of operation, the temperature inside the submarine would rise to as much as 50 degrees centigrade. Considering the high humidity, the *Ictíneo*'s interior must have felt like a sauna—with a jackhammer inside going full tilt. According to Pascual, test immersions that made use of the underwater engine only achieved depths of a few meters before having to return to the surface to cool off.

Monturiol could see that there were two possible solutions to the problem. The first would be to build a whole new submarine. Such a submarine would be made of metal, a far better conductor of heat than wood, and would house the engine in a separate climate-controlled space. Needless to say, this solution was entirely unrealistic given the budgetary circumstances. The second and more practical solution would be to install a cooling system in the existing submarine. A series of bronze pipes could be used to move seawater around the interior cabin and so carry off the excess heat. Such a solution would clearly work. Unfortunately, it would also be rather expensive. In the race between submarine glory and money, money had just gained a crucial few steps.

Monturiol's dream was reaching the last moments before dawn. In the final months of 1867, he wrote this note to himself:

> The moment is approaching when I will be able to say that the submarine world belongs to us. What will matter then all the toil, anguish, and tribulations through which I must now pass?

After twelve years of single-minded passion, he had already built the most advanced submarine of his time anywhere in the world. It was a submarine capable of descending to great depths, of moving about under its own power, of interacting with the ocean environment, and of sustaining human life indefinitely in the deep. All it lacked was a way to keep the crew cool while they were down there.

But what if he failed to secure the last measure of funds necessary to realize his dream? In the same note to himself, Monturiol left the question unanswered:

> Poor, scorned by the powerful, forgotten by those who made me conceive of hopes of support, threatened by imminent bankruptcy—what will become of me and my *Ictíneo*, if I do not succeed in completing my work in these few months or perhaps days of truce that remain to me?

Twenty-nine

Prometheus Bound

On December 23, 1867, the bank account of La Navegación Submarina finally hit rock bottom. Not a single peseta was left. At the same time, the corporation's principal creditor, the shipyard of Navegación e Industria, filed a motion in court to reclaim the 4,000 duros it was owed. With a trembling heart, Monturiol laid off all workers and suspended all activities.

On January 12, 1868, he chaired an emergency session of the submarine association. For an hour or so he recounted the many achievements of the *Ictíneo*: its successes in making controlled descents, in propelling itself under artificial power, in generating a life-sustaining environment in its interior. Then he described the financial woes of the corporation. Before, we were just flat broke; now we are in hock up to our necks, he said. (His actual language was somewhat grander.) He vowed to fight on, whatever it took. Hoping to entice more investment, he offered to give up most of his claims to future profits. He closed with a rhetorical question: "Could I abandon the project that is the soul of my life and without which my earthly existence would have no purpose?"

After twelve years of throwing money into the sea, however, Monturiol's shareholders could all too easily imagine life without the submarine. Tired of a venture whose noble ideals seemed only to empty their pockets, many failed to turn up for the meeting. Among those who did, many had been ruined themselves in the course of Barcelona's ongoing economic malaise. The shareholders offered Monturiol a few words of regret but no money. La Navegación Submarina was well and truly bankrupt.

Monturiol himself laid the blame largely on an evil with which all of humankind is well endowed:

> There is in society a mass of men who are capable only of con-
> serving what exists; so mean are they, that they will sacrifice
> none of their present wealth in order to build a better future;
> and in order not to appear so mean and miserable, they deny the
> very possibility of a better future, and attack those people who
> attempt to achieve progress. Such is the vulgar mass of men.

It may also be that the vulgar mass was loath to help Monturiol in particular, given his checkered record as a social revolutionary. His idealistic past indeed represented a heavy claim on the future. The arrests of 1866 and 1867 had interrupted his work for several months at critical moments and were perhaps the immediate cause of his predicament. The same revolutionary spirit that had made the conception of the submarine possible in the first place came back to threaten its very existence.

In retrospect, one could also have laid the blame on simply being in the wrong place at the wrong time. Monturiol arrived on the scene twenty years before the development of the electrical technology that would eventually provide a safe and comfortable source of power for underwater locomotion. And he showed up in Spain, not a propitious locale for a prospective submarine inventor. Spain in the late nineteenth century was a banana republic in the making. Its navy would receive its comeuppance for techno-logical backwardness at the end of the century, when the United States would take away the poorly defended island nation of Cuba.

If to be Spanish was a misfortune, to be Catalan smacked of care-lessness. Because of his regional origins—and despite his evident lack of separatist sentiment—Monturiol was caught between the suspicion of central government bureaucrats in Madrid and the narrow-minded provincialism of the burghers of Barcelona.

But Monturiol's predicament had more to do with the way in which his project was organized and funded. Once set on the course of creating a true submarine, the inventor's only real hope was in fact to receive support from either the government or disinterested visionaries like himself. In the absence of government support and given the dearth or relative poverty of disinterested visionaries, his only other option was to present the submarine as a business opportunity. And yet, in a fundamental way, this involved a serious misrepresentation. A coral-fishing diving bell might have made a decent investment proposition, but his submarine wasn't really a business. Monturiol's vision was of a pure technology—the *true* submarine—and the potential pecuniary rewards could always only be a vague and hoped-for consequence of such a technology.

The benefits of any pure technology are often unforeseeable, both in their potential extension and in their respective beneficiaries. Inasmuch as the main contribution of such a technology is the advance of scientific knowledge and the expansion of human horizons, its principal beneficiary in fact is the public at large. Private capital by its nature does not seek such vague and diffuse benefits, however valuable they may be to society as a whole. To be sure, the pursuit of private gain produces much that is of public good; but not all public goods can be the product of the pursuit of private gain. In describing his own case, Cerdà put the matter succinctly, in words that apply with equal force to Monturiol's submarine: "There are *private* inventions that offer in themselves or through some privilege an appropriate reward; and then there are inventions with primarily public utility, inventions that are and should be acquired by the state."

In other words, Monturiol was right when he argued that the advance of subaquatic science and technology would ultimately be a boon to humanity; but his investors were also probably right in figuring that it would be a bane to their wallets. Monturiol's dream belonged to that special category of human endeavor that would lift the fortunes of everyone without favoring anyone in particular.

The failure to secure support from the state demonstrated only that Monturiol's aspirations exceeded the capabilities of the social system within which he found himself. He was condemned to envision a future that his countrymen were ill prepared to see. The thread of his life story twisted in the gulf that separates the visionary genius from ordinary humankind.

In the final analysis, the explanation of Monturiol's fate must eventually come to rest with the man himself. The Catalan inventor made many concessions to the status quo along the way to realizing his dream—he sought to do business with a corrupt queen and her dictatorial generals, he humored bad poets, he offered his scientific vessel to the gods of war—but the one thing he never compromised was his vision of the true submarine. And, in the end, that was the cross to which he was nailed.

Of Robert Fulton, the steamboat inventor and thwarted submariner, a eulogist said, "Like the self-burning tree of Gambia, he was destroyed by the fire of his own genius." No apter words describe the fate of Monturiol. The fire of his genius shone brightest in the flame he kindled underwater, the miraculous chemical steam engine—a technological marvel that was not strictly necessary for a coral-fishing operation but essential to the idea of the true submarine, and that added two years and all the money he did not have to his submarine project.

Had he not insisted on developing the ideal form of underwater locomotion, very likely he would have reaped the short-term profits his project needed to survive. He acknowledged as much in his later writings: "Perhaps it would have been better if I had not let myself be seduced by the great advantage that the motor offered me." Had he not insisted on the purity of his vision, however, he would not have been Narcís Monturiol, and he would never have conceived of the true submarine in the first place. In the agony of retrospection, he consoled himself with this knowledge: "I could not have done otherwise." Character is fate, as the ancient philosopher Heraclitus said. Monturiol's end had its beginnings in the very nature of the man that he was. He was destroyed by the fire of his own genius.

◆ ◆ ◆

On February 21, 1868, La Navegación e Industria secured a court order for the seizure of all assets of the submarine association. The only asset was a submarine. Through a friend, Monturiol approached the CEO of his corporate creditor. The friend asked the man, a Mr. Alexandre de Bacardi, whether he had any patriotic sentiments at all. Mr. Bacardi responded that indeed he had none; he wanted his debt paid, and that was that. He had his own reason to be upset with Spain: the government's earlier decision to cancel the new fleet had left his shipyard high and dry, forcing him to cut wages and sell landholdings to keep his own business from failing. On February 23, La Navegación e Industria took possession of the *Ictíneo II*.

The submarine association met again a few days later. Desperate, Monturiol promised the shareholders that if they could come up with the funds to buy back the submarine, he would take them all fishing for coral by summer, and by autumn they would be rich. He concluded his words with a plea: "This will be either a day of solace for me or the saddest day of my life. May your resources correspond to your desires, and may this not be the last time we meet!" But it was indeed to be the last time the submarine association met, and it was the saddest day of Monturiol's life.

Mr. Bacardi sold the submarine to a businessman named Antoni Palés. At first, Monturiol hoped that Palés might wish to exploit the vessel for his own use in fishing for coral. It was not to be. The coup de grâce came, appropriately, from the government. At the time, the government was in the habit of levying a tax on all seagoing vessels. When it came to the attention of the authorities that the *Ictíneo* was in fact a seagoing vessel, they promptly issued a tax bill. Palés figured it would be more profitable to scrap the submarine than continue to pay the tax. He ordered the *Ictíneo* hauled up onto dry dock and dismantled.

Monturiol could only watch helplessly, like a Prometheus bound, as the vultures feasted on the vital organs of his creation. They stripped the copper skin screeching from its sides and broke off its pincer arms. They plucked out the nineteen crystal eyes—

for eventual use in remodeling a bathroom. They twisted off the pipes and valves of its artificial lung and sold them as scrap. Then they snapped the vessel's wooden bones and ripped out its throbbing heart, the twin-engine system. They dragged the surface motor off to a textile factory, where it lived out its days chained to the shop floor, spinning out the fabric of Barcelona's industrial revolution. When at last they reached the mysterious underwater chemical motor, the fire of his genius, they wrenched off the pieces that had resale value and tossed what was left into the sea.

Within days, the *Ictíneo* was no more. Only the detailed mechanical drawings of Joan Monjo, the lengthy treatises by Monturiol, and the scattered impressions of the many who participated in or witnessed the rides of the *Ictíneo* remained as proof that, once upon a time, a true submarine had plied the waters of Barcelona and had taken humankind safely on a voyage under the surface of the sea.

Twelve years had passed since that day on the rocky shores of the Cape of the Crosses when Monturiol evoked the vision that would define the meaning of his life. "Poor heart that trembles, desist not from your cause!" he told himself in the early days, full of hope and fear. For twelve years his heart endured. He snatched the torch of victory from the hostile indifference of the sea. Now he saw the fire of his knowledge and the meaning of his life extinguished before his eyes, and it was too much to bear. His poor trembling heart finally—mercifully—broke.

Part III

Monturiol Redux

A portrait of the inventor as an old man

Thirty

The Ictíneo *in Words*

General Narváez died in his bed in April 1868, shortly after the somewhat less reactionary General O'Donnell expired. With the passing of the old guard, the season for change arrived. As the summer of 1868 turned to autumn, revolution swept across Spain like a front of thunderstorms rolling over the plains. When the progressive General Prim stepped off his boat in the southernmost Spanish port of Cadiz on September 19, and declared himself for "Spain with honor," there was no doubt about just whose honor he was calling into question. Ten days later, the lascivious Queen Isabel II was seen scurrying across the French border, never to set foot in Spain again. In the heat and dust of the revolutionary moment, few had a thought to spare for an erstwhile submariner and his recently deceased fish boat.

The sudden collapse of his submarine dream threw Monturiol into a crushing depression. A full year after the seizure of the submarine, he confessed to his wife, "The death of the *Ictíneo* has left me listless. I can't stop thinking about it." He felt so oppressed, he said, he could barely breathe. Adding to the burden were the calumnies whispered by many who had lost money in the venture—in particular by those who had never imagined that the project was more than a way of generating a certain percentage return for their portfolios. Heaviest of all, though, in the years that stretched ahead, was the weight of oblivion. Soon the rest of the world, save for a dwindling band of friends and family, forgot entirely that there ever had been a submarine and that it had successfully navigated under the surface of the waters of Barcelona and Alicante.

Monturiol told Emilia that he longed for the days of his youth, days of "activity and energy," "unlimited hope," and "confidence in his own powers." His only consolation, he said with his customary humility, was that in view of his modest talents, he had accomplished "more than could have been hoped of me." "What am I to do now?" he asked himself. "I have not yet found an answer to this question." And again: "Always the *Ictíneo* before me. Nothing more for today."

For a time, he could not even speak of the *Ictíneo*, and his friends learned to tread carefully around the subject. When at last he broke the silence, the "fire of a profound passion illuminated his eyes," says Puig Pujadas, and one could see in his face "the internal fluttering of an idée fixe, the secret vibration of a mind obsessively seeking the definitive solution to all sides of the problem that obsessed it."

Monturiol slowly recovered his spirits through a kind of writing therapy. During 1869 he labored on his magnum opus, the 300-page *Essay on the Art of Underwater Navigation*. The book surveys the early history of submarine technology, argues for the many potential applications of submarines in science, industry, and defense, and summarizes the contemporary knowledge in the relevant sciences: oceanography, meteorology, chemistry, biology, and so forth.

Most importantly, the *Essay* includes a complete set of instructions for building an *Ictíneo*. It provides diagrams for the second *Ictíneo*; describes the mechanisms it used for buoyancy control, balance, and maneuvering; explains how the motor worked; prescribes a variety of chemical recipes for underwater locomotion; and discusses at length the various means of purifying the internal atmosphere of a submarine and generating oxygen. The book, in brief, is everything but the submarine itself. It was without question the most comprehensive and sophisticated treatment of the subject in the history of submarines to that time. Unlike any previous submarine inventor, Monturiol was determined to make his dearly acquired knowledge part of the public domain. "Herewith twelve years and one hundred thousand duros expended," he said frankly in the preface, "without any other fruit—if fortune continues to be adverse—than the writing of this *Essay*." The book was his last bid for redemption.

He signed the preface to the *Essay* on January 1, 1870. In it he expressed his hope that the growing success of and appreciation for science in the world would soon overcome the "social resistance" that had sapped his strength and thwarted his submarine designs. He reaffirmed his faith that the submarine would eventually have "a transcendence capable of influencing human destiny." He asked that his *Essay* be considered one small contribution to the grand edifice of human progress. Now all he needed was a publisher.

He didn't find one. From time to time in the years to come, he would approach potential benefactors and high officials, not stopping short of the king of Spain himself, to ask for help in financing the publication of his book. No luck. For the rest of his life, the compendium of his submarine knowledge and with it his contribution to the potential salvation of the human race would remain confined to a sheaf of papers stuffed inside his desk.

In the meantime, the ex-submariner and his family faced the prospect of a descent into poverty. Toward the end of his own life, Cerdà, thinking mainly about himself, wrote in his diary: "He who has taken upon himself in a passionate way the development of an idée fixe that, in his understanding, will have a great impact on the destiny of humankind, finds himself gripped and forced, despite himself, to abandon completely the care of his own private interests in order to consecrate himself without reserves of any kind to the realization of this idea." Cerdà's apt words tell the story of Monturiol's life. For the sake of his transcendental mission, the utopian inventor had abandoned completely the care of his own private interests. Now he was penniless and unemployed.

In hopes of turning a quick profit, he once again rolled out his cigarette machine. Financial security appeared on the horizon when in early 1872 the Spanish national tobacco company accepted the machine for use in its factory in Madrid. At the time, the factory employed hundreds of cigarette girls, who, predictably, were none too keen on Monturiol's labor-saving device. They plotted to sabotage the machine, and their plot succeeded on June 7, 1872. Monturiol claimed an indemnity from the company, which he received two years later in the amount of 16,940 pesetas—not a fortune to retire on, but enough to pay off debts and keep the family fed and clothed for a time.

Thirty-one

Adelaida and Delfina

Monturiol had always been a family man, and in the brooding years after the death of the *Ictíneo* he found solace in the company of his wife and children. Whenever he was apart from them, he exchanged intimate letters with each member of the family, as often as every day. Many years earlier, in his first revolutionary journal, *La Madre de Familia*, he announced that family "is the most sacred thing." Now, a letter to Emilia reaffirmed it. "For me, my wife and my children are and have been and will continue to be the sky of my existence." In another letter to his wife, he added, "Our fate may be more or less adverse, but at least we have the good fortune of loving each other."

But fate—not satisfied with the outrageous desolation of his submarine dream—had yet more slings and arrows in store for the benighted submariner. In the summer of 1871, Adelaida—the daughter born in the heat of the revolution of 1854—began to cough blood. Within two months she was dead of tuberculosis. The disease spread to her adoring younger sister and playmate Delfina—the daughter born in the year of the launch of the first *Ictíneo*. Emilia took Delfina to the countryside near Vic, where the mountain air, it was hoped, would speed a cure.

Devasted by the loss of one daughter, Monturiol did what he could to cheer up the ailing thirteen-year-old Delfina. In a letter of April 1872 he starts to describe the excellent lunch her brothers and her older sister shared the other day: a paella of rice, fish, sausages . . . but then he stops, saying that he can tell from a conversation he is overhearing among her brothers that they are already describing the feast in *their* letter to her. Still, he cannot resist mentioning that Anita prepared an *excelentisima crema*— a Catalan version of custard—and that she promises to make another "equally good" *crema* when her little sister returns from the hills. He tells Delfina that now that she is in the country she must taste the famous sausages and ham of Vic. He also recommends raw meat—finely chopped and dressed with a *piquillo* of salt, a small clove, and cinnamon "according to your taste." His old friend Dr. Letamendi came to visit him, he tells her, and the good doctor insisted that she take two tablespoons of cod-liver oil every day and as much raw meat as possible, making sure to cut out all the fat and tendons.

Despite the raw cures, Delfina's condition deteriorated. That summer, Monturiol joined mother and daughter in Vic. On the evening of August 2, 1872, he stayed by his daughter's side through the night, as her fever grew worse. "Father, shouldn't you be going to sleep? Father, go to sleep," she told him. *"Pobre papa,"* he remembered her saying. He gave her morphine from time to time in small doses to alleviate her suffering. She died the following morning at eleven o'clock.

Monturiol's letters to his wife trace a trail of grief through the remaining years of his life. Although three of their other children had died previously, they had died as infants, and so their deaths had not marked him in the way that those of his two teenage daughters did. One year after Delfina's death, he wrote to his wife about their daughters' "beautiful and generous souls," and then, addressing those souls directly, added, "your memories, painful as they are, are our good fortune." Two years later he wrote, "I spend most of the day alone in my room, waiting for time to pass. . . . I spend many hours thinking about . . . the daughters we have lost. I shed a few bitter tears and I console myself that I did what I could. . . . The images of Adelaida and Delfina accompany me everywhere, everywhere I see them." In 1880 he wrote: "Nine years have passed; the sharpness of the pain has dulled, although from time to time it returns; but those times, despite the catastrophe that befell me and my great and daring enterprise, will always be the most beautiful of my life. You, Adelaida and Delfina, you adored your mother and me."

Recurring throughout Monturiol's correspondence of those years was a word and a concept that is very Catalan (though Monturiol, like most Catalans of the day, wrote everything in Castilian): *enyorança*. It's like nostalgia, only the pining and the sense of irrevocable loss are amplified, to the point where every virtue added to the imaginary idyll of the past only serves to deepen the inconsolable grief felt in the present. To be Catalan is to have lost something: in the fourteenth century, to have lost an empire; in the eighteenth century, a state; in the twentieth century, but for strenuous resistance, a language. But the language has survived and remains more than willing to put the loss into words.

One year after the death of Delfina came some welcome news on the family front. The submarine engineer Josep Pascual i Deop finally got up the nerve to ask for the beautiful Doña Anita's hand in marriage. She accepted, and the pair soon provided Monturiol with his first grandchild.

Thirty-two

The Submariners' Republic

In the wake of the uprising of September 1868, the republican movement, having spent twelve years underwater, once again bubbled to the top of national political life in Spain, where it would remain for the next six years.

The most powerful benefactor of the submarine cause, General Dulce, emerged from exile in the Canaries to join Prim and his plotters. As a reward for his efforts, he was appointed captain general of Cuba once again. At the time, Cuba was undergoing a revolution of its own, fighting for independence from Spain. Dulce offered the islanders freedom of the press, freedom of association, free elections, and an end to slavery. But all that only seemed to make matters worse. After five weeks, he gave up on reforming Cuba and returned to Spain in failing health. He retreated to a spa town in France for a cure, but it didn't work; he died in early 1869 at the age of sixty-one. Sadly, Monturiol's other great benefactor, the well-living Don José Xifré i Downing, saw even less of the revolution. He died of tuberculosis in Paris in October 1868 at the age of forty-six—a mere two months after his doting mother, Judith Downing, passed away.

Meanwhile, after cleansing Spanish soil of Isabel II and her cultish court, General Prim—who remained a royalist at heart—scouted around for a new king. Eventually he settled on a man named Amadeo, whom nobody else liked very much. Shortly after Amadeo ascended to the throne, however, Prim was assassinated.

Over the subsequent years, while Spain's national political life was in turmoil, liberal forces made decisive gains amid the confusion. It was a good time for the members of the submarine club (or at least those who were still alive). Francesc Sunyer i Capdevila, the ex-communist doctor and subaquatic poet, made a splash in 1869 with a booklet titled *God*, in which he defended his uncouth belief that there isn't one. In 1871, he took up a position as vice president of the Barcelona Provincial Council. Elected president of the same council was Monturiol's singing comrade, Josep Anselm Clavé. After some misunderstandings with other ruling bodies—during which time the Provincial Council was effectively dismembered—Clavé resigned his position as president. Taking over as acting president was that old utopian Ildefons Cerdà.

Under Cerdà's guidance, the Barcelona Provincial Council initiated a series of reforms intended to build the structures within Catalonia that would allow for an increasing level of autonomy from Madrid. Cerdà figured that some kind of decentralization was the best way to create a more progressive and representative form of government. He also pursued some of his own pet projects, such as a rather fanatical continuation of the Extension grid up the impossibly steep slopes of Montjuic and the resurrection of some of his zoning concepts. The Provincial Council was just one of many bodies competing for power at the time, however, and Cerdà had little success in advancing his urban plans.

On February 11, 1873, the unloved Amadeo abdicated the throne, and for the first time since anyone could remember, Spain was without a crown. That same day, a republic was declared. The progressives believed their time had come. The people were sovereign at last. Elections for a new national congress were scheduled for April 7.

After the republic was declared, the submariners chalked up even more impressive gains. Antonio Altadill set aside his career as a pulp-fiction writer to become governor of the province of Guadalajara, for a brief period, and then governor of the province of Murcia. Pascual Madoz, the former mayor of Barcelona and Monturiol's chief fund-raiser in Madrid, became the civil governor of Madrid. Joan Tutau, the former president of La Navegación Submarina, put in a stint as minister of finance. The first president of the republic of Spain was Estanislau Figueras, the deputy to congress who had so warmly embraced Monturiol in his victory tour through Figueres twelve years earlier. The second president—who took office after the first president's distressingly short term of a couple of months—was Francisco Pi i Margall, the elder brother of the congressional deputy who had taken Monturiol to the opera and otherwise entertained him during his earlier stays in Madrid.

The decisive role played by ex-submariners and their friends and relations in the creation of the republic provided eloquent testimony to the progressive political nature of Monturiol's underwater project. Through twelve years of reactionary rule, his work (along with that of a number of others) kept alive the circles of ideas and friendships that made possible the emergence of a more representative and democratic government.

Soon enough, Monturiol himself received the call. The progressives put his name forward as their candidate to represent the town of Manresa in the congressional elections of April 7, 1873. He won the election easily. After the victory party, unfortunately, it became apparent that there was no money to pay for his trip to Madrid, the site of the national congress, and Monturiol lost a couple of months scrounging for funds among republican sympathizers. He eventually raised enough to pay for the ticket and set off for the capital that summer.

In order to provide their fellow submariner with some income while serving as a representative in Madrid, his political allies arranged for his appointment as director of the National Stamp Factory, a position he held from September 1873 to January 1874. There was also some talk of naming Monturiol the ambassador to Switzerland. But by the time talk turned to action, the revolution was over.

The first Spanish republic unraveled in a comedy of errors. The factions in congress were never sure just who was who in the new political order. They each wanted to change the world, but they couldn't agree on just how to do it. Some wanted a centralized state, others a federalized one; some were conservative by nature, others were unrepentant communists. Pi i Margall, the republic's second president, championed a federal communism: that is, a Spain divided into hundreds of communist cantons. His favorite political philosopher was Proudhon, the French anarchist most famous for the slogan "Property is theft." Pi advocated the separation of church and state, state control of the army, free and compulsory education, and an end to slavery in Cuba. In other words, he wanted to upend just about every pillar of the status quo. With such a radical program, it was perhaps not so surprising that his presidency lasted only five weeks. Two more presidents would come and go before the republic faded from view. Monturiol wrote that he longed for an Abdó Terrades, the great socialist leader of his youth, to bring order to the progressive cause.

Reactionary forces took advantage of disarray on the left. On January 3, 1874, a military coup in Madrid ambushed the squabbling democracy. Carlists arose from a slumber of more than thirty years and besieged towns and villages throughout Spain. The remnants of the republic fizzled until all that was left was the flat, stale brew of the old order. By the end of the year, the monarchy was restored, complete with a new boy king, Alfonso XII, Isabel's son.

In the aftermath of the republican debacle of 1874, Barcelona's submariners dispersed to pursue new paths to personal and political fulfillment. The submarine movement once again went underground, where it set to work reinventing the culture of Barcelona.

Josep Anselm Clavé died in 1874, but death proved no impediment to his career. His own music became a central element of the so-called Catalan *renaixença*, or renaissance. The tropical rhythms he imported from Cuba eventually felt their way into a variety of traditions of Spanish music, not least the *havaneres*: plaintive songs describing the fate of the many Catalans who sought their fortune in Cuba and returned home when the island was lost. The Wagnerian howls he had brought from Germany defined Barcelona's operatic tastes for decades to come. Most importantly,

Clavé's choirs continued to multiply across Catalonia, and during the coming decades thousands of workers would sing their way to happiness, if not necessarily freedom from all oppression. His mustachioed visage and portly frame—figuring in dozens of commemorative portraits, monuments, and posters for upcoming events—became an icon for the new Catalonia.

Dr. Letamendi became president of the Ateneu and led it to ever greater heights of cultural awareness. The Ateneu served as the focal point for the creative individuals and their bourgeois sponsors who would remake Barcelona. Letamendi's own achievements in the mathematics of medicine, on the other hand, were less enduring. At best, one could say that he was a precursor of what today we might call holistic or mind-body medicine. A more somber epitaph, however, comes from the *Dictionary of Spanish Scientists*: "His enthusiasm for free speculation and his love of rhetoric led him to formulate a brilliant and spectacular doctrine that time has shown was nothing more than a bonfire of artifice without any foundation." He did, however, make enough of an impression on his fellow Barcelonans to get a spacious plaza in Cerdà's Eixample named after him.

Ramón Martí i Alsina, Monturiol's friend and portraitist, struggled to gain critical recognition after having rejected the academy and everything it stood for. As usually happens in such cases, he was reduced to painting portraits of wealthy burghers for a living and received the attention he craved and deserved only after his death. His naturalism encouraged many artists to leave their studios and paint the great outdoors and thus helped inaugurate a new sensibility in the visual arts.

Antonio Altadill and his brother Carlos—who wisely chose to write in Catalan, unlike Antonio—formed part of the movement to develop a national literature. Their work contributed to the *renaixença* of Catalan letters of the 1870s and 1880s.

Some of the former submariners, inevitably, sold out. Francisco J. Orellana, Monturiol's collaborator on the translation of the *Voyage to Icaria*, seems to have gone over entirely to the industrial establishment, achieving respectability as the leader of the association of big businesses of Barcelona.

Joan Monjo, the chief engineer of the *Ictíneo II*, stayed true to his path of hard work and harder luck. He lost all his savings in the submarine adventure. Wretched and broke, he totaled up the ruinous losses—unrecovered back pay and worthless shares—and wrote a memoir titled "Moral Sufferings the *Ictíneo* Caused Me." Then he headed to a beach town north of Barcelona, where he set up a college for the merchant marines. Certain that his misfortunes were as cruel as they were undeserved, he nonetheless continued to seek redemption through unstinting toil. He wrote all the textbooks for his school—on grammar, on geometry, on accounting (two volumes)—and taught most of its courses. He died in 1884. His grandson, Enrique Monjo, became a famous sculptor.

The hardest journey was that of Ildefons Cerdà. Sent packing at the end of the first republic in 1874, he buried himself again in writing the definitive exposition of the new science of urban planning. His thoughts extended to over four volumes and, in retrospect, constitute one of the most original and clear attempts ever to understand the nature of urbanization. With his typical bad luck in public relations, however, Cerdà managed to publish only the first two volumes during his lifetime, and these were the driest, most analytical of the set. The other two would be a century in coming, by which time Cerdà's rightful place as history's first and possibly greatest urban theorist had been ceded to others who, unknowingly, trod the ground he had broken long before.

By 1874, Cerdà was stuck in a deep financial rut. He had always funded his work out of his large inheritance. Another man might have used his inside knowledge of future urban developments in order to amass a private fortune. Cerdà, however, seems to have gone to the other extreme; his sense of moral duty to his fellow citizens led him from riches to rags. Now there was nothing left. He filled his diaries with obsessively detailed estimates of his expenditures over the years and sent a number of bills to the city for past services. These were never paid. Instead, city authorities continued to ride roughshod over Cerdà's innovative plan. After erasing most of the green spaces and ignoring the egalitarian zoning rules, they allowed developers to build higher and deeper than Cerdà had ever intended, thus re-creating in the new town the unbearable population density of the old. Cerdà's vision of a freely moving and centerless city, everywhere the same for every citizen, was fading fast.

Cerdà's health gave out in 1875, and he retreated to a spa in northern Spain. According to a friend, he spent his final months "doubting justice, doubting friendship, doubting the future, doubting his work, doubting everything except God." Cerdà himself wrote, "I can say in good faith that I have striven to do my utmost for the city of Barcelona, despite harboring deep inside me the conviction that it will never know how to thank me for it." He died in 1876 at the age of sixty-one.

After his death, Cerdà's family lost all connection to its ancestral homeland. His eldest daughter married an Englishman, the second married an American, and the third died young. His fourth (illegitimate) daughter changed her name to Esmeralda Cervantes, became a famous harpist, and today has a bridge connecting Brazil and Uruguay named in her honor. Cerdà's grandchildren ended up in Australia, Argentina, California, Great Britain, Malaysia, and elsewhere. None, ironically, made their home in the city that Cerdà had so thanklessly reinvented.

After the coup of 1874, Monturiol remained in Madrid for several months. His days were filled with loneliness. He complained about the weather, which he compared unfavorably to the temperate climate of Barcelona. He lost his job in the stamp factory, and, in order to economize, he told Emilia, he stopped going to the cafés. He said he was tired of life in the capital, where "my heart finds only light affectation, weak sympathies, and mistrustful friendships."

Emilia, too, showed signs of strain. She wrote to tell her husband that she wandered about "stupefied," as if she were "living in a dream," and that she felt a "weakening in her bones." No doubt the tragedy of Adelaida and Delfina still weighed heavily on her mind. Perhaps she was also suffering from the cumulative toll of twenty-five years of marriage to an incorrigible dreamer, years that despite his high-minded aspirations and extraordinary achievements had brought more than their fair share of poverty, enforced separation, exile, and social opprobrium.

Monturiol wondered for the first time whether their separation now was only physical, or if the sharp edges of experience had not opened up a silent rift between them. He wrote to patch things up: "I love you so much, Emilia! How good I feel with the sweet expression of your affection! Do not be severe with me; consider that my enthusiasm for all my affairs is not just my life, but the life of your love, and that without this enthusiasm I would be insipid, I would not speak, and you would not find in me the sweet companion of your life, who will love you as long as he lives."

Monturiol's political thought matured during the republican experience. The red and the black of his youth gave way to shades of gray. Now he took a much more skeptical view of revolutionary action. In a letter to Anita he explained his change of heart. Throughout history, he said, humankind has been divided into the strong and the weak. The weak periodically band together to rebel against the strong, and they call it "revolution." But their lack of experience in government gives rise to reaction and to the return of the strong. Politics, he suggested, consists mainly of convulsions from below followed by convulsions from above.

Yet, even within this seemingly fatalistic worldview, Monturiol found hope for progress. Progress would still take humankind forward into a brighter tomorrow, he believed, but it would do so much more deliberately than he had imagined in his revolutionary days. "The science of government consists in the establishment of laws that tend to favor the development of its powers," he argued. "To govern, then, is to conserve the treasury of knowledge, virtues, and acquired riches and facilitate means for new acquisitions." In other words, good government is the gradual and painful accumulation of "the right ways of doing things." The improvement of the human condition depends on the development of the infrastructure of know-how—or what the gurus today might call "knowledge capital." Although his revolutionary ardor had obviously cooled, Monturiol remained faithful to the Icarian-Platonic ideal of a social order based on wisdom: "Government should be the patrimony of the wise, but until now it has been the patrimony of the strong."

The rise and fall of the first Spanish republic, in Monturiol's mature view, was not an unmitigated disaster. Rather, it represented one small and painful step on a very long journey toward a more just society. History has since confirmed that this was the sensible view. It was not until the final quarter of the twentieth century, after the last of the warlords passed away, that Spain established a liberal democracy on a solid footing. It might well have taken even longer, had not the progressives of the nineteenth century, like Monturiol, created the ideas and traditions that would serve as the foundations of a representative state.

Monturiol's mature insight was the lasting fruit of his submarine labors. In the struggle to realize his submarine dream, as he well knew, he had sacrificed pieces of his utopian ideals in order to win the acceptance of a less-than-perfect social system: he had exchanged his pacifism for military support, communism for capitalist backing, and internationalism for provincial partisanship. He would never have achieved as much as he did without such concessions to the establishment. Even then, it was not enough. Not until society caught up with his vision would it be possible to build a true submarine in a manner befitting such a grand enterprise.

Progress is slow, Monturiol realized, much slower than we tend to think. However brilliant a technological achievement may be, its utility and its beneficence depend very much on the nature of the world that is around to receive it. Without broad support in the knowledge base and practices of a society, a new invention will have no use. Without the cultivation of the wisdom to use it well, it will do no good. Society moves forward only as fast as its slowest element. Humboldt was right: Universal education is the foundation of liberty, and liberty is the foundation of progress. A lone inventor and his submarine cannot carry a people to freedom. The best he can hope to do is show them the way.

Thirty-three

A Life of Invention

Upon returning to Barcelona in the spring of 1874, Monturiol once again faced the struggle for subsistence. Now fifty-four years old, he had no official position and no income. For the next five years, he scraped together a living by taking odd jobs as a writer and editor.

Under the pseudonym M. Draper he published a popular work on *Historical Scenes from the Most Remote Ages to the Present Day*. With a partner, he wrote a compendium of biographies of *Celebrated Men and Women*. Among the celebrated were Galileo, Watt, Newton, Napoleon, William Tell, and Héloise and Abelard. On behalf of a local club of republicans, he gave a series of lectures on physics, astronomy, and geology—or pretty much everything that was known about the universe at the time. The lecture notes he wrote out in neat longhand on old stationery from La Navegación Submarina. To earn spare change, he translated works from French and copyedited manuscripts. It was hack work, yet Monturiol's prose remained purposeful and lucid throughout.

At one low point in 1878 he took up an administrative job with a new daily paper called *La Corona*—ironically, a mouthpiece for Barcelona's monarchists. In the same year, a friend who acquired some property in west Africa suggested that Monturiol go and live there to supervise it. The inventor gave it some serious thought, but Emilia must have put her foot down.

Monturiol's economic woes finally drove him into the clutches of a brokerage house, where he accepted a day job as a clerk in

1879. The following year, at the age of sixty, he worked his way up to cashier—the trade for which he had trained thirty-five years previously as a student in Madrid. The brokerage house became a full-service bank; in 1882, Monturiol became editor of the bank's newsletter. He retired in September 1883.

"It is hard to have to stoop to occupations of this class, when my head has produced the art of underwater navigation," Monturiol lamented in 1874. He was disgusted with himself for wasting energy on "small things that I also fail to achieve." And yet, even as outrageous misfortunes fell upon him, even as the humiliations cut deeper because they were moving so slowly and deliberately, Monturiol's passion to improve the world by means of new inventions marched on implacably, constrained only by the narrowing grooves of opportunity laid out by the necessities of life. By day he was a congressman, an editor, a hack, or a bank cashier; but on candlelit evenings and weekends he was still Monturiol the visionary inventor.

During his four months as director of the stamp factory in 1873, he invented a machine for the rapid and effective drying of sticky paper. He bequeathed the device to the factory, presumably out of a misplaced hope for improved efficiency in the Spanish public sector.

After the reactionary coup of January 1874, with Carlist forces besieging small towns across the country, Monturiol turned his mechanical genius to military weaponry. He conceived of an inexpensive portable artillery piece that could be used to keep the reactionaries at bay—a mortar. It was to be, he emphasized, "a weapon to annihilate the Carlists." The prototype weighed 80 kilograms (Monturiol claimed it could be carried on one's shoulders, though that seems a stretch), and it had a projected range of 2,000 meters. In April he went out into the wilds around Madrid to give the mortar a try. When he fired the weapon, unfortunately, the ammunition cartridge got stuck halfway up the tube—an eventuality that "had never entered into my plan," he explained to his wife—and the mortar exploded, leaving behind a half-length rump. He went searching for the missing half but could not find it, because "the place where we performed the test was too uneven."

Back in Barcelona, Monturiol applied his imagination to finding inexpensive ways to supplement the family diet. (Since the early days when he put out an article on cooperative kitchens for workers, Monturiol had always taken an interest in the matter of feeding the masses.) He took to raising rabbits and then, in order to keep costs down, invented a rabbit food whose main ingredient was sawdust. The bunnies were none the wiser, and apparently they did not have a woody taste when eaten. The woodwork got Monturiol thinking about glues, so he invented a wood glue that he claimed was more effective than any previous ones. The wood glue in turn inspired him to find a better way to shine his shoes. He came up with a shoe-polishing paste that creates a shine "with the mere application of the brush." The experience with cleaners led him to develop a method for fabricating soap in the cold. The next apparently random act of invention was a pocket telescope.

At the time, Monturiol's son-in-law Pascual had a respectable job as an industrial engineer. Over lunch one day he told his father-in-law of a seemingly intractable problem his firm faced in the design of a new steam engine. In the following weeks, Monturiol reinvented the regulator used on the steam engine in question and solved the problem. The work drew his attention to a problem with most steam engines of the day: the scandalous loss of energy in the hot gases escaping through the chimney. So he invented a device for capturing the energy that otherwise went up in smoke.

Even the most mundane tasks inspired Monturiol's inventive mind. While serving as a clerk at the bank, he noticed that a considerable amount of time was spent in copying out correspondence. So he devised a mechanism for copying letters as they were written. After discussions with a banking client in the stone quarry business, he developed a superior way of cutting rocks at right angles.

In his final years, Monturiol turned his creative energy back to the theme of food, seeking a safe and palatable way to preserve meat. He suspected that external agents—those *animalillos*—were to blame for the rotting of meat, and he concocted various coatings to defend the meat against this outside threat. Some of the chemical solutions, no doubt, were leftovers from his submarine days. In February 1883 he recorded that "today we tried a small hake" that was seven days old and conserved in a special formula. The smell was good, he noted, but the taste a little off—it was a bit chewy, not quite as delicate as fresh fish. In April 1883 he claimed that meat two months and five days old looked just like fresh meat and was perfectly edible, although the gelatinous coating of antiseptic chemicals left an aftertaste that was "not agreeable to the palate." By the end of the year, after much grudging assistance from members of the household and polite visitors, Monturiol believed he had found a formula that worked. He wrote an enthusiastic letter to his friend Martí Carlé, who had emigrated to Argentina in search of work, in hopes of setting up an intercontinental meat-shipping business.

This invention, like all its predecessors, produced no cash for Monturiol. The source of the problem was not the idea itself but rather the inventor's astonishing inability to turn a great idea into a good business. Monturiol himself diagnosed his own handicap well: "I do not know how to market anything, I do not know how to conquer the hearts and minds of men so that they may come to my aid."

In no case was this lack of business acumen more evident than in his meat-preservation invention. After the successful experiments in the chemistry of meat, a man named Josep Llovera, posing as a chemist and engineer, approached the inventor with a proposal for helping him market his product. Monturiol, whose confidence in the good nature of the human race never faltered, gladly supplied Llovera with the secret formula. Instead of helping him negotiate with local meat companies, however, Llovera absconded with the recipe to London, where he set up his own intercontinental meat-shipping business, making use of Monturiol's invention. He built a fleet of fifteen steamships and, in the days before refrigeration, transported meats in Monturiol's chemical stew from as far afield as New Zealand, Australia, and Argentina. On his death in 1909, Llovera left a fortune estimated at

£2.5 million. A Spanish newspaper ran the story under the headline NARCÍS MONTURIOL, MILLIONAIRE?

Yet a millionaire Monturiol is all but inconceivable. The inventor of underwater navigation would always be a dreamer, and even as he fabricated one gizmo after another, his mind raced ahead of practical realities and latched on to far more ambitious and speculative designs. A companion wrote that in his later years one of Monturiol's great pleasures consisted in "locking himself in a room on Sunday afternoons in the company of a close friend, usually another dreamer, and passing the hours launching his imagination through the universe of possible inventions searching for new ideas and daring developments."

Always fascinated by the phenomenon of magnetism—one argument he made for the submarine was that it would serve to test the behavior of magnetic fields under the sea—Monturiol theorized about ways in which the earth's magnetic field could be put to use for human benefit. He also contemplated the possibility of aerial navigation—in his mind, the natural twin of underwater navigation. He examined birds, alive and dead, and observed that, pound for pound, they had much greater muscle power than humans. However, he left no designs of flying machines for us to judge. Perhaps his most intriguing suggestion for an imaginary invention comes in a letter to Anita, where, after listing the various projects on which he is working—the meat preservative topping the list—he says he has had a brilliant idea, one that outshines all the rest by far: a means for converting the light of the sun into a source of power for locomotion.

Monturiol's dreams usually began that way: contemplating some elemental feature of the world and then imagining the unlikely ways it might be put to use for the benefit of humankind. Whether in solar power, aerial navigation, or submarines, the dreams usually ended in a place hopelessly ahead of his time. Monturiol was the kind of visionary who is impossibly prescient, forever condemned to foresee a future in which he can never participate.

All the while, deep under the surface, Monturiol still carried a torch for his submarine. From time to time, he secretly plotted the resurrection of the *Ictíneo*. Ten years after its demise, he confided in a letter to Anita that he was busy figuring out the exact timing and method of his submarine comeback. But the "social resistance" to his costly underwater ventures remained unyielding, and his friends and family politely dissuaded him from pursuing the dream further.

Monturiol's talent for invention was exceptional; he was, in the words of historian Lluis Permanyer, "a machine for generating ideas." And yet, according to Monturiol himself, "We are all, more or less, inventors." For an inventor is just "a poor apprentice of an art that does not yet have a master," and we all labor like amateurs to invent our particular lives, an art for which there is no master. About his own accomplishments, Monturiol wrote: "As a printer, I did not stop until I could print paper in a roll; as a smoker, until I could make cigarettes mechanically; as a man, until I created the submarine chamber, adequate to sustain life in inhospitable environments, whether in the ocean or elsewhere; as a physicist I have created the submarine motor, the aerial motor, etc." Invention was the way he invented himself. It was the way he became what he was.

Thirty-four

Twilight of a Submariner

The lectures Monturiol gave in the 1870s bear some curiously grandiose titles: "Geosophy," "On the Comets," and, most impressively, "A General Idea of the Universe." They should have been trite discourses, aimed at a lay audience, performed in exchange for hourly wages. But they weren't that at all. In these and other writings from the last third of his life, scattered in notes and letters, Monturiol was striving for nothing less than a comprehensive theory of the universe. And this is why the long twilight years after the death of the *Ictíneo* are the most remarkable of his life. Despite adversities that should have overwhelmed him and forced a bitter retreat from life, he never lost his faith in scientific progress but, rather, strove unceasingly against increasing odds toward a more perfect future for humankind.

In his lecture on the "General Idea of the Universe," Monturiol reaffirmed his long-standing conviction that the old ideal of God must be replaced with the new ideal of science. He cited Laplace's famous dictum—that God is an unnecessary hypothesis for explaining the system of the universe—and then added:

> What should capture our attention in the study of nature is not the act of creation [of the universe] or the passage from nothing into being, since neither reason nor observation, as Humboldt says, can give us an idea about such things; but rather the study of life and of the forces that animate the universe. What matters to us [that which] will always be an enigma, the essence of

things, before the grandiosity and utility of the laws of its development, of the succession of forms in which it appears, of the relations of bodies with each other . . .?

True to his Humboldtian creed, Monturiol tossed metaphysics out the window along with the old deities and demanded that we focus our attention on the panorama of real experience.

Monturiol wanted to concentrate on the phenomenal world— a world consisting of matter, light, forces of nature, and organic life. But within that world he reserved a special place for human intelligence. In his 1874 lecture he said:

> Very great is the world; but very great as well is the human intelligence that comprehends it, that describes it, and knows how to use the cosmic forces in benefit of progress.

Human intelligence, in Monturiol's world, arises from nature and yet has the potential to transcend its origins. In his lecture "On the Comets," he elaborated:

> These millions of meteors that we see announce the death that awaits the earth—the laboratory of organic life—that has created our intelligence and endows it every day with more power so that it may dominate and direct the forces of nature and perhaps one day arrive as the free power that it is to put itself above all other powers.

Monturiol's commitment to scientific progress had its cosmic side. It was about more than creating laborsaving devices and novel forms of transportation; it was about the realization of the essence of human intelligence, which was in turn about the coming of age of the universe as a whole.

In a letter to Anita, Monturiol described the ultimate destination of universal progress. We are "free and powerful in creating machines," he said, but other beings "more complex than we" will someday create "organisms far superior to man." The process can end only in the advent of a "truly free Power." Thus, God awaits us in the future, at the end of time, and not in the past, at the beginning of time, as humankind has vainly believed. This is why his *Ictíneo* had to be so like a fish: it was to be the first step in the creation of a truly free form of life, the first step in the transformation of man to god and the total liberation of the universe.

At the heart of all Monturiol's passion, despite or perhaps because of its rigorously scientific orientation and its obsession with the minutiae of the workings of the physical world, there was this mystical moment, a vision of a perfect union with the cosmos—the same vision he had on the shores of Cadaqués, one that would stay with him, drive him forward, haunt him, and always remain just out of reach. Maybe every work of pure technology has something equally mystical and unapproachable at its core.

In the same letter to Anita, Monturiol acknowledged just how far short of his ultimate goal he had fallen. "We do not know how to create anything more than mechanisms and so, naturally, we are mechanics; others will come who are by nature biologists, and others . . . others whom we cannot imagine." A merely mechanical device, a wood-and-copper submarine, he recognized, could hardly take humankind all the way to a perfect union with the cosmos. Even so, he said, it was worth the effort. Monturiol found his ethical bearings within the grandest context imaginable. As he explained to Anita, our duty is to "cultivate our morality and intelligence, and in that way we contribute with all our best efforts to the advent of truly free Powers." And that, in fact, was precisely what the inventor had done throughout his life.

The Promethean struggle to bring forth a new form of life is also a struggle against death. Visions of a union with the infinite cosmos are, in essence, attempts to overcome the finitude of the human condition. In his later years, Monturiol's religion of progress became a way for him to make sense of the greatest tragedy that befell him, the death of his two teenage daughters:

> I continue to believe that the psychic elements, that is, the moral and intellectual elements of those two beings, improve

the world. We all give what we have, and, just as all matter radiates heat, light, and gravity, so I believe that man radiates what constitutes his essence, and that when this essence disaggregates and disperses at death, its parts enter into new combinations and contribute to new formations, that would be less perfect if they lacked the human elements. Thus, my daughters were not born in vain; they were perfect as products of progress; their elements were not extinguished, but rather continue to live, improving the new aggregates of which they form part.

It was a truly Hegelian feat of synthesis: to unite the death of his daughters, a positivistic understanding of science, and the ideal of progress into a meaningful whole. More striking still is the remarkable resilience of Monturiol's faith. Despite overwhelming evidence that fate did not always favor the cause of progress, and that history was a catalog of outrageous and senseless acts, the submariner never deviated from his course of true belief.

In September 1883, Monturiol retired. His sixty-fourth birthday occasioned some melancholy reflections on the course of his life:

> How the time has flown: I arrive at the end of my journey leaving for others that which I should have done myself. How many years, year after year, so miserably lost! Since '69 everything is merely aspiration; no reality except the tears for those two we lost for ever.

Other moments, though, found him in better cheer. Just before retiring, he journeyed to Figueres and Cadaqués in the company of Anita. In Figueres he strolled along the streets and reminisced about the glorious reception he had received more than twenty years earlier. "At last, we are happy," he whispered to his daughter. In Cadaqués he visited his old friend Lito, the farmer who once offered to sell his vineyard to help finance the *Ictíneo*. As he walked the rocky shores for the last time, he seemed reconciled to the weatherbeaten form his life had assumed.

Throughout 1884, Monturiol's health deteriorated. He suffered from emphysema—surely the effect of all those cigarettes, although one wonders if breathing in the confined spaces of his submarines didn't speed the process. By June 1885 he was gravely ill. The family moved him to Anita's house in Sant Martí de Provençals, a village on the outskirts of Barcelona. The change in location rejuvenated him, but only for a while. One day, his friend Damás Calvet, the engineer who had recited an ode to Monturiol over lunch many years earlier, paid him a visit. Monturiol said to him, "I die without having completed any of my works." And yet, according to Calvet, he said it with uncommon serenity, perhaps acknowledging that his work was of the kind that never quite reaches its destination. In his last four days, Monturiol lost the ability to speak, although he was still able to write tender and plaintive notes to his family. He died at eleven o'clock on the morning of September 6, 1885, in the presence of his wife and children.

Monturiol was buried in a private ceremony in a grave alongside his deceased children. The tombstone there already read:

Emilio, 12 months, in 1849
Filomena, 4 years, in 1854
Luis, 23 months, in 1864
Adelaida, 17 years, in 1871
Delfina, 13 years, in 1872
The older they were, the greater our grief. May your remains improve the world, and our pain improve Humanity!

To which was added:

Here lies Narcís Monturiol, inventor of the Ictíneo, *the first submarine boat, in which he navigated through the depths of the sea in the waters of Barcelona and Alicante in 1859, 1860, 1861, and 1862*

Death came not without irony. A few miles from Monturiol's grave, the steam engine that had powered his submarine served as the throbbing heart of a new textile factory. Also, around the time of his death the world's newspapers ran a story about the Swedish inventor Nordenfeldt, whose recently launched submarine, they averred, was the first of its kind. It was left to Monturiol's son-in-law, the ever-loyal Josep Pascual i Deop, to remind readers, in a subsequent letter to the editor, that Monturiol had built a submarine twenty-six years previously, and that, in a detailed comparison between the new Swedish boat and the *Ictíneo*, "the advantage was decidedly on the side of the Spanish invention."

Thirty-five

Redemption

Barcelona came of age in 1888, the year it hosted its first World Fair. The fair lasted thirty-five weeks, lured one and a half million visitors from around the world, and almost bankrupted the city, but it put Barcelona on the map. More importantly, it sparked a kind of civic self-recognition. In the four decades between that fair and the next one, held in 1929, Barcelona reinvented itself as the home for a unique culture, with a unique set of responses to the challenges of modernity.

The World Fair changed the face of Barcelona—literally. The first great architectural symbol of the era was the café built for the fair in the park of the Ciutadella by Domènech. If the style was new, the elements of which it was composed were not. The entrance to the café boasted an exceptionally long and low arch of the kind for which Catalan architecture had always been famous. Overhead, some windows showed playful allusions to Arab motifs. What was new about Domènech's café, paradoxically, was its use of ancient materials. The exposed brick and iron harked back to the traditional Catalan country house. Previously this would have been considered déclassé and possibly barbaric—every decent building hitherto covered its raw innards with classical facades of stone—but in Domènech's hands the scandalous and titillating use of such earthy materials became part of a new, distinctively modern aesthetic.

The organizers of the fair also saw fit to erect a monument to Christopher Columbus, which still occupies the circle at the sea-

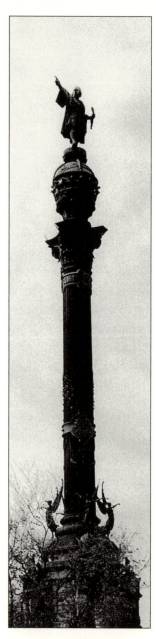

Barcelona's Columbus monument. There is some difference of opinion concerning which way he is pointing.

ward end of the Rambles. Since Columbus was a great man, they reasoned, he must be Catalan. The Catalan Columbus stands high atop a column and points a bronze finger out to sea, toward the New World. Given the position of Barcelona with respect to the sea, he is actually pointing somewhere in the direction of his actual birthplace in Italy, in the Old World.

The fictional Columbus of the Catalans was a perfect symbol for the twin-headed nature of the new culture of Barcelona. It was a culture that thrilled at the idea of the new and yet all the while pointed very much in the direction of the old. The foundations for the reinvention of Barcelona were laid during the 1870s and 1880s, in the so-called *renaixença* of Catalan culture. This *renaixença* wasn't so much a rebirth as a feverish hunt through a cemetery for signs of life. Its poets and novelists were desperate to locate the essence of Catalonia, which they were sure was buried somewhere in meadows or mountains or in the backyard of a country manor. Barcelona in its renaissance was merely in the throes of labor, a labor that would soon give birth to a genuinely original culture.

In the wake of the World Fair, the *renaixença* evolved into a more sophisticated movement called *modernisme,* usually bracketed in the period between 1888 and 1910. To the old stew of Catalan nationalism, *modernisme* added an international cosmopolitan flavor and a fascination with the modern. At bottom, *modernisme* was a response to the problem of modernity in Barcelona. Through the second half of the nineteenth century and beyond, Barcelona's industrialization accelerated. The Extension filled up and soon it too was bursting at the seams. By 1900 over a quarter of Catalonia's population, nearly half a million people, lived in its capital city. New technologies—cars, electricity, trains, ships, factory machines—continued to invade everyday life. The fundamental premise of *modernisme* was that modern technology could be, and indeed would have to be, turned around in order to produce a new and better version of ancient human realities.

In art, *modernisme* meant absorbing the latest lessons from French Impressionism and living in the best bohemian style. Picasso spent his early youth in Barcelona around this time and

Statue of Antoni Rovira i Trias in his plaza. Despite losing the battle to design the Extension to Cerdà, the much-loved and well-connected Rovira got his plaza long before Cerdà got his. The bronze Rovira clearly remains convinced that his bronze plan for the Eixample is far superior to that of his rival.

tested his brush against the Catalan artists who frequented a favorite café, Els Quatre Gats. In literature, *modernisme* meant reading Wilde and sundry Parisians and then attempting to capture extraordinary and hallucinogenic experiences in words. In music, it meant Wagner; Catalans thrilled so much to Wagner's legends of a heroic past that they were sure the operas were meant to be set somewhere in the misty mountains of northern Catalonia. But *modernisme* left its biggest mark in architecture, in the new style that began with Domènech's café in the park and soon decorated the more fashionable parts of the Extension with exuberant and often outlandish visual spectacles. Above all, *modernisme* would come to mean Gaudí—although, truth be told, Gaudí was so extraordinary and idiosyncratic that to some extent he was a movement unto himself.

It was the wide avenues falling from Cerdà's utopian calculus that literally set the stage for the show of *modernisme*, creating the platform on which the city's architects could compete to represent the new face of Barcelona. In 1890, some thoughtful Barcelonans proposed that a plaza be named in honor of the man who had designed their Eixample. But the city authorities—apparently feeling that thirty years was not long enough to hold a serious grudge—shot the proposal down. Instead, they saw fit to name a plaza in Gracia in honor of Antoni Rovira i Trias, Cerdà's great rival. In the plaza they placed a statue of the defeated architect, seated on a bench, looking disapprovingly down the hill in the direction of Cerdà's Eixample. Laid out on the ground before the miffed Rovira is a bronze version of his own starburst plan, the future/past that never came to be.

The *modernistes* themselves showed equally monstrous ingratitude to Cerdà. They complained of the "monotony" of his grid, oblivious to the fact that Cerdà himself had already answered the charge of "monotony"—he argued that the supposedly monotonous grid provides the level playing field on which individuals can differentiate themselves and compete for glory—and that the very work of the *modernistes* substantiated his argument. Yet the Cerdà-bashing continued. Josep Plà, the most widely read Catalan writer of the early part of the twentieth century, summed up the conventional wisdom when he dismissed the urbanist as "a man of mathematical education and of deliriously bad taste."

Nonetheless, it was Gaudí's Casa Milà, situated on the Passeig de Gracia at the epicenter of Cerdà's Eixample, that became the crowning glory of Barcelona's experiment with *modernisme*, the most universal symbol of the movement. When construction on the Casa Milà began in 1906, wags likened its twisted steel framework variously to a recent train wreck in which dozens died and to an aerial parking lot for blimps. When it was completed in 1910, its undulating stone exterior earned it the enduring sobriquet La Pedrera—the rock quarry. In fact, the new apartment block on the corner of the Passeig de Gracia and the Carrer Provença looks— and was clearly intended to look—rather like the surface of the ocean on a windy day. An imaginary gale has whipped the white limestone to a matte finish and carved surreal curves and ghostly shapes into the stone. Iron strands of seaweed, iron driftwood, iron clams, and other unidentifiable ferrous creatures of the deep have been tossed up by make-believe surf to act as balconies in front of the submarine holes wherein the tenants reside. Hallucinatory sculptures sprout from the undulating curves on the roof. Flattened images of a nautilus, an octopus, and a starfish grace the hexagonal tiles strewn over the entry floor. (The city, by the way, took a fancy to the tiles and paved the sidewalks of the entire Passeig de Gracia with them.) Salvador Dalí, the Empordàn painter who rode the bewitching winds of the *tramontana* to surrealistic heights, summed up La Pedrera thus: "It is a house built following the forms of the sea. . . . It's not about deceptive metaphors. It's about real buildings, a true sculpture."

There was something very modern about the Casa Milà. After seeing the first automobile cruising the streets of Barcelona in 1903, Gaudí added circular ramps spiraling up an interior light shaft to his design, so that residents could drive to their apartment doors. When the ramps proved too steep and cramped for cars, he kept them as pedestrian walkways and installed Barcelona's first parking lot in the building's basement. But there was also some-

The Casa Milà

thing very archaic about Gaudí's stone quarry. In modeling his design on the sea, he was reaching back deep into the past, to a time before the abstract principles of classical European architecture imposed straight lines and regular curves all over the landscape. He wanted to build a new Barcelona out of purely organic forms, forms taken from some ur-original human experience of life in a natural shelter, surrounded by plants and animals, subject to the force of the wind and the waves.

Gaudí's masterpiece spoke of a longing for an originary Eden unspoiled by abstract principles, a space measured to the dignity of the human organism. It represented the synthesis of the old opposition that had bedeviled Catalan culture since its first encounters with industrialization, the opposition between the pragmatic rationality of *seny* and the mystical passion of *rauxa*.

Gaudí was his own kind of genius; but the vision inscribed on the stormy wave front of the Casa Milà drew on cultural raw material that was first fabricated by another—specifically, by Narcís

The tiles of the Passeig de Gracia

Monturiol. Gaudí's vision was a reproduction of Monturiol's sub-aquatic utopia. Like Monturiol's submarine dream, it was a vision that, with its steel frames and automobile ramps, embraced modernity. Yet, like the boat that would have become a true and living fish, it was also a vision of something archaic. Gaudí was, in effect, attempting to realize in his own way Monturiol's project of combining scientific *seny* with utopian *rauxa*. Gaudí even tapped into the reservoir of Monturiol's imagery. The vision of a shelter safe from the winds in the very heart of the sea borrowed directly from the pictorial vocabulary of the submarine dream.

It should come as no surprise, therefore, that Monturiol, who died in utter obscurity in 1885, was reborn a few years later, at the moment when Barcelona embarked on its adventure with *modernisme.*

Monturiol's resurrection and ascension into the pantheon of Catalan culture took place in 1890. In September of that year *La Vanguardia,* Barcelona's leading newspaper, produced a special

Sunday supplement that included a dozen articles on Monturiol and his incredible submarine. Another paper, *La Tomasa*, devoted an entire issue to the inventor. The city authorities commissioned a portrait of Monturiol and hung it with great ceremony in the Gallery of Illustrious Catalans in the chamber of the city council. In a companion volume on the twenty or so most illustrious Catalans, they honored the submariner with his own chapter. And, finally, the inventor's magnum opus, his *Essay on the Art of Underwater Navigation*, saw the light of day. The employees of the Compañia Transatlantica, Barcelona's leading maritime passenger service, banded together to fund its publication in 1891 and sent a copy to the British Library, presumably in hopes of spreading the word about Monturiol far across the globe.

One of the reporters of *La Vanguardia* wrote, "If humanity erected statues in public places to *good* men"—as opposed to the merely famous or powerful, he meant to say—"then Monturiol would have his." Some years later, the city of Figueres took him up on the suggestion. They exhumed their hometown hero from his pauper's grave on the outskirts of Barcelona, transferred his remains to the Figueres town square, the site of his ecstatic reception so many years before, and erected a monument there in his honor. They also graced a street with his name. Soon there were streets and secondary schools across Catalonia bearing the name of the great Catalan inventor. Even Joan Monjo, Monturiol's hapless chief engineer, got a street in Barceloneta, not far from the shipyards where the *Ictíneo* was built.

It was not until the second half of the twentieth century that Cerdà's name received favorable mention in polite society. By then the city had a point of comparison with which to understand just what its pioneering urbanist had accomplished. In the postwar years, Barcelona had continued to expand beyond the limits of the Eixample. But the latest additions to the city amounted to a grotesquely unplanned sprawl. In this third belt the ratio of road area to built area declined to the claustrophobic levels found in the

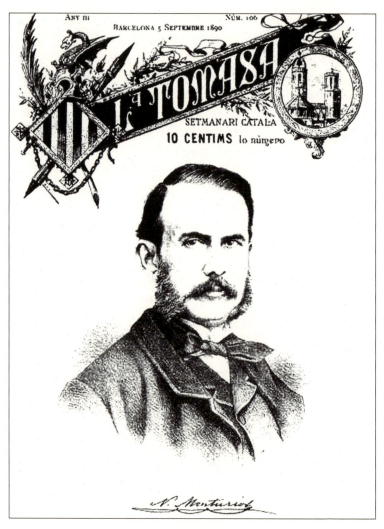

Cover of La Tomasa

old city. The new hieroglyph of Barcelona declared unambiguously that there is no guarantee of progress in this world, unless some individual or individuals take the steps necessary to ensure that it comes about. Even stripped of many of the best features of Cerdà's design—such as the garden spaces and the zoning rules—

the old Eixample suddenly looked pretty good. In fact, considering that it was laid out four decades before the arrival of the automobile, it looked remarkable.

In 1959 the city organized an exposition of Cerdà's work, and the man who designed the better part of Barcelona finally got his plaza. Actually, it's more like a traffic circle. The location is not great—it's far out on a congested end of the Gran Via—but at least it's big. Cerdà's treatises also finally emerged into the daylight and began to receive the scholarly attention they deserved. Many now agreed that Cerdà had been one of the most original minds ever to tackle the problem of urbanization and that his work was—and ought to have been, as one commentator recently put it—"fundamental and foundational" in his discipline.

Today the fortress of Montjuic is a museum, its guns silent except for the graffiti, and on a sunny day it offers the best views of the city and the mountainous coastline stretching to the north. A tranquil park and Barcelona's zoo have replaced the ominous fortress of the Ciutadella. The shanty wooden fry bars of Barceloneta have given way to upmarket restaurants serving an international clientele. In preparation for the 1992 summer Olympics, Barcelona suddenly discovered that there were miles of sandy beach tucked away behind a line of factories and plenty of space among the piers and loading cranes for boardwalk bistros and fashion boutiques. In the same pragmatic spirit with which it built the textile powerhouses of the nineteenth century, Barcelona has embraced the sea.

But the old longings are still there, not so far below the surface. The new Barcelona recently went fishing in the waters of its imaginary past and reeled in Monturiol and his amazing submarine. Here and there in the new city one finds remnants of the great inventor's work, scattered like small bits of treasure trawled up from the deep. A sculpture in his honor graces the Avinguda Diagonal. It shows a bronze model of his fish boat piercing the bronze slab of the deep. A full-scale mock-up of the *Ictíneo II* lolls on a grassy spot near the new harbor. Hoarded in the Maritime

The Ictíneo II *model. Enjoying a sunny day on the new pier, the submarine keeps an eye on the harbor.*

Museum is a stash of fragments from the real *Ictíneo*: a flag, a couple of portholes, the pressure gauge, the odd piece of machinery that presumably had no resale value.

Over on the new beachfront, an undulating copper mesh designed by Frank Gehry mimics the curves of a giant fish. It looks like the work of a Gaudí with a laptop and is the latest nonlinear facsimile of the *Ictíneo* to attract the eye of Barcelona. The city planners chose the name New Icaria for the adjoining neighborhood developed for the Olympic athletes. The new utopia has a shopping mall. The mall comes complete with an excellent multiplex cinema that shows movies in the original version. One film that played recently was a fictionalized documentary celebrating the exploits of Monturiol.

But the real monument to the great submariner is the city itself. Like the "psychic elements" he ascribed to his dead daughters—the fragments of a life that scatter after death in order to form parts of new combinations of things—so Monturiol and his amazing submarine dispersed and then reassembled in the afterlife to shape the new city of Barcelona. The shaved corners

Submarine sculpture by Josep Maria Subirachs

Cerdà added as a final flourish to his blocks have become the octagonal trademark of the city, recording the distant echo of a call for the open spaces within which a freedom of movement and association is possible. The exuberant facades of the Eixample's architectural gems, like the sculptural model of Monturiol's *Ictíneo*, register the homegrown synthesis of Dionysian passion with the exigencies of Apollonian form. In its recent opening to the sea, Barcelona has merely followed the directions indicated by its pioneering submariner. Icaria was neither lost nor found, just woven into the fabric of civic life. In the tranquil patterns of this city by the sea, Monturiol eventually earned the redemption he so desperately sought in life. His work helped Barcelona find an answer of sorts to the problem of modernity, although—as usually happens in such cases—it wasn't quite the answer he had in mind.

Every July on the freshly painted beachfronts of Catalonia, crowds gather to down shots of flaming rum and hear sailor-

An artificial fish for the postmodern generation

suited guitarists sing *havaneres*. The melancholy tunes take the listeners back to a time over a century ago, when Spain—for lack of a
submarine—lost Cuba, a time when many Catalan adventurers
returned home singing these gentle Afro-Caribbean songs, songs
that took them back to the island paradise they left behind, where
they sang these same songs to remind themselves of the land and
the love they left behind to go to Cuba in the first place. It's a triple
play for that yearning sense of *enyorança*. The inescapable logic of
the situation is that everything good in life is just a memory, and
memory itself is loss. And this is why the ultimate failure of Monturiol's submarine dream only makes it all the more representative
of the place that made it possible.

Like its patron genius Gaudí, Barcelona has always striven to
build something radically new as a way of retrieving something
that is radically old. It never loves the modern more than when it

may be safely consigned to history. It rushes into an idealized future while clinging tightly to an imaginary past, and so it strews in its wake a surfeit of unrealized dreams and failed visionaries. At an elemental level, the longing for the deep that Monturiol inspired in his compatriots was as much a pining for a submerged past as it was a desire for the conquest of a new world. In the paradoxical calculus of Barcelona's crablike walk into modernity, it was inevitable that Monturiol should have succeeded only after he failed. He had to be forgotten, so that he could be remembered and cemented into the city's story of itself.

There is something maddening about this city's hopelessly backward-looking march into the future. But there is a measure of wisdom in it too. Barcelona has learned never to take its utopias too seriously. It knows how much of paradise it can afford and rarely goes over budget. It still mixes its mysticism with a healthy dose of pragmatism. It absorbs what it can from its visionaries and saves the rest for historical entertainment. It knows how to embrace the modern without forsaking the good food, the ample sunshine, the warm seashore, and the inalienable sense of well-being with which it has been endowed. So it avoids the tyranny of the ideal in favor of a republic of the possible and converts the potential terror of utopia into comedy. From time to time, Barcelona struts and frets for recognition on the world stage, yet it never lets itself get carried away. Deep down, it knows that it is a province, that its idiosyncrasy is irremediable, and that its genius lies only in the small things, in whatever doesn't move or translate well.

It is this kind of generosity in the face of shortcomings that makes the story of Monturiol and his amazing submarine universal. We all sometimes want to reach for the stars, yet we also know that often all we can bring back is a fistful of the same earth on which we stand. For every hero, we rightly suspect, there is an anti-hero; for every history, there is an anti-history; and for every world capital, there is an anti-capital where the better part of reality happens. Everyone who is not self-deluded harbors inside some small measure of failure, some compromising secret of the past, something hopelessly provincial. And every effort to make this world a better place falls short of the ideal. The noble and passionate life of Monturiol reminds us of why we keep trying anyway.

Epilogue

The Post-Monturiol Era
of Underwater Navigation

The submarine came of age in the 1880s. In Britain, France, the United States, and Spain itself, a fresh crew of inventors harvested the seeds planted by Monturiol and his predecessors. John P. Holland, an Irishman in America; Thorsten Nordenfeldt, a Swede in Britain; Simon Lake, another American; and Maxime Laubeuf in France were some of the great names in the springtime of the submarines.

In 1889 a Spanish naval officer and inventor named Isaac Peral y Caballero (1851–1895) built one of the most advanced boats of the day, notable for its pioneering use of an electric motor for underwater propulsion. After completing successful test runs of his new vessel, Peral received congratulatory messages from groups around Spain and the rest of the world. Upon receiving a commendation from a group of Catalans, Peral responded:

> I cannot but recall, and recall with greatest pleasure, that great Catalan, the illustrious Monturiol—the man who took one of the most giant steps in the resolution of the problem of underwater navigation. If that genius, as full of abnegation as talent, had lived in the present era of scientific and industrial advance, the congratulations with which you so greatly honor me would have gone—no doubt with greater merit—to him.

It was a graceful acknowledgment, and a highly unusual one in the competitive and secretive world of submariners. It was also among the last that Monturiol would receive. As subaquatic technology advanced, Monturiol's name receded into history. Largely oblivious of his achievements, submariners of the future would reinvent many features of his designs and then move on.

By the turn of the century, the submarine had become part of the furniture of the modern world. The future of underwater navigation, however, did not take the shape that Monturiol anticipated. When war broke out in Europe in 1914, there were several dozen submarines in the world, with the largest concentration under the command of the Royal Navy. By the end of the war there were over 400 submarines in the world's navies and another 300 or so littering the bottom of the world's oceans. German submarines sank 11 million tonnes of shipping during the war, representing approximately 5,000 surface vessels and an uncounted number of lives. The most notorious submarine adventure of the war was the sinking of the passenger liner *Lusitania* in 1915, in which 1,200 drowned.

As the century progressed, the body count increased. During the Second World War the submarine destroyed millions of tonnes of shipping and hundreds of thousands of lives on all sides of the conflict. The postwar world witnessed the arrival of the nuclear-powered ballistic-missile submarine. A single submarine now had the capacity to destroy most of civilization. It seemed for a time that Monturiol was correct in predicting that the art of underwater navigation would one day exert a "transcendent" influence on human destiny, but that he was quite in error about the nature of this influence.

In retrospect, it seems obvious that the vision Monturiol glimpsed on the Cap de Creus in 1856 could have borne only a tangential relationship to the course of future events. He could not have anticipated how the nature of his own submarine would change as it confronted the political realities of his time. Much less could he have foreseen the direction that subaquatic technology eventually would take. It was perhaps inevitable for his creation, like Dr. Frankenstein's monster, to have escaped his control and wreaked destruction on the world. The course of submarine development after Monturiol would appear to count as a refutation of his idea of progress.

✦　　✦　　✦

But the story of underwater navigation after Monturiol is not all about machines of war. Although heavily outweighed and outgunned by the military tradition, the scientific side of the history of submarines has nonetheless registered decisive advances over the past century. (Often the scientific work piggybacked on military requirements: deep-sea exploration received its greatest boost with the sinking of several nuclear submarines on both sides of the Cold War.) Monturiol's dream of a vessel capable of reaching the very bottom of the world's oceans was eventually realized in 1960, when the bathyscaphe *Trieste*, piloted by Jacques Piccard, finally brought humankind to the bottom of the very deepest part of the ocean—the 11,000-meter-deep Marianas Trench.

Scientists have since come back from the bottom with remarkable discoveries—discoveries that underscore the significance of the questions that first impelled Monturiol on his journey. Monturiol asked, for example, whether the ocean floor was composed of the same mix of minerals as dry land. It is now clear that the ocean floor is indeed made up of an unusual combination of minerals, a result of the processes of formation of the earth's crust that take place down there. Deep-sea research thus helped confirm the theory of continental drift, which provides that the continents sit atop massive tectonic plates that float and move on the hot liquid magma beneath the earth's crust.

Monturiol's fascination with ocean currents and with the "source of all stormy seas" also turns out to have been prescient. Subsequent research has shown that the ocean currents have a massive impact on the earth's climate. Models used in predicting the fate of the global climate, and in particular the possibility of global warming, rely crucially on an understanding of the role of the oceans in weather systems.

Monturiol wondered whether there was much life in the deep and, if there was, how it differed from surface life. Through the early twentieth century, many scientists assumed they had an answer: the bottom of the ocean was a desert, inhospitable for life, they said. Deep-sea exploration has since revealed that the ocean depths harbor an extraordinary abundance and diversity of life. Phosphorescent fish, tubular animals that live like plants on the bottom, gelatinous colonies of symbiants, and other bizarre monsters populate the eternal darkness. Perhaps the most remarkable of these newfound creatures are the microbes that derive their living energy not from the light of the sun or from other living matter but from the hot chemical stews found near volcanic vents on the ocean bottom. They represent a form of life that is not only utterly different from anything seen before but may also be more archaic than life as we know it. Some scientists believe such microbes may even help explain the origin of life on earth.

There is yet another branch of contemporary undersea activity that resonates with Monturiol's submarine dream. Monturiol put those nineteen portholes on his *Ictíneo* because he just wanted to see what was down there under the surface. There was always something simple and childlike in his wonder. Today there are millions of amateur scuba divers who, for an hour or two at a time, can swim just like fish and experience firsthand the wonders of the watery world. This new form of access to the deep has undoubtedly stimulated awareness of the beauty and value of the undersea environment.

With the origin of life and the future of the global environment still in play, it seems there may be some hope for Monturiol's dream after all. In his vision on the Cap de Creus, he got the timing and the details mostly wrong, as history demonstrated with its customary cruelty and indifference. But possibly he got the big picture right. Maybe one day a submariner will save the world. When asked about the historical consequences of the French Revolution, a Chinese politician famously said, 200 years after the event, "It is too soon to tell." Likewise, when asked about the ultimate significance of Monturiol's dream, we should only say: It is too soon to tell.

History does not have a plot. It is a story whose end recedes in time, always changing shape, always demanding revisions of what came before. But sometimes someone shows us a fixed point on the horizon, an ideal, like a beacon in the distance, that can help us get our bearings for a time. The ideal of progress for which Monturiol lived is still the farthest point that we can see, still the brightest light on the horizon. And the voyage is far from over. Progress is neither predictable nor inevitable. It does not follow inexorably from the logic of history. It is much slower than we tend to imagine. Yet it happens nonetheless. Its foundation is enlightenment. And it is the work of individuals—individuals like Narcís Monturiol.

Acknowledgments

In researching this book I depended on the assistance of a number of Catalan institutions. I would like to thank the invariably helpful staff of the Athenaeum of Barcelona, the Historical Archives of Barcelona, the Library of Catalonia, the Municipal Archives of Figueres, the Museum of the Empordà, and the Museum of the History of Barcelona. Most important, as the many illustrations and the bibliography will attest, I owe a considerable debt to the excellent Maritime Museum of Barcelona.

I would also like to thank my agent, Andrew Stuart, for his early faith in the project, and my friend Richard Kaye, for his insightful comments on the manuscript.

I performed much of the research for this book while enjoying life in Barcelona during the late 1990s and then again in the winter and spring of 2002. During that time I incurred a great debt of gratitude to family and friends there. For advice and assistance I relied on my uncle Josep Montserrat and my aunt Jessica Jacques, both on the faculty of the Autonomous University of Barcelona, as well as my uncle Albert Montserrat and family. My thanks are due also to Agustí Nieto-Galan for taking the time to discuss the project with me. Much of what I know about the excellence of Catalan cuisine and Catalan family manners I learned at the table of Beatriu and Eduard Castellet. The rest I acquired from my friend Antoni Canyelles i Mateu, whose mind is a storehouse of instructive anecdotes from the history of Barcelona and other sources of Catalan wisdom.

Acknowledgments

Those whom I can never thank enough are my mother, Myo, who had the good sense to be born in Barcelona; my wife, Katherine, whose love and support made this book possible; and my daughter, Sophia, who made it all seem worthwhile—and who cooperated magnanimously in our temporary relocation to Barcelona, despite being only four months old at the time.

Notes

Page 6 One day on the shores: Joan Sardà, a personal friend of Monturiol, has Monturiol saving the coral diver in *La Vanguardia* (1890). In Monturiol's own version of events (1891), the identity of the diver's savior is hidden behind a passive voice. The biographer must therefore decide whether Sardà invented the tale or Monturiol covered up his role out of characteristic modesty.

7 "of an irresistible penetration": Puig Pujadas (1918), p. 101.

7 "of great virtue": Eusebi Corominas, cited in Puig Pujadas (1918), p. 52.

7 "a modesty so natural": Ibid., p. 102.

8 "one of the most noble": Ibid., p. 15.

8 "a Christian": Ibid., p. 52.

8 When he discovered: Joan Sardà, *La Vanguardia* (1890).

8 Cervantes' novel: Ibid.

11 "Fiery are my cares": Poem dated November 17, 1858, Barcelona, cited in Puig Pujadas (1918), pp. 115–16.

22 The past with its traditions: Cerdà (1999), pp. 36, 54.

25 "cannot be described": For this and following citations from Cerdà, see Cerdà (1994), pp. 38*ff.*, and Cerdà (1991).

26 "Rare is the Barcelonan": Eduardo Mendoza (1986), p. 196.

27 One historian famously observed: Jaume Vicens i Vives (1995), p. 33.

28 "magnificent sight": For this and following, see Cerdà (1999), pp. 53*ff.*

39 "masterpiece of tenderness": Joan Sardà, *La Vanguardia* (1890).

PAGE 39 "Even more than a father": del Castillo (1963), p. 27.

45 "Isolation and selfishness": Monturiol (1850).

45 "freshness and vigor": Joan Sardà, *La Vanguardia* (1890).

46 Josep Anselm Clavé: For biographical details on Clavé, see Caballé (1950) and Poblet (1973).

46 Ildefons Cerdà: For biographical details on Cerdà i Sunyer, see Cerdà (1968–1971), vol. 3, especially Appendix by Manuel Angelón, as well as Cerdà (1999) and Cerdà (1994). Cerdà's diaries are available in the Arxiu Històric de la Ciutat de Barcelona and are mostly published in Cerdà (1991).

49*ff.* For biographical details on Cabet and the history of the Icarian movement, see Johnson (1974), Prudhommeaux (1907), Shaw (1972), and Sutton (1994).

65 "No, my dear Emilia": Letter of June 27, 1848, to Emilia, cited in Puig Pujadas (1918), p. 64.

66 "What I suffer": Puig Pujadas (1918), pp. 61ff.

71 "the working classes": Roure (1925), p. 82.

86 For more on Martí i Alsina and his links to Monturiol and Cerdà, see Museu d'Art Modern (1994).

93 "Great effects do not always arise from great causes": Cerdà (1999), p. 27.

94 "I am both a revolutionary": Cerdà (1994), p. 136.

96 an account of the ramblers' conversation: Puig Pujadas (1918), p. 95.

97 "just as if": Monturiol (Dec. 1860), p. ii.

98 "Its form is that of a fish": Monturiol (1858).

98 "For those who do not accept": Monturiol (Dec. 1860), p. ii.

100 "The hour has come to explore the abysses": Monturiol (1858).

100 "The Universe is subject to laws": Monturiol (1891), p. 14.

103 "Great is the enterprise of submarine navigation": Monturiol (1891), p. 24.

104 "In vain has man": Letter to Anita Monturiol, in Puig Pujadas (1918), p. 95.

111*ff.* For more on the history of submarines in general, see Further Reading, p. 325.

126 Possibly he knew: *El Museo Universal*, April 1, 1859, mentions the work of one "Lodner Philips."

Page 128 "All of these inventors": This paragraph and the following citation on diving bells originally appear in the *Dictamen* of the Ateneu of 1860 and are repeated in Monturiol (1891), p. 10. Whoever the words belonged to, the ideas certainly came from Monturiol.

131 "stimulates men to noble actions": Aristotle, *Nichomachean Ethics*, VIII, 1, 15ff.

133 Nuevo Vulcano: See del Castillo (1955) for an interesting history of Barcelona's largest shipyard, including discussion of the construction of Monturiol's submarine.

135 *Obsession*: *Webster's New World Dictionary of the American Language*, 2nd ed. (1980).

150 "I mean those gases": Monturiol (Dec. 1860), p. 19.

158 "The silence that accompanies the dives": Monturiol (1861).

162 "The *Ictíneo* descends and ascends": Monturiol (1891), p. 17.

163 The description of the *Ictíneo*'s first public launch is based on a lengthy article in the *Diario de Barcelona*, September 24, 1859.

165 "The enthusiasm": Roca y Ferreras (1894), p. 86.

170 "[E]verywhere immense sums are deployed for war": Cited in Puig Pujadas (1918), p. 177.

175 A leading light: For more on Letamendi, see Calbet (1982).

177 October 21, 1861: Letamendi recorded the following in an article reprinted in *Estrany* (1915).

180 "Fortunate is the genius": Lobo (1860).

184 Don José Xifré i Downing: For biographical details on Xifré (father and son), see Ramón de San Pedro (1956) and Vicens i Vives (1958).

198 According to his contemporary: For Roure's description of Antonio Altadill, see Roure (1925), vol. 2. p. 80.

220 For the life of Joan Monjo i Pons, see Vilà i Galí (1997).

233 "This enterprise": Letter to Dulce cited in Puig Pujadas (1918), p. 180.

236 "To the water!": Cited in Puig Pujadas (1918), p. 188.

237 "I was intimately familiar": *La Vanguardia* (1890).

241 "The *Ictíneo* had a simple and safe process": *La Vanguardia* (1890).

245 "And for this I received blame": Monturiol (1891), p. 21.

PAGE 249 One chronicler of the times: Roure (1925), vol. 2. p. 221.

249 "As it is very long": Monturiol's letter to the U.S. secretary of the navy and the secretary's reply are preserved in the U.S. National Archives.

258 "It is a true pleasure to find oneself hermetically sealed": Monturiol (1891), p. 88.

263 "Like the self-burning tree of Gambia": Sale (2001), p. 173.

270 "fire of a profound passion": Puig Pujadas (1918), p. 277.

280 "His enthusiasm for free speculation": López Piñero (1983).

289 "locking himself in a room": Joan Sardà, *La Vanguardia*, 1890.

292 "free and powerful in creating machines": Letter to Anita Monturiol, in Puig Pujadas (1918), p. 253.

313 "I cannot but recall": Cited in Estrany (1915).

Further Reading

Texts by Monturiol

The only comprehensive collection of Monturiol's submarine writings may be found in the archives of the Museu Marítim of Barcelona. The biography by Puig Pujadas (1918) includes selections of key texts.

Un reo de muerte. Las Ejecuciones y los espectadores. Barcelona: Tomás Carreras, 1844. Reproduced in Riera i Tuèbols (1986).

Reseña de las doctrinas sociales antiguas y modernas. Barcelona: Juan Capdevila, 1850.

Proyecto de navegación submarina. El Ictíneo o barco-pez. November 6, 1858. Barcelona: Narciso Ramirez, 1858.

Memoria sobre la navegación submarina por el inventor del Ictíneo o barco-pez. February 10, 1860. Barcelona: Narciso Ramirez, 1861.

Memoria sobre los Ictíneos de guerra. December 1860. Manuscript. Museu Marítim.

Monturiol a la prensa periodica. May 16, 1861. Madrid, 1861.

A la prensa periodica: a propósito de la construcción de un ictíneo de guerra. Barcelona: Narciso Ramirez, 1862.

El Ictíneo y la navegación submarina. Barcelona: Narciso Ramirez, 1863.

A los interesados en el Ictíneo y a cuantos han contribuido a su desarrollo. Ramirez y Ca., 1866.

Memoria leida por el Gerente Industrial de la Navegación Submarina en la junta general del 22 de abril de 1866. Ramirez y Ca., 1866. Reproduced in Puig Pujadas (1918).

Navegación submarina. Memoria leida por el inventor del Ictíneo en la junta general del 8 de diciembre de 1866. Ramirez y Ca., 1866.

Notes for a final meeting of *la Navegación Submarina.* Reproduced in Puig Pujadas (1918).

Idea general del Universo. December 19, 1874. Manuscript. Museu Marítim.

Meteoros ígneos. January 1875. Manuscript. Museu Marítim.

Geosofía. April 1875. Manuscript. Museu Marítim.

Ensayo sobre el arte de navegar por debajo del agua. Barcelona: Alta Fulla, 1982 (1891).

Assaig sobre l'art de navegar per dessota l'aigua. Versió catalana de Carles Rahola. Barcelona: Consell de Pedagogia, 1919.

Contemporary Accounts of the *Ictíneo*

Ateneu Barcelonés. *Dictamen que acerca del Ictíneo de Monturiol emite una comission de la sección de Ciencias Exactas, Físicas y Naturales del Ateneo Catalán en noviembre de 1860.* Barcelona: Narciso Ramirez, 1861.

Diario de Barcelona. Esp. September 24, 1859; September 28, 1860; June 10, 1861; June 11, 1861.

Dictámenes científicos acerca del Ictíneo o barco-pez para la navegación submarina. La Habana: Librería El Iris, 1863.

Estrany, Jerónimo, ed. *Narciso Monturiol y la Navegación Submarina. Juicios críticos emitidos sobre los importantisimos trabajos realizados por este sabio inventor catalán.* Barcelona: Gustavo Gili, 1915.

Lasso de Vega, Jorge. *El Ictíneo o barco-pez. Juicio facultativo.* Barcelona: Narciso Ramirez, 1861.

Lobo, Miguel. "Invento del Ictíneo o sea del Barco-Pez para la navegación submarina por D. Narciso Monturiol, natural de Barcelona." *El Museo Universal* 4:354–55 (November 4, 1860).

Monjo i Pons, Joan. *Sofriments que m´ha causat l'Ictíneo.* Barcelona: Diputació de Cultura, 1985 (1869).

Servat, Joaquim. Collection of unpublished poems and other items of interest concerning Monturiol. Biblioteca de Catalunya.

El Telégrafo, September 10, 1864.

La Vanguardia, September 28, 1890.

La Verdad, May 11, 1861.

Secondary Literature on Monturiol

Ainaud de Lasarte, José Maria. "Monturiol, un héroe romántico." *Historia y Vida* 6:64:57–75 (July 1963).

Bellmunt, Frances. *Monturiol: El Senyor del mar.* Screenplay of film by same name. Lleida: Pages, 1993.

del Castillo, Alberto. *Narciso Monturiol: Inventor del submarino "Ictíneo" (1819–1885).* Barcelona: La Mutua Metalurgica de Seguros, 1963.

Moreno Rico, Xavier. *El Vaixell-Peix de Narcís Monturiol: mite i realitat.* Sabadell: Fundació Bosch i Cardellach, 1999.

Nieto-Galan, Augustí. *La seducción de la máquina-vapores, submarinos e inventores.* Madrid: Nivola, 1999.

Passarell, Jaume. *L'Inventor Narcís Monturiol.* Editorial Barcino, 1935.

Puig Pujadas, J. *Vida d'heroi. Narcís Monturiol, inventor de la navegació submarina.* Imprenta i Llibreria l'Avenç, 1918.

Riera i Tuèbols, Santiago. *Narcís Monturiol: una vida apassionant, una obra apassionada.* Generalitat de Catalunya, 1986.

Roca y Ferreras, José. *Galería de Catalanes Ilustres.* Barcelona: Esplugues, 1894.

Techel, H. "Der Ictineo von Narciso Monturiol. Beitrag zur Geschichte des Unterseebotes." *Schiffbautechnisches Gesellschaft,* Berlin (February 16–17, 1941).

Torrent i Orri, Rafael. "Narcís Monturiol: l'inventor de l'Ictíneo." *Hora Nova,* 1985.

Vilà i Galí, Augustí. *Joan Monjo i Pons: Un exemple de la tenacitat.* Barcelona: Oikos'tau, 1997.

History of Submarines

Interestingly, no English-language history of submarines mentions the work of Monturiol.

Bak, Richard. *The C.S.S. Hunley: The Greatest Undersea Adventure of the Civil War.* Dallas: Taylor Publishing, 1999.

Ballard, Robert D. *The Eternal Darkness: A Personal History of Deep-Sea Exploration.* Princeton University Press, 2000.

Broad, William J. *The Universe Below: Discovering the Secrets of the Deep Sea.* New York: Touchstone, 1997.

Burgess, Robert Forrest. *Ships Beneath the Sea: A History of Subs and Submersibles*. New York: McGraw-Hill, 1975.

Compton-Hall, Richard. *The Submarine Pioneers*. Stroud: Alan Sutton, 2000.

Field, Cyril. *The Story of the Submarine: From the Earliest Ages to the Present Day*. London: Sampson Low, Marston, 1908.

Harris, Brayton. *The Navy Times Book of Submarines: A Political, Social, and Military History*. New York: Berkley Books, 1997.

Morris, Richard Knowles. *John P. Holland 1841–1914: Inventor of the Modern Submarine*. Columbia: University of South Carolina Press, 1998.

Preston, Anthony. *Submarine Warfare: An Illustrated History*. San Diego: Thunder Bay Press, 1999.

Poluhowich, John. *Argonaut: The Submarine Legacy of Simon Lake*. College Station: Texas A&M University Press, 1999.

Sale, Kirkpatrick. *The Fire of His Genius: Robert Fulton and the American Dream*. New York: Free Press, 2001.

Villon, A. M. *La navegation sous-marine*. Paris: B. Tignol, undated.

Zim, Herbert Spencer. *Submarine: The Story of Undersea Boats*. New York: Harcourt, Brace, 1942.

Ildefons Cerdà

Cerdà, Ildefons. *Teoría general de la urbanización y aplicación de sus principios y doctrinas a la reforma y ensanche de Barcelona*. 3 vols. Madrid: Instituto de Estudios Fiscales, 1968–71.

Cerdà, Ildefons. *Teoría de la construcción de las ciudades y otros trabajos conexos. Cerdà y Barcelona*. 2 vols. Madrid: Instituto Nacional de la Administración Pública and Ajuntament de Barcelona, 1991.

Cerdà, Ildefons. Unpublished papers. Arxiu Històric de la Ciutat de Barcelona.

Cerdà: Urbs i Territori, una visió del futur. Catàleg de la mostra Cerdà. Also available in English translation. Fundació Catalana per a la Recerca, 1994.

Soria y Puig, Arturo, ed. *Cerda: The Five Bases of the General Theory of Urbanization*. Trans. Bernard Miller and Mary Fons i Fleming. Madrid: Electa, 1999.

Further Reading

Other Works of Interest

Alemany i Llovera, Joan. *El Port de Barcelona: història i actualitat*. Barcelona: Port Autònom de Barcelona, L'Avenç, 1984.

Altadill, Antonio. *Barcelona y sus misterios*. 1860.

Artola, Miguel. *La burguesia revolucionaria (1808–74)*. Madrid: Alianza, 1974.

Balaguer, Victor. *Las calles de Barcelona*. Barcelona, 1865.

Balcells, Albert. *Historia dels paisos catalans*. 3 vols. Barcelona: Edhasa, 1980.

Benet, J., and C. Martí, *Barcelona a mitjan segle XIX. El moviment obrer durant el bienni progressista (1854–1856)*. 2 vols. Barcelona: Curial, Documents de cultura, 1976.

Caballé y Clos, Tomás. *José Anselmo Clavé y su tiempo*. Barcelona: Freixenet, 1950.

Cabet, Étienne. *Voyage en Icarie*. Paris: Au bureau du Populaire, 1848.

Calbet, J. M., and J. Corbella. *Diccionari biogràfic de metges catalans*. 3 vols. Fundació Casajuana amb la collabouració del seminari Pere Mata de la Universitat de Barcelona, 1982–84.

Carr, Raymond. *Modern Spain 1808–1939*. Oxford University Press, 1966.

del Castillo, Alberto. *La Maquinista Terrestre y Marítima, personaje historico: 1855–1955*. Barcelona: Maquinista Terrestre y Maritim, 1955.

Fernandez-Armesto, Felipe. *Barcelona: A Thousand Years of the City's Past*. Oxford University Press, 1992.

Fontana, J. *La revolució liberal (política y hacienda, 1833–1845)*. Madrid: Instituto de Estudios Fiscales, Ministerio de Hacienda, 1977.

van Hensbergen, Gijs. *Gaudí: The Biography*. London: HarperCollins, 2001.

Hughes, Robert. *Barcelona*. New York: Alfred A. Knopf, 1992.

von Humboldt, Alexander. *Cosmos: A Sketch of the Physical Description of the Universe*. 2 vols. Baltimore: Johns Hopkins University Press, 1997.

Johnson, Christopher H. *Utopian Communism in France: Cabet and the Icarians*. Ithaca, N.Y.: Cornell University Press, 1974.

López Piñero, José M. *Diccionario histórico de la ciencia moderna en España*. Barcelona: Peninsula, 1983.

Mendoza, Eduardo. *Ciudad de los prodigios*. Barcelona: Seix Barral, 1986.

Museu d'Art Modern del MNAC. *Cent anys de paisatgisme català:*

centenari de la mort de Lluís Rigalt, Ramón Martí Alsina i Joaquim Vayreda. Barcelona, 1994.

Paredes, Javier, ed. *Historia contemporánea de España (siglo XIX).* Barcelona: Editorial Ariel, 1998.

Permanyer, Lluis. *Historia de l'Eixample.* Barcelona: Plaza & Janes, 1990.

Poblet, Josep M. *Josep Anselm Clavé i la seva época.* Barcelona: Dopesa, 1973.

Prudhommeaux, Jules Jean. *Icarie et son fondateur, Étienne Cabet: contribution à l'étude du socialisme experimental.* Paris: E. Cornély & Cie, 1907.

Ramón de San Pedro, J. M. *Don José Xifré Casas. Industrial, naviero, comerciante, banquero, y benefactor. Historia de un indiano catalán (1777–1856).* Madrid, 1956.

Ribot y Fontseré, A. "El Coral." *El Museo Universal* 3:115–18 (1859).

Risques, Manel, ed. *Història de la Catalunya contemporània.* Barcelona: Pòrtic, 1999.

Roure, Conrad. *Recuerdos de mi larga vida.* Barcelona: El Diluvio, 1925.

Ruiz Cortés, Francisco. *Diccionario biográfico de personajes históricos del siglo XIX español.* Madrid: Rubiños-1860, S.A., 1998.

Shaw, Albert. *Icaria: A Chapter in the History of Communism.* Philadelphia: Porcupine Press, 1972.

Soler Vidal, J. *Abdó Terrades. Primer apòstol de la democràcia catalana (1812–1856).* Barcelona: Edicions de La Magrana, 1983.

———. *Pels camins d'utopia.* Mexico: Club de Llibre Catala, 1958.

Sutton, Robert P. *Les Icariens: The Utopian Dream in Europe and America.* Urbana: University of Illinois Press, 1994.

Ventura i Subirats, J. "Icaria, Vida, teorías y obra de Étienne Cabet, sus seguidores catalanes y experimentos comunistas icarianos." *Cuadernos de Historia Economica de Catalunya,* vol. 7. Barcelona, 1972.

Vicens i Vives, Jaume. *Industrials i polítics.* Barcelona: Teide, 1958.

———. *Noticia de Catalunya.* Barcelona: Edicions 62, 1995.

Vilar, Pierre, ed. *Història de Catalunya.* Barcelona: Edicions 62, 1988–.

Index

Figures in *italics* indicate captions; "M" indicates Monturiol.

Index

Index